"Corporations are managed by men; and men, never forget, manage corporations to suit themselves. Thus, corporate calamities are calamities created by men. And, as we shall see in fifteen case histories, the basic cause of the business disaster is greed, human greed, simple and unadulterated. In most cases, the greed crossed over the line into corruption."

Isadore Barmash in
Great Business Disasters

GREAT BUSINESS DISASTERS

Swindlers, Bunglers and Frauds in American Industry

(Revised and Updated Edition)

Edited by

Isadore Barmash

BALLANTINE BOOKS • NEW YORK

BALLANTINE BOOKS, INC.
201 East 50th Street, New York, N. Y. 10022

Contents

Acknowledgments

"The Metamorphosis of Philip Musica" by Robert Shaplen originally appeared in the October 29, 1955 issue of *The New Yorker*. Reprinted by permission. Copyright © 1955, The New Yorker Magazine, Inc.

"The Decline and Fall of Billie Sol Estes" originally appeared in *Time* under the title "The Billie Sol Estes Scandal." Reprinted by permission from *Time*, The Weekly Newsmagazine. Copyright © 1962, Time Inc.

"The Soybean Scandal" originally appeared in the December 8, 1963 issue of the *New York Herald Tribune*. Copyright © 1963, New York Herald Tribune Inc. Reprinted with permission of W.C.C. Publishing Co., Inc.

"The Fate of the Edsel" by John Brooks. Copyright © 1959, 1960, 1961, 1962, 1963, 1964, 1965, 1966, 1967, 1968, 1969 by John Brooks. From *Business Adventures* published by Weybright and Talley. Reprinted by permission of David McKay Co., Inc.

"Real Estate's Humpty-Dumpty: Bill Zeckendorf After the Fall" by Elliott Bernstein originally appeared in the September 23, 1968 issue of *New York*. Copyright © 1968 by the New York Magazine Co. Reprinted with the permission of *New York* magazine.

"Pennsy: Bad Management or Ailing Industry Debated" by Robert E. Bedingfield originally appeared in July 1970 in the *New York Times*. Copyright © 1970 by The New York Times Company. Reprinted by permission.

"Bailing Out—Penn Central Officials Sold Stock as Carrier Was Nearing Disaster" by Fred L. Zimmerman originally appeared in the July 14, 1970 issue of the *Wall Street Journal*. Reprinted with permission of The Wall Street Journal.

"Long Haul Ahead—Penn Central Faces Lengthy Legal Snarls Under Bankruptcy Law" by W. Stewart Pinkerton, Jr. originally appeared in the June 30, 1970 issue of the *Wall Street Journal*. Reprinted with permission of The Wall Street Journal.

Great Business Disasters

Introduction

In case there was any doubt about it, there needn't be anymore. The early Seventies will surely be considered the watershed years in the history of the American business calamity. Early in 1973, one of the most startling scandals in the history of American business, the discovery of more than $20 million in fictitious insurance policies on the books of Equity Funding Life Insurance Company, rocked the business community, leading to potential losses of about $300 million in common stock by investors and sparking a number of regulatory probes.

Only the Watergate scandals involving the Nixon Administration and the charges that businessman Robert L. Vesco bought favors in Washington through illegal political contributions drew more attention in the press. But it would be a long time before businessmen and the public would forget Equity Funding. The case involved once again the use of insider knowledge on Wall Street and drew a cloud of suspicion over the activities of the local insurance man.

All this further strained the public's faith in American business, already reeling under the 1972 housing frauds in four American cities, the latest phases of the unbelievable Penn Central bankruptcy, the irrational hoax of a Howard Hughes non-autobiography, and the strange relations between the Nixon Administration and the International Telephone & Telegraph Company.

For some years, the country's youth had been demonstrating against such corporate achievements as napalm, pollution and racial intolerance in employment practices. Now the revelations of graft-ridden housing shenanigans, which acted to increase the central-city blight, cheat the low-income home buyer and bilk the taxpayer, prompted adults to wonder if youth simply hadn't been more alert to what was really going on. Do the young then really see things more clearly?

What was even more disturbing perhaps were the sudden disclosures of the frailties, involvement and apparent irresponsibility of a number of heretofore untouchable American institutions. What then was left to believe in? Family, religion, the human ethic? But all these, too, were undergoing their own upheavals.

Stung into indignation by the housing scandals on top of all the others, the *New York Times* in a lead Sunday editorial in April 1972, entitled "The Business of America," asserted:

"Even for people who regard themselves as knowledgeable about the facts of business and political life in the United States, the cumulative impact of the recent series of business and government scandals has been stunning. . . .

"Coming on top of a series of other scandals during recent years involving the largest railroad in the nation, the largest conglomerate corporation, the largest defense contractor and many companies in these and other fields, one is forced to ask whether a new rot has infected the American political-economic system or whether this is just a recurrence of the oldest story of all—the greed that periodically is exposed when the greedy become a bit too careless and flagrant. . . ."

But greed is as old as man, and so the history of business disasters goes back a long time—as long as there have been men in business.

In America, the saga of business scandals had one of its more infamous, early chapters in the corruptions of the Tweed ring a century ago. William Marcy Tweed was a chairmaker and bookkeeper who showed considerable political acumen by advancing himself from New York City alderman in 1852 to grand sachem of Tammany Hall by 1868. This rise gave him control of the city administration, during which he and his cohorts stole something like $200 million from New York City.

It became clear too that some of the city's most prominent businessmen, such as John Jacob Astor II, were allied with the crooked politicians. By use of bribes and other sweeteners, they deprived the city of tremendous sums in real estate and taxes. Tweed died in prison, a pauper. His city controller absconded with six million dollars and died abroad. But the wealthy magnates and entrepreneurs who were the silent partners retained their loot in the form of real estate, utility franchises, property rights and exemption of taxes. These, such is the irony of birthright, became the legacy to their descendants, who emerged as some of the nation's wealthiest families.

As the country's economy prospered, pushing gross national product into the trillion-dollar level, so did the corruption level in the boardrooms and executive suites.

One of the most corrupt of all was Jay Gould. Born to a poor Yankee farming family in Roxbury, New York, the dark, furtive Gould seemed in his avaricious, charmed life to have heels of lightning. He always managed to outrun both the marshals and his business competitors. His career, for example, began with his milking profits from a Pennsylvania tannery to which he had been assigned as manager. A partner committed suicide when he learned how badly Gould had duped him. But when the marshals were sent to apprehend him, Gould got the local residents to fight them off long enough for him to escape.

A year or two later, he married the daughter of a wealthy grocer. His father-in-law helped him to get control of a decrepit New England railroad for ten cents on the dollar. But Gould, by various means, turned what had begun to look like a disaster into a $100,000 profit.

This was to be his first link in a scheme that he had dreamed of as a boy, to forge a railroad line across the country. Cornelius Vanderbilt, another financial buccaneer, had the same dream. Big as a bear and as brutal, Vanderbilt, however, found he was no match for the tiny, ferretlike Gould. Together with Daniel Drew and James Fisk, the first a rapacious railroad speculator and the other a beefy ex-peddler who had made it big as a playboy and supersalesman, Gould acquired control of the Erie Railroad. They bested Vanderbilt, who had sorely wanted the road as the final stretch in his coast-to-coast rail network. Then the two dumped 100,000 illegal shares of stock on the market, causing the usually wily Vanderbilt to pick up quickly seven million dollars of it.

Process-servers came after the three con men, but they made it just in time across the river to Jersey City, out of the jurisdiction of the New York police. Soon afterward, Gould bribed members of the New York legislature to make his stock legal and to foreclose the possibility of a merger between the Erie and the New York Central owned by Vanderbilt.

In 1869, Gould and Fisk combined in another effort of the type that a century later was to be cutely called a "caper." They drew up a scheme to corner the country's gold by kiting the value of their purchases. The result was Black Friday of September 24, 1869, a day of tumbling commodity and stock prices and personal ruin for many.

But even that wild scheme seems to pale when compared to what John Pierpont Morgan tried and almost succeeded in pulling off in 1889. The heavy-set, hulking scion of a successful financier father, J.P., or "Pip," as he was called as a youth, was browbeaten by his parent until he was 20. But afterwards the young man stepped out on his own and far outdistanced his father in both attainment and skulduggery. He not only vanquished Gould and Fisk in a scheme but emerged for a time as a popular hero. He became the greatest financier of his time, with perhaps the most questionable ethics of his time.

The 1889 exploit began quietly, even surreptitiously. The day after New Year's, three of New York's largest investment bankers "confidentially" summoned the country's biggest railroad magnates to J. P. Morgan's Manhattan townhouse. Morgan spelled it out simply. What he suggested to the group was an airtight combination (monopoly) that would declare a moratorium on competition among its members and effectively give them control of the American railway system.

The bankers who had gathered the group together guaranteed that they would prevent the negotiation of any securities that would invite competition. Thus the combine would control the building of parallel lines or the extension of lines. It was a direct violation of some of the high statutes of the land, but no one present objected.

The scheme almost came to realization when James J. Hill, who controlled the Great Northern Railroad, and Edward H. Harriman, who controlled the Union Pacific, worked out an agreement to acquire jointly the Chicago, Burlington & Quincy line. Instead of fighting each other for the line, they would split up its territory and together keep out competition.

J. P. Morgan was named arbitrator of the plan. And why not? His firm held a big block of shares in Northern Pacific which, in turn, owned a large interest in Chicago, Burlington & Quincy. But Morgan didn't stop at being the arbitrator. He became instead the mastermind behind the plan. Morgan sold all the major parties the concept of organizing the Northern Securities Company. This vast holding company would take title to both Great Northern and Northern Pacific, with the latter's big interest in CB&Q. And so the new company would own all three lines.

But there was a bitter outcry from those who feared such an anticompetitive combination. The federal government brought a suit against Northern Securities and the U.S. Supreme Court decided that the holding company was an illegal corporation.

If the reversal severely affected Morgan, it did not seem to bother him for long. That same year, he began negotiating the formation of the U.S. Steel Corporation, and when it was put together in 1901, it became America's first billion-dollar corporation.

In those formative years of the world's mightiest economy, when the rules of corporate propriety and behavior were still weak (are they strong now?), the advent of the trusts was simple and their exploits went largely unchallenged. John D. Rockefeller, Sr., the first American to amass one billion dollars, formed a partnership with two others in Cleveland to corner the Ohio petroleum industry. This involved secret rebates from the railroads and conspiracies against the smaller refineries. In due course, Standard Oil Company of Ohio was formed, mushrooming into a colossus which controlled more than 90 percent of the country's refining capacity. It ground into the dust hundreds of refiners before the Supreme Court blew the whistle and ordered dissolution of the holding company and the separation of its entities.

And then there was the Sugar Trust that worked an immense fraud on the U.S. Government—some $30 million worth. From at least 1800 through 1909, the American Sugar Refining Company stole from five to ten percent from the duty on every cargo of raw sugar it imported. The method was simple. By bribing customs officials to underweigh its sugar imports, the Sugar Trust carried on its plundering for years. As the *Sun* of New York, as it was then known, put it:

"Shippers of sugar the world over knew of this robbery. Carriers knew it. Weighers knew it. Officials within the Custom House itself must have known it. The Sugar Trust silenced revelations. . . ."

But it wasn't to last. The government, aroused by the rumors and by the *Sun*'s front-page disclosures, obtained a judgment against the complex of 121 sugar plants that the deceased Henry O. Havermeyer (he died two years earlier in 1907) had forged under the name of the American Sugar Refining Company. But it was a pitiful settlement that the government accepted— $2,134,411.03 for thefts of $30 million.

The American trust, that power-locked group that kills competition and usually buries its tentacles deep into the seat of government, ran into greater disasters in the ensuing years than did the Sugar Trust and its members.

The Match King formed one. Ivar Kreuger, a Swedish engineer and financier, came to the United States in 1893 and engaged in construction activities. He also operated in South Africa and France before returning to Sweden in 1907, where he organized a new construction company. But between 1913 and 1917, he formed a match trust—the United Swedish Match Company and the Swedish Match Company. The combination eventually controlled 250 factories in 43 countries, as well as forests and mines. Eventually it became a huge international finance agency.

Kreuger, as it turned out, was not only pathologically ambitious but a dealer of the most devious kind. Financing big loans to war-torn countries for reconstruction, he obtained industrial concessions in return. Much of his funds came from naïve American investors. Speculations and fraud, however, caught up with him, and the economic crisis that began in 1929 brought the collapse of the "match-stick empire." After his suicide in 1932, it was found that many of his financial manipulations were based on falsified balances. The upshot was heavy losses to stockholders around the world.

Then there was the "Utilities King," Samuel Insull,

and his public-utilities trust, which climaxed a set of amazing exploits in 1932.

Born in London in 1859, Insull emigrated to the United States in 1881 and became a secretary to Thomas A. Edison, America's great inventor. For a while, he was instrumental in managing industrial holdings. But he too was ambitious, finding his life with Edison too static for his taste.

In 1907, after settling in Chicago, he involved himself in the hot public-utility competition and beat his way to control of the city's transit system. Through one merger after another, he expanded throughout the state and its neighbors. By 1912, he had developed a vast, interlocking directorate operating more than 300 steam plants, 200 hydroelectric plants and many other power plants throughout the country.

But his jerry-built structure swayed and collapsed in the Depression. He left his three-billion-dollar empire and took off for Greece and then Turkey. Extradited to the United States in 1934, Insull had to face charges of using the mails to defraud investors and of grand embezzlement. The case was the most celebrated of its time. He was acquitted and died in 1938, a controversial man-of-mystery to the end.

And then there was Philip Musica, the swindler who took a dying drug-wholesaling company, McKesson & Robbins, and—But that is where our volume begins. The double life led by Musica, surely one of the most complex of American con men, probably is a fitting opener.

In legal circles these days, it is estimated that ten billion dollars will pass hands in any current year in American business as a result of conflict-of-interest relationships, kickbacks, payoffs and commercial bribery in general. Representing only about one percent of the gross national product, the estimated take in business corruption is probably a very conservative one.

Thirty years ago, when the GNP was substantially

less, the estimate was that one billion dollars a year was kicked back in commercial bribes alone, according to Herbert Robinson, a New York lawyer often involved in prosecuting business fraud.

"Thus, the great growth in the American economy has undoubtedly been paralleled, if not exceeded dollarwise, by an equivalent increase (inflation) in conflict of interest and commercial bribery," he said.

But corruption, much as we would like to attribute most business calamities to it, is only one of several major causes. There are no statistics, of course, but besides the corruption that often lies at the heart of every disaster-maker, there are also stupidity, mismanagement and greed.

Sometimes, all three are represented in a particular disaster. Question: At what point does the profit drive turn into pure greed?

What can one conclude led to the Edsel fiasco? Or the debacle of the computer venture by RCA? Or the bubble-deflation of National Student Marketing? Or the smell of the salad-oil scandal? All were hardly cases of mismanagement.

In the case of Billie Sol Estes, it was simply corruption and greed—and perhaps a large measure of self-deception.

In the case of the Atlantic Acceptance bankruptcy, one is forced to say it was stupidity and almost nothing else. In the case of Edward M. Gilbert, it was greed pure and simple. But what is one to say about William Zeckendorf, who tried to out-Walt Disney Disney in the Freedomland disaster and emerged instead more like an oversize Mickey Mouse? Somehow, though, the big, bluff realtor comes off being liked and perhaps somewhat excused as you might excuse an erring, blundering but happy-go-lucky uncle.

And what of Penn Central, the biggest merger of all that turned into the biggest bankruptcy of all? All the possible reasons seem to fit here, but perhaps the most apt one was that it was a marriage that should never have been.

If one were to track all the reasons in all the 15 prime business disasters described in this book, it is probable that one pragmatic common denominator would emerge: uncontrolled expansion that raced away like a prairie fire.

With several exceptions, all the original sources for the disasters that are unfolded here were selected because they were on-the-spot, contemporary journalism, containing the feel, the excitement, the pertinence, the topicality and the flavor of the calamity and the events that led up to it. Any drawbacks presented by the fact that some of the pieces lack information of what came afterward, after the apprehension, the bankruptcy, the litigation, are hopefully offset by the brief introductions. Each offers, so to speak, both a preamble and a postscript in advance.

And now—brace yourself—a gallery of business horrors.

ISADORE BARMASH

A Study in Bamboozlement

2

In the annals of the American con artist, Philip Mariano Fausto Musica occupies a high perch. Stocky, about five feet, eight inches tall, with flattened dark hair on a broad forehead, a squarish face that bore a calm, almost serene expression, he resembled Mussolini and in his nattiness and demeanor even looked somewhat like Caruso in the opera singer's heyday. But Musica's mind was like a computer dedicated to bilking the public, and he had the kind of self-righteousness that allowed any end to justify the means, especially if the means was to bamboozle a naïve society.

He was definitely a creative artist. Who else could swindle two companies out of millions, then join the investigative forces, disappear for five years and then surface again to resurrect a third concern and then swindle that one into near-ruin?

As *Who's Who* indignantly proclaimed in a special 1942 volume, entitled *Who Was Who in America*: "COSTER, Frank Donald. The sketch of the then president of McKesson & Robbins, Inc., published in Volume XX under this name, is the only instance—during nearly five decades of continuous publication involving over 77,000 biographies—of a fictitious biographee foisting himself on the editors of *Who's Who*. . . . This impostor became so qualified on being elected president of the important drug house of McKesson & Robbins, Inc. He had for years successfully hoodwinked banks, boards of directors, famous clubs' admission committees, trade organizations, stock exchanges and scores of leading businessmen and officials. It later developed he had had falsified birth certificates filed which apparently substantiated his biographical data, to which he added fraudulent educational information. Although buried as Coster, he was actually Philip Musica, an ex-convict. . . ."

In his amazing 43-year business career, Musica made several mistakes. But the one that brought about his ultimate downfall and suicide in the bathroom of his Fairfield, Connecticut, estate was a basic one. He had forgotten to have his face lifted. Going as far as he did, it seems, he should have gone one step further. For someone casually glancing through a newspaper decided that the face of F. D. Coster, the distinguished pharmaceuticals entrepreneur, bore a striking resemblance to that of Philip Musica, the convicted swindler. This suspicion caused the fingerprints of each to be compared, and then it was all over.

The meeting of the Manhattan-born swindler and the then 100-year-old McKesson & Robbins came at a time when the conservative old drug firm was clearly headed for the rocks. After five years in the red, a split developed between the two families that controlled the business. This resulted in the McKesson side taking over the manufacturing of chemicals and the Robbins side being left with the dwindling pharmaceuticals business. The latter decided to sell out. And Coster-Musica was there, already back on his own with a Connecticut chemical business, Girard & Co., that he had founded.

Enthusiastically backed by a group of Bridgeport bankers that he had completely fooled, Musica spearheaded the offering of a stock issue of about $1.5 million to buy the old McKesson & Robbins and revitalize it. In the winter of 1926, Coster-Musica put down a check for one million dollars, merged Girard with McKesson & Robbins, and thus one of the biggest corporate swindles of modern American business was started.

Robert Shaplen's brilliant piece is actually the second of two articles on Coster-Musica. The first covered the Musica phase while the one reprinted here narrates the McKesson & Robbins episode and has more pertinence. It is, without question, a classic and telling account of a corporate swindle, both as a journalistic and sociological narrative. But, it is something else too. In its detail and story-thrust, it offers an effective admonition against our traditional American habit of "assuming"—assuming that all is well, that every decision is receiving appropriate action, that every invoice is being paid, that each does indeed represent a legitimate purchase, that each purchase represents an actual shipment and, above all, assuming that corporate executives are not dipping into the corporate till.

The Metamorphosis of Philip Musica

by Robert Shaplen

Shortly after nine o'clock on the evening of Monday, December 5, 1938, five nervous men gathered in a sixth-floor apartment of the Sherry-Netherland occupied by Sidney Weinberg, a prominent Wall Street broker and a director of some thirty large corporations. One of the companies Weinberg was most interested in was McKesson & Robbins, Inc., a century-old drug concern that had started out as a small pharmaceutical house on Maiden Lane and in the past decade had zoomed to the top of the national whoesale drug field under the presidency of F. Donald Coster, a small, owlish-looking man of fifty-four. Weinberg's four visitors were all McKesson & Robbins executives. They had hurried over from their homes or from dinner parties to attend the meeting, which had been hastily called because of a mystifying report that only a few hours before a Federal Court judge in Hartford, Connecticut, had without warning granted a petition to throw the huge drug firm into receivership. The grounds for the action were astounding. It was charged that the company had misled the public by claiming fictitious assets "in excess of ten million dollars."

Weinberg, a bustling man who was ever on the move, had been attending a private dinner with some other businessmen in a suite of the Waldorf-Astoria when he was called to the telephone and told what had happened in Hartford. His informant was Wilbur L. Cummings, a member of the McKesson & Robbins' executive committee and a partner in Sullivan & Cromwell, the law firm that represented the company. Cummings had been unable to reach Coster in Fairfield, Connecticut, where McKesson & Robbins had a plant and where Coster lived, but he had been in touch with three of the other directors before he called Weinberg, who now suggested that they all meet at his place in the Sherry-Netherland. "I'll get there myself as soon as I can," he promised. One of the other guests at the dinner Weinberg was attending was John M. Hancock, the chairman of the important stock-list committee of the New York Stock Exchange. This committee was about to consider an application by McKesson & Robbins for permission to list three million dollars' worth of debenture bonds on the Exchange. Returning to the table, Weinberg, who was himself a governor of the Exchange, whispered his startling news to Hancock. Only eight months before, Richard Whitney, a former president of the Exchange, had been sentenced to prison for embezzlement, and the scandal had left Wall Street severely shaken. Both Weinberg and Hancock devoutly hoped they were not in for another such mess. McKesson & Robbins had about forty million dollars' worth of stocks and bonds outstanding and available for trading on the market, and its well-regarded common stock was selling at seven dollars and fifty cents a share. The receivership action, it was clear, not only meant postponing or cancelling the new bond issue but raised the grave question of whether or not to suspend all trading in McKesson & Robbins securities.

By the time Weinberg reached his apartment, the four other McKesson & Robbins executives—Charles F. Michaels, executive vice-president; William J. Murray, Jr., first vice-president; Julian F. Thompson, treasurer; and Cummings—were already feverishly discussing the situation. The news of the receivership had stunned them all, but one of them was slightly less stunned than the others. That was Thompson, and he was telling an unbelievably strange story. It had to do with the company's crude-drug department, an international buying-and-selling agency of McKesson & Robbins that Coster had built up and had been supervising singlehandedly from Fairfield. For some time, Thompson had been privately and apprehensively looking into the operations of this department. Now, in the face of the Hartford development, he was frankly telling all present that he was unable to locate twenty-one million dollars' worth of assets—crude-drug inventories and accounts receivable—being carried on the company's books. Thompson eased the tension in the room a little when he went on to qualify this revelation by saying that while there was undoubtedly something odd going on, he couldn't bring himself to believe that these assets were completely nonexistent; it was more likely that they had got lost in bookkeeping procedures and were only temporarily unaccounted for. This, he added, was why he had been reluctant to speak up about the matter until he had learned more. His dismayed listeners were glad enough to go along with his tentative theory that Coster, who had always operated rather secretively, was probably engaged in some big speculative venture that he was keeping to himself. However unorthodox, and even inexcusable, this way of running a large corporation might be, it was a lot more pleasant to contemplate than the possibility that a substantial fraction of the company's value simply did not exist. With this happier thought in mind, Weinberg telephoned Coster, who by then had returned home.

"This is a frightful thing, Donald," Weinberg said with his usual friendly gruffness. "What the hell is it all about?"

Coster, who apparently had a bad cold, protested that he knew nothing about the receivership. "Here I'm living right in Connecticut, Sidney, and nobody has told me a thing about it," he said. He promised that in the morning he would come to New York, where the company had its executive offices, and discuss the matter.

The directors poured themselves a round of stiff drinks, and then Weinberg called the home of George May, the senior partner of Price, Waterhouse & Co., which was the accounting firm McKesson & Robbins retained to audit its books. May was in bed, but Weinberg persuaded him to get dressed and come over to the hotel. He arrived around midnight and assured the group that, as far as he knew, the company's books were in order. This news was additionally reassuring, but, even so, since the receivership *had* been granted and since the whereabouts of millions of dollars' worth of supposed assets *was* unknown, Weinberg made two more calls, between one and two o'clock. He got Hancock, his dinner companion of that evening, out of bed at the Union League Club, told him the gist of what he had just heard, and asked him if he would telephone the other officers of the Stock Exchange to make sure a trading ban was imposed on McKesson & Robbins securities the next morning, so that all investors might have equal protection. Hancock agreed to do this. Then Weinberg telephoned Washington, where he got still a third man out of bed—William O. Douglas, who was then chairman of the Securities and Exchange Commission. Weinberg told Douglas that he and the other McKesson & Robbins directors would welcome the Commission's help in investigating the peculiar position in which their corporation had so suddenly found itself. Douglas sleepily promised to do something about it when it was daylight, and hung up, whereupon the group at the Sherry-Netherland disbanded. Looking back on that evening recently, Weinberg said, "If we'd known what amazing things were about to happen, we sure as hell would have stayed up all night."

Probaly no man in the history of financial skulduggery was ever more tragically put upon than Thompson, the McKesson & Robbins treasurer. His acquaintance with Coster dated back to 1925, when Coster was running a chemical firm in Mount Vernon called Girard & Co. and Thompson was working for Bond & Goodwin, a big investment house in Wall Street. Coster wanted to acquire some capital for expansion, and Thompson, after a look at the company's books, wrote such a glowing analysis of the firm's prospects that Coster was able to raise the money and move Girad & Co. to a bigger plant, in Fairfield. Over the years during which Thompson helped Coster buy up McKesson & Robbins, and then became his treasurer, he had not the slightest occasion to doubt Coster's integrity; the man was a financial genius whose operations, though at times inscrutable to lesser financiers, were invariably successful. It is not surprising that the thought of fraud never crossed Thompson's mind when he had his first misgivings about the crude-drug department. And then, as the chronicle of mismanagement— at the very least—continued to unfold, Thompson found it almost impossible to grasp the extent to which Coster, whom he had for so long regarded as a friend as well as a business associate, had been using him as a foil. The treasurer was later criticized for not having made known his suspicions at once, but he had little opportunity to defend himself, because four and a half months after the emergency meeting in the Sherry-Netherland he died of influenza—the result, many felt, of a weakened physical condition brought on by mental suffering.

At the time of the debacle, very little was known by

anybody about Coster. It was believed in Wall Street
that he owned about ten percent of McKesson & Robbins' common stock, and that for some years—especially before the market crash of 1929, when he lost at
least a million dollars—he had been a heavy private
investor. But there was nothing conspicuous about him.
He always kept to himself and was hardly ever seen in
the financial district. And in Connecticut, where Mc-
Kesson & Robbins operated one of the state's largest
and most affluent business enterprises, there were relatively few people, either in Fairfield or elsewhere, who
knew Coster, or had even heard of him. He appeared to
dislike New York and to have a strong aversion to
spending the night in town; whenever business made an
overnight trip necessary, he stayed at the Roosevelt,
only a couple of blocks from the McKesson & Robbins
executive offices, at 155 East Forty-fourth Street, and
even closer to Grand Central, to which he would hurry
as soon as he could get away, and take the first train
back to Fairfield. (Whenever he had to go to Washington, he followed much the same procedure; if it was
impossible to return home at night, he would put up
at a small hotel just across the street from Union Station.) Sometimes, when Coster's associates knew that
he was spending the night in Manhattan, they would
propose going out and taking in a night club, but he
always refused; at the very most, he would consent to
join them in a bridge game at a private club on the
upper East Side. Until his luck ran out, his desire for
seclusion was accepted without question. His salary over
the twelve years that he controlled McKesson & Robbins
fluctuated between twenty and sixty-eight thousand
dollars, depending on profits, and averaged about
thirty-five thousand. Neighbors guessed that it cost
well over a thousand dollars a month to run the house,
and that Mrs. Coster, to judge by her considerable ward-
robe, spent about five hundred a month on clothes. Like
most men of means, Coster had a costly hobby. He
owned a two-hundred-and-eighty-four-ton, hundred-

and-thirty-four-foot, twin-screw seagoing yacht—
named the Carolita, after his wife—which he bought
in 1934 from John Hays Hammond for forty thousand
dollars and on which he spent an additional eighty-five
thousand dollars rebuilding the hull and quarters, in-
stalling mahogany furnishings, souping up the engines,
and putting in powerful two-way radio equipment. (After the showdown came, there were those who thought
that he might have had some idea of using the Carolita
to make an emergency getaway to a foreign country,
but if he did have that idea, it turned out to be im-
practicable, because in December, 1938, the yacht
was in drydock.) The Carolita, which had a crew of
six, was the center of Coster's circumscribed social life;
every now and then, he would invite a few McKesson
& Robbins executives or Connecticut politicians—and
perhaps a Fairfield butcher or hardware dealer—to join
him on a fishing party on Long Island Sound. On other
occasions, the yacht put in at Newport, Gloucester,
Marblehead, and Nantucket, and sometimes it went as
far north as Maine and as far south as Florida. Once
aboard his yacht, Coster would unbend somewhat and
drop the stiff Teutonic manner that characterized his
workaday life. Sometimes he even forgot about his ul-
cers long enough to take a drink or two. "After a couple
of highballs, he wasn't a bad guy," one of his guests
has recalled. "He had a real belly laugh." An experienced fisherman who went along on a couple of the
Carolita's weekend cruises was bemused to find that
his host insisted on having a member of the crew take
over a guest's line at the first sign of a nibble and haul
it in. Among the guests who signed their names in the
Carolita's leather-bound log was Sidney Weinberg; after his name he scrawled, "I'm for McKesson & Robbins and Coster, that's all." Coster, according to his sail-
ing companions, never liked to talk business on the
yacht; he preferred politics, and frequently assailed
President Roosevelt. (He was given to writing long letters criticizing the New Deal and mailing them, special

delivery, to the White House.) During one cruise, he fell to talking about the career and suicide of Ivar Kreuger, the Swedish match millionaire who turned out to be an international swindler. "It's a terrible thing when a man like that goes back on himself," a member of the party remembers his saying.

There appeared to be a sound basis for the respect that Coster's associates had for him as a businessman and for the faith that thousands of investors had in Mc-Kesson & Robbins securities. Under his leadership, the rise of the drug firm was undeniably phenomenal. Coster bought the firm in 1926 for a million dollars; by 1937 the company's sales were listed at a hundred and seventy-four million, its earnings at four million, and its assets at eighty-seven million. What Coster had acquired for his million was little more than a fine name. McKesson & Robbins had once been one of the biggest drug distributors in the country, but in the nineteen-twenties it had been losing money and curtailing its operations to such an extent that, physically, there was nothing left for Coster to take over except an obscure factory in Brooklyn that was desultorily engaged in turning out a moderately popular tooth powder and a few less well-known products. Coster closed the Brooklyn plant down, moved its equipment to the Fairfield plant of Girard & Co., and put out a number of new products under the McKesson & Robbins label. What was more important, in October, 1927, he organized a Canadian affiliate—McKesson & Robbins, Ltd.—which had little trouble selling nearly a million dollars' worth of stock to an investing public that in those days was eagerly snapping up anything. In this venture he had the financial help of the officers of the Bridgeport-City Trust Company, who had also backed his purchase of the Brooklyn firm. The Bridgeport bankers simply couldn't get over Coster's brilliance. "We were impressed by the tremendous dynamic power behind this man," Horace B. Merwin, the president of the Bridgeport-City Trust, said later. "He completely took our breath away. We country boys figured that we better let go the tail of the bear." But Merwin and his associates did not let go; on the contrary, they kept tightening their grip. At the end of 1927, when Coster was able to show them earnings of six hundred thousand dollars and came forward with a breathtaking proposal to merge all the nation's leading regional drug firms into his company, they, in conjunction with an investment firm in Waterbury, Connecticut, and two large New York investment houses—Goldman, Sachs and Bond & Goodwin—agreed to go along with him to the extent of underwriting a thirty-six-million-dollar issue of new stock and bonds. Thus buttressed, Coster during the next few years brought into the McKesson & Robbins fold as subsidiaries almost all the large regional wholesale drug houses in the country—sixty-six of them, in as many cities—by persuading their owners to exchange their private, family-owned stock, which would create terrifying inheritance-tax problems for their heirs, for more readily negotiable McKesson & Robbins securities, which would not be likely to depress the market severely if sold in large blocks to pay inheritance taxes. In addition, the owners of the private firms became salaried vice-presidents of the parent concern. In all these negotiations, Coster remained pretty much behind the scenes; it was Thompson, his invaluable front man, who not only cajoled Wall Street bankers into backing the enterprise but went out on the road and lined up the first fifteen wholesale houses to throw in their lot with McKesson & Robbins.

To a considerable degree, Coster's success in putting over this extraordinary series of mergers can be attributed to the precarious condition of the drug market in the United States at the time he came on the scene. The growth of such mammoth chain-store organizations as Walgreen's and Liggett's was threatening to choke out small retail druggists, and this, in turn, was threatening to choke out the regional wholesalers. What

Coster offered the individual wholesaler was local autonomy, centralized manufacture, and the advantage of being able to supply the druggists in his territory not only with his own products, under his own label, but with the products of all the other drug houses in the McKesson & Robbins orbit, under their various labels. This arrangement made it possible for the wholesaler to compete with the big chains, and by the end of 1929 the combined wholesale outlets were selling drugs at the rate of a hundred and forty million dollars' worth a year. While only about ten per cent of these drugs bore McKesson & Robbins labels, all the profits were funnelled into a holding company called McKesson & Robbins, Inc., a Maryland corporation, which Coster created as the financial nerve center of his far-flung interests. From its offices in New York, it controlled McKesson & Robbins of Connecticut, McKesson & Robbins of Canada, McKesson & Robbins of London (an insignificant offshoot), McKesson Wholesalers, Inc., the McKesson Development Corporation, and Isdahl & Co., a Norwegian manufacturer of cod-liver oil. It was of this colossus that Thompson was treasurer, presiding over its gigantic stock offerings, bond dealings, and bank loans.

Although he was extremely active in setting up subsidiaries, Coster prudently let men more familiar than he was with the intricacies of American drug wholesaling run the show. He devoted his own attention to an entirely separate branch of the business—the international buying and selling of crude drugs. One of the things about Coster that impressed Thompson was the learning he professed. Coster let it be known that he held both a Ph.D., in chemistry, and an M.D. from the University of Heidelberg, and that in the course of his studies there, he had become an expert on crude drugs the world over. Consequently, it seemed only logical that he should make a specialty of trading and speculating in such pharmaceutical ingredients as Spanish saffron, balsam of Peru, balsam of fir Canada, oil of dillseed, oil of orange, oil of peppermint, oil of lime, oil of ginger, oil of juniper berries, oil of geranium rose Algerian, oil of sandalwood East Indian, oil of snakeroot, oil of lavender flowers, dragon's-blood powder bright, Mexican vanilla beans, and benzoin of Siam. As his associates understood the setup, Coster, working through agents, would place an order to buy a consignment of one or another of these exotic products in a country where the price was low, and then store it until he could find a buyer who was willing to pay more for it. The company's books showed an average profit of ten per cent on these deals. Coster was much respected by the other directors of McKesson & Robbins for his comprehensive knowledge of conditions in the world crude-drug market. "I think I could get a better price at Mitsui," he might remark at a board meeting, or, "Now is certainly the time to send someone to Chile to look into iodine." Not only did this sound good but the company's books showed that it *was* good, in dollars and cents; according to them, the crude-drug department never lost money.

Coster ran the department from the Fairfield plant —quietly, with a small, personally chosen group of assistants. Its day-to-day operating head was George Dietrich, a ten-thousand-dollar-a-year assistant treasurer, who signed all the Connecticut company's checks, occupied an office adjoining Coster's, and maintained a closer business relationship with him than anyone else. Dietrich, like Thompson, had been associated with Coster since Mount Vernon. Dietrich's younger brother, Robert, who was purchasing agent for the shipping department of the Fairfield plant, was also active in the operations of the crude-drug division; whenever George Dietrich was out of his office, Robert would sit in for him. Except for a few members of the billing and shipping departments, no one besides Coster and the two Dietrichs had any idea of exactly how the crude-drug department operated; except for Coster, all the officers of the corporation worked in New York. The way the department did operate was this: Purchases of crude drugs were made through a group of five wholesale houses in Canada, which would be asked to quote a price when Coster wanted to place an order for a certain commodity. After looking over the quotations, George Dietrich would decide which one to accept, and Robert would prepare a formal purchase order in quadruplicate on regular McKesson & Robbins blanks. He would give these to his brother, who would keep the original and send the three copies through the firm's usual bookkeeping and accounting channels. All McKesson & Robbins mail at Fairfield was sorted out by George Dietrich into a rack installed in his office, and whenever an invoice announcing a Canadian purchase showed up, he would extract it and put it in his files. The invoice from Canada would eventually be followed by a debit advice from a firm identified in the McKesson & Robbins files as Manning & Co., a private commercial bank in Montreal, indicating that the Canadian wholesaler who had bought the drugs for McKesson & Robbins had been paid for them by Manning on behalf of the Fairfield firm. The amount of this debit advice would be entered on the McKesson & Robbins cashbooks in Manning & Co.'s favor.

When it came to disposing of crude drugs, all sales were handled by the Montreal office of W. W. Smith & Co., Ltd., which was known around McKesson & Robbins as a Canadian and British sales agency owned by the Manning bank. On one of its business forms, the Smith firm described itself as "commission merchants, purchasing, forwarding, steamship agents"; as having been established in London in 1857; and as maintaining offices in Hamburg, Genoa, Liverpool, Marseille, Melbourne, Colombo, Bombay, Hong Kong and Brooklyn, as well as Montreal. When a sale was made—always in a foreign country, and usually in some part of the British Empire—a sales order would be filled out in quadruplicate in Fairfield; one copy was sent to the customer, to inform him that the goods had been shipped, and the others went to the bookkeeping and accounting departments in Fairfield. Presently, the sales order would be followed by a bill addressed to W. W. Smith & Co. for collection; copies of this were also routed through channels. When a bill was paid, a credit slip would arrive in Fairfield from W. W. Smith, stating that the sale had been carried out and that the proceeds had been deposited with Manning & Co. The Manning account on the McKesson & Robbins books in Fairfield would then be adjusted to reflect this credit. McKesson & Robbins paid Manning & Co. an annual fee of twelve thousand dollars for its services; W. W. Smith & Co. received a commission of three-quarters of one per cent on all crude-drug sales and a flat fee of fifteen hundred dollars a month, all of which averaged out to about a hundred and fifty thousand dollars a year. As a matter of course, McKesson & Robbins always listed as part of its assets both the inventories of crude drugs being held in its name in Canada and the accounts receivable from crude-drug buyers.

Although the Dietrich brothers seemed to be close to Coster during business hours, and although they and their wives lived nearby, the Costers remained aloof from them socially. George Dietrich was essentially a family man; he and his wife, Claire, an extrovert blonde, had five children and lived in a large, friendly house that was full of gadgets and games. As a sideline, George and his wife dabbled, with some success, in local real estate. Robert Dietrich, who was married to a quiet, re-tiring girl named Anne, and had two children, was ex-tremely civic-minded. He was an enthusiastic Mason, helped run the McKesson & Robbins baseball team, played the neighborhood Santa Claus at Christmas, and took an active part in the local government. Once, during a company ball game, an office clerk happened upon Coster and the two Dietrich brothers in the locker room of the company's gymnasium and overheard Coster say something to the others in Italian. Later in the day, the clerk, carried away by the democratic spirit of the occasion, ventured to ask his employer where he had learned Italian. Coster, looking as if he considered the question unduly familiar, baseball game or no baseball game, replied curtly that while he was a boy he had spent some time in Rome, where his father had been stationed as a member of the German diplomatic service. Ordinarily, McKesson & Robbins employees who valued their jobs did not ask Coster needless questions, and some of them privately considered him a martinet. "If you asked him one question he'd get sore, and if you asked him two he'd fire you," a man who worked there has recalled. Among themselves, his employees called him "the Duke." Coster, in turn, referred to his employees behind their backs as "the maggots," and he had very strong ideas about their conduct. "I have experienced no difficulty personally in having publishers of trade journals, curiosity seekers, and manufacturers keep away from making inquiries," he once wrote in an office memorandum. "All of these have come to me at some time or other, but only once. Then they have kept away from me thereafter. . . . If each of us tends to his own 'knitting' faithfully and conscientiously . . . the organization as a whole automatically is bound to be a success, and where success lies, fear of criticism ends."

One of the few persons who felt they could talk to Coster freely was Thompson. Physically, the two men were an oddly matched pair. Thompson was tall and thin, with a long, ascetic face and the general air of an intellectual, which was not lessened by the pince-nez he wore. Coster, on the other hand, was small and plump and poker-faced, with deep-set dark-brown eyes that glittered behind thick-lensed tortoise-shell spectacles; he wore a trim graying mustache that paralleled the downward slant of his eyebrows, giving him a rather dour expression. Coster was always formal with Thompson, but there seems little doubt that he genuinely admired him. A graduate of Princeton and a one-time student at Oxford, Thompson not only was highly thought of in Wall Street but was a gifted playwright;

indeed, his best-known effort, "The Warrior's Husband," produced in 1932, gave Katharine Hepburn her first starring role. Once or twice a week, Coster took a train to New York (if the weather was cloudy, he would carry a well-worn raincoat and an ancient umbrella with a crooked handle) and went to his office on East Forty-fourth Street. "He looked so different from the other men—so old-fashioned," a secretary of one of the directors there later recalled. As a rule, Coster didn't have much business to transact in his office and would be out most of the day, presumably conferring with his brokers. Sometimes, however, he and Thompson and two or three other officers of the company would lunch together, and on the way to and from the restaurant, Coster would walk by himself, a few feet ahead of the others. His companions were mildly amused by this habit. "At first, we thought he was being standoffish, or just plain rude," one of them said later. "But then we guessed he was simply absentminded and thinking of something else." It never occurred to any of them that the president of McKesson & Robbins, as he sauntered along the sidewalk by himself, seemingly abstracted by the problems of running a big and legitimate business, was perhaps the most frightened man in New York.

A routine part of Thompson's job as treasurer of the company was to keep an eye on how much money each department was making in proportion to the amount of capital invested in it. He was aware that the crude-drug department, while showing commendable large profits on the books, was plowing every dollar of them back into buying fresh inventory, instead of diverting part of them to help defray the expenses of management, and late in 1936 he mentioned the matter casually to Coster. Coster replied that since the department was obviously making a lot of money, this was no time to put a crimp in its operations. After all, he pointed out, McKesson & Robbins had extended considerable credit to a number of retail drugstores during the depression, to keep them from going under, and in doing so had inevitably taken some losses (Coster himself, with the disapproval of the other directors, had insisted on this munificence); now, with things getting better, the crude-drug department, if imaginatively operated and not tied down by corporate formalities, was in a position to help compensate for those losses. Thompson agreed that this reasoning made sense, and turned his attention to other matters. Early in 1937, however, the subject came up again, when the board of directors decided that the time had come to reduce the amount of the company's long-term bank obligations. As a means of raising the cash to pay off the banks, the directors ordered a company-wide four-million-dollar reduction or sale of inventories, and levied one million of the total on the crude-drug department. But at the end of the year, Thompson found that in spite of this order the department had added another million dollars' worth of crude drugs to the stocks that its books showed were stored in the Canadian warehouses. "That bothered me," Thompson said later. "I decided I'd just find out as much as possible about this thing."

Thompson began finding out in March, 1938, by sending for the company's copy of its contract with W. W. Smith & Co. Except for Thompson, Coster, and the two Dietrich brothers, no one at McKesson & Robbins knew anything about the Smith firm, and all Thompson actually knew about it was that Coster had always dealt with it. Thompson had never met a representative of the concern, but because it was a foreign one, he did not think this specially significant; through the years, he had become so familiar with the name that he had developed, as he afterward put it, "a feeling of continuity" that was tantamount to respect for the firm. From the contract that was now brought to him, he learned to his surprise that the Smith firm appearing on it as a signatory was not a Montreal but a New York corporation, and that performance of the contract was guaranteed by W. W. Smith & Co. of Liverpool, evidently the parent corporation. Apprehensively, Thompson walked down the block to Grand Central Station and consulted a Montreal phone book. He was reassured to find "W. W. Smith & Co., Ltd." listed in it, as well as the various Canadian warehouses where the records showed that McKesson & Robbins was storing drugs. Back in his office, Thompson sought to reassure himself further by consulting the Dun & Bradstreet reports on W. W. Smith and the Canadian warehouses—like practically every big company, McKesson & Robbins subscribed to the business-information service. He knew that these reports were in the files because he remembered glancing through them every year as they came in, but he hesitated to send for them; he desperately wanted to avoid stirring up rumors, and he suspected that his clerical staff might think something odd was afoot if he followed up his request for the Smith contract by an immediate request for more data on the firm. So, instead, he called a lawyer in Long Island city, a former college roommate of his, and asked him, as a personal favor to get hold of duplicate reports and send them over. When these arrived, Thompson was shocked to read in them that the Montreal office of the Smith company, which was supposedly selling a million and a half dollars' worth of drugs each year for McKesson & Robbins alone, was merely "a small space" put at the disposal of "persons travelling from Liverpool." The news about the Canadian warehouses was equally depressing. "There apparently was no business done at those addresses that amounted to anything," Thompson later told the Securities and Exchange Commission. "I again got this elusive situation—that they were just mailing addresses." Thompson next made a check on the Smith company's Liverpool office, and this time was not greatly surprised to get word that it was only an "accommodation address," and that in Liverpool the main Smith office was believed to be in Montreal. "I was terribly anxious to find out where the Smith people banked, because a volume of business *must* have been going through," Thompson subsequently told another hearing, this one conducted by the State of New York. "So I made a bank check in Liverpool, and again got a report back that they were unknown in banking circles there."

Having ascertained this much through clandestine investigation, Thompson now found himself, as he told the State hearing, "in a tremendously delicate and embarrassing situation." He went on to say, "I felt that if I went to the president with a suspicion but with no knowledge and he just explained the whole thing to me, I would either have to accept it or say, 'I think you are lying to me.' I could not prove he was lying to me, and I decided that the thing for me to do was just inform myself outside in every way I possibly could." Proceeding "tactfully and unostentatiously," Thompson asked several McKesson & Robbins employees what they knew about the firm's crude-drug business in general and about the Smith company in particular, and one of them—John McGloon, the McKesson & Robbins comptroller—revealed that he, too, at one time had had misgivings about Coster's conduct of the crude-drug department. "[McGloon] told me that he had taken it up with Coster some two years ago and that Mr. Coster had satisfied him . . . that everything was in order," Thompson recalled at the State hearing. (McGloon later elaborated on this episode, and considerably altered its significance, by saying that he had been sharply rebuffed by Coster for his inquisitiveness, and informed that further questions on the subject would be as unwelcome as they were unnecessary.) Thompson was more persistent than McGloon. "My responsibility to the stockholders was simply tremendous if anything was wrong," he told the State hearing. "I had helped put the thing together. I had helped sell securities in the beginning. It was inconceivable to me that there wouldn't be any assets. Mr. Coster was, in my opinion, too intelligent and too capable a man ever to let him-

self get into a position where he'd falsify books. . . .
So I said to myself, 'There must be some assets there.
For some reason that I don't know, he's kept this from
me and masked this thing.' "

Still trying to get to the bottom of Coster's relationship with the Smith firm, Thompson wrote to a well-
known British chemical house that, according to the
records, had bought a large order of McKesson & Robbins crude drugs from Smith. He received no reply.
He then enlisted the aid of an inquiry agent in London
to find out about another sale that Smith had supposedly
made to a British firm, and received the thoroughly up-
setting reply that the firm "knew nothing" of McKesson
& Robbins. It was now summer, but Thompson was
in no mood to take a vacation; instead, he stepped up
his private investigation, devoting to it "my odd moments on the side, every time I got a chance." At one
of those odd moments, some time in the middle of
October, he dug out a batch of records of the McKesson
& Robbins Connecticut company—records that he, in
his position as treasurer of the Maryland company, had
never before had occasion to inspect; as he told the
New York State hearing, "It wasn't my function to sit
down and analyze the details of accounting or the details of handling any particular department." As he
went through the records, however, it didn't take much
analyzing of accounting details for him to discover that
the large commissions W. W. Smith & Co. was receiving for the business it transacted for McKesson & Robbins were being paid in cash from the McKesson & Robbins treasury in Fairfield, and not, as he had
presumed all along, from the profits of the crude-drug
department. The implications of this were truly
ominous. As Thompson said later, it was his first indication that "real cash was moving out of the funds
of the manufacturing end of the business in Connecticut."

Learning from the same records that McKesson &
Robbins paid commissions to Smith with checks signed

by George Dietrich and issued on the Guaranty Trust Company, in New York, Thompson went to the bank and prevailed upon its officers to let him see some of the checks as they came through—after they had been cashed by the Smith company and before they were cleared and routed back to Dietrich, in Fairfield. The first two checks he was shown (one for a commission and the other for clerical expenses incurred by Smith while making a sale) led him to the discovery of two Smith bank accounts—with the Chase National Bank and with a New York correspondent of the Royal Bank of Canada. Neither account, it developed, was large or active. Thompson also found that Manning & Co. had a small, inactive account with the Chase bank. Since he had hoped to find a big and vigorous account, representing the large sums that he had assumed were pouring into the Manning bank from the sale of drugs abroad, this was the last straw. In Thompson's words, "I felt I had evidence enough and I'd have to do something about it immediately."

On Sunday morning, November 27th, Thompson went up to Fairfield and called on Coster at his home. The ostensible reason for the visit was to talk over the three-million-dollar bond issue that Coster was eager to put out, but as soon as the two men were alone together, Thompson asked for a full explanation of the W. W. Smith & Co. account. Coster promised to set it all down in a detailed memorandum, and then he switched abruptly to the subject of the bond issue, for which he needed the treasurer's approval. Thompson kept trying to get back to the question of Smith's sales of crude drugs, and Coster kept putting him off with promises that the memorandum would make everything clear. "I left with the feeling that I had been stalled," Thompson told his questioners at the State hearing, and they could see how he might have. The next day, Coster came to New York, and, at Thompson's suggestion, they had lunch together. In the restaurant, Thompson, clearly offended by his old friend's attitude, said he felt that Coster was holding something back from him. Coster smiled, and, as Thompson later recalled it, replied, "I want to smoke you out." When Thompson asked what he meant by that, Coster said "Well, there's something back of this. It must be a conspiracy of people in the New York office or something." Thompson then changed his tone and said severely, "There *is* a conspiracy in the New York office. In fact, it's right in your treasurer, and I will let you smoke me out." Coster got angry, accused Thompson of bad faith, and bluntly asked if the treasurer actually thought there were no assets in the crude-drug department. "You're too too smart not to have assets," Thompson replied. "But I've got to know what they are." Coster promised to produce some receipts for sales of drugs abroad. Thompson told him that as far as he had been able to discover, McKesson & Robbins hadn't bothered to insure its large stocks of crude drugs, and asked why. Coster, after a moment of fluster, replied that W. W. Smith & Co. had always taken care of that. After he had assured Thompson that he would go over the whole crude-drug operation with him in detail in the very near future, the two men left the restaurant. Neither had felt like eating much.

Thompson tried to get in touch with Coster the following day—Tuesday, the twenty-ninth—but was told that he was in bed with an attack of tonsillitis. At this point, the workings of the treasurer's mind became for a moment a matter of conjecture, but it is conceivable that as he fretted over the stymie posed by Coster's illness, it occurred to him that what he had read in the Dun & Bradstreet reports his friend in Long Island City had sent him did not jibe with his vague recollection of the contents of the reports in his files. In any event, he now decided that things had progressed too far for him to worry about what conclusions his staff might draw, and he ordered a secretary to get him his own set of Dun & Bradstreet reports from the files. When they were brought to him, he found, to his dismay, that they did not correspond at all with the reports he had received from his friend; the W. W. Smith & Co. they pictured was a busy concern, with a staff of nine hundred and strong financial backing. Having reached the stage where any kind of chicanery seemed possible, Thompson felt it would be unwise to remove the set belonging to McKesson & Robbins from the office, so he had photostats made and took them down to the Dun & Bradstreet headquarters, at 290 Broadway. There he made still another discovery—the most shocking thus far. A Dun & Bradstreet official put in a call to the firm's Montreal office, where the information about W. W. Smith & Co. would have been assembled, and was told that nothing corresponding to the Smith entries in Thompson's reports had ever been forwarded from there. The Smith entries, said Montreal, must be forgeries. Montreal was correct. The entries, it later developed, were prepared, at Coster's direction, by a man who had worked for Bradstreet before it merged with R. G. Dun & Co., and was employed by McKesson & Robbins at the time. After drawing them up in what was actually the old Bradstreet style, according to subsequent expert testimony, he had had them typed out on Dun & Bradstreet stationery and had then given them to Coster, who had sent them through channels as the genuine article.

There are people who feel strongly in retrospect that the time had come when Thompson was no longer justified in keeping what he knew to himself—after all, a forgery is a forgery—and that he should have alerted the McKesson & Robbins board of directors, and perhaps the Securities and Exchange Commission as well. (As a matter of fact, at some time during the previous few days, the treasurer had confided a little of his apprehension to two members of the board—just how much it is impossible to say, for they, too, have since died—and they had advised him against making any public disclosure that might prove unwarranted and that would certainly do great injury to McKesson &

Robbins. As Thompson later told the S.E.C., "The important thing was to get something tangible. . . . This was all negative information and not positive. . . . I was absolutely convinced that there were assets somewhere that Coster had set up a screen to hide, that he was doing some other sort of business, I didn't know what.") Whatever the proprieties involved, two or three days after Thompson made the discovery about the fraudulent Smith reports he paid another call on Coster, who was still in bed, his throat apparently so sore that he could hardly speak. Thompson brought up the matter of the forged records, at which Coster became visibly perturbed. "Why, there is something wrong here—something wrong at Dun & Bradstreet!" he whispered hoarsely. After he had calmed down, he turned to the treasurer and asked, "Thompson, what do you want?" Thompson replied that he wanted to go to Montreal and have a look at the contents of the warehouses. Coster asked him instead to write out a list of questions covering all the information he wanted, and promised to get immediate answers by telegraph from W. W. Smith & Co. in Montreal or from the offices of the warehouses themselves. Again he urged Thompson to approve the new bond issue, and when Thompson refused to, Coster suggested that he "step down" as treasurer. As the conversation drew to a close, Coster grew angrier than Thompson had ever seen him. Shaking a finger, he said, "If you do anything to wreck the credit of McKesson & Robbins, you are going to regret it." He followed this up with another threat. "If you're not careful," he croaked, "I'll throw the company into receivership and wipe out the common stockholders!" Thompson pointed out how foolish that would be. "Why, you're the biggest common stockholder," he said. "You'd be the greatest sufferer."

The next afternoon, Thompson, feeling utterly wretched, went over to 1 Hansen Place, in Brooklyn, the address listed in the telephone book for the Brooklyn branch of W. W. Smith & Co. His spirits rose slightly when he found the building was an impressive one and that a directory in its lobby listed not only the Smith company but the Manning bank. Upstairs, on the glass panel of a door leading to a two-room suite, the names of both firms appeared below the name George Vernard. Vernard turned out to be a medium-sized, pudgy man, whom Thompson recognized at once. Ten years earlier, when Thompson had been preparing the analysis extolling the financial soundness of Coster's drug firm in Mount Vernon, Coster had given the Smith company as a reference and sent Thompson around to see Vernard, its local agent. At this second meeting, Thompson found Vernard as evasive as Coster had been; when Thompson asked what warehouses in Canada were storing McKesson & Robbins drugs, Vernard replied that he was merely the New York representative of the Smith and Manning outfits—his only staff was a secretary—and that any such information would have to come from their Montreal offices. When Thompson persisted, Vernard became incoherent, and the treasurer realized that he had been drinking.

Early in the afternoon of Monday, December 5th, Thompson called Coster, who was still sick at home, and told him flatly that he was going to bring the whole mysterious matter to the attention of the McKesson & Robbins executive committee without further delay. Coster muttered something unintelligible. At seven o'clock that evening, feeling relieved at the prospect of sharing his heavy burden, Thompson arrived at his apartment on Park Avenue just as the *Wall Street Journal* telephoned to inquire about the significance of the receivership that had been granted late that afternoon in Hartford. For a moment, Thompson was speechless with incredulity; then he remembered Coster's threat of a few days before. Two hours later, he told his associates about it at the emergency meeting in Sidney Weinberg's Sherry-Netherland apartment, and after they had heard the whole of Thompson's story, they concluded that Coster must in some way have instigated the court action, which would mean impounding the company's papers and thus hindering further investigation.

This conclusion turned out to be right. The receivership action had got quietly under way two days before, when one of Coster's attorneys visited Thomas J. Spellacy, the Mayor of Hartford and a well-known lawyer and businessman, and asked him for "advice." Without mentioning Coster, whom Spellacy had never met, the visitor said that "an officer" of McKesson & Robbins had told him that about twenty million dollars' worth of the company's assets "were not only now nonexistent but never had been in existence." After discussing the situation confidentially with some other lawyers, Spellacy suggested a temporary equity receivership —a standard legal formality to stop a company from doing business, while a court prepares for a full investigation of its affairs—and asked the city's corporation counsel to act as the petitioner; he himself agreed to be one of the two receivers. On Monday evening, at about the time the meeting in Weinberg's apartment began, the other receiver, a lawyer named Abraham Weissman, went over to the McKesson & Robbins plant in Fairfield and changed the combinations on the locks of the company's safe and vault. He was unaware that a large number of company files had already been removed from the office.

The morning after McKesson & Robbins was thrown into receivership, Coster turned up at his Fairfield office, arriving a little later than usual, and did something he had never been known to do before while at work. Opening a bottle of Martin's V.V.O. Scotch, a brand the company distributed to liquor retailers, he had a drink. Then he telephoned his New York office to say that he could not come to town, as he had agreed to do when Weinberg called him the night before, because he had been instructed by the receivers to stand by in Fairfield. Thompson, accompanied by three other Mc-

Kesson & Robbins officials, went up to Fairfield during the day to see the receivers and, according to his later testimony, found Coster "just sitting there, doing nothing. No one spoke to him and he didn't speak to anybody." While sitting in silence, Coster suffered an acute nosebleed. At eleven-thirty that morning, the Board of Governors of the New York Stock Exchange met and ordered an indefinite suspension of trading in McKesson & Robbins securities. The suspension, it was made clear, was voted not because of what the governors knew but because of what they did not know. In over-the-counter trading that day, McKesson & Robbins bonds broke from 103 to 57 and its common stock from 7½ to 1¼. In midafternoon, it was announced that William O. Douglas, in line with his promise to Weinberg on the telephone the night before, had ordered the New York office of the S.E.C. to investigate the case, and early the next morning, December 7th, two of its agents—Hector J. Dowd and Irving J. Galpeer—appeared at Coster's house in Fairfield to question him. He told them very little ("He was a beaten dog in a total fog," Galpeer reported), but he did say that he had probably placed "too much confidence" in George Dietrich. The S.E.C. men tried to question Dietrich, too, but he refused to talk before consulting an attorney. However, both agents noticed something that, if it had been noticed before by others, had not been commented on: Dietrich and Coster looked alike. Meanwhile, back in New York, Thompson, and Wilbur Cummings, the McKesson & Robbins lawyer, were appearing, before the Stock Exchange's stock-list committee to outline the background of the case as it had been disclosed by Thompson's detective work. Speaking of Coster's crude-drug department, Cummings made the most ominous observation any of the directors had thus far publicly voiced. "It may be that the whole thing is just a hollow balloon, just a shell," he said.

The next eight days were eventful and harrowing as,

one after another, a dozen federal, state, and local agencies began to investigate McKesson & Robbins, each after its own fashion. On Thursday, December 8th, the McKesson & Robbins executives in New York obtained a superseding receivership under the Chandler Act, a new law providing for an independent trustee in bankruptcy with strong investigative powers and a minimum of interference from stockholders' committees. William J. Wardall, a tall, bushy-browed man who was known for his ability to handle complicated corporate reorganizations, was appointed trustee of McKesson & Robbins and immediately moved into Coster's office on Fortyfourth Street. Meanwhile, the securities bureau of the New York State Attorney General's office had subpoenaed the Price, Waterhouse & Co. files on McKesson & Robbins and the records of the Smith company, and started to hold a series of informal hearings. Vernard, who appeared as the first witness, claimed to be in the real-estate business and said he merely acted "on the side" as a representative of W. W. Smith & Co. Far more important was the testimony of Albert B. Ritts, a senior accountant of Price, Waterhouse, who declared that while he and his staff had regularly gone over the records of McKesson & Robbins' crude-drug business, they had never asked its customers if they had actually bought the drugs, and had never inspected any warehouses to see if the physical inventories were what the records stated them to be. The company had not requested these services, both of which would have been very expensive, Ritts said, and it was not general accounting practice to make even a spot-check without a specific request. (As it was, McKesson & Robbins had paid Price, Waterhouse nearly a million dollars, over the years, for preparing its annual financial statements.) "Accountants are not competent to judge physical inventory," Ritts added. "They could show me a barrel of drugs and say it was thus and so, but I wouldn't know." Two more agencies entered the case over the weekend—the United States Attorney's office, which summoned a federal grand jury to consider evidence presented by the S.E.C., and the office of District Attorney Thomas E. Dewey, which was interested in ascertaining whether grand larceny in New York County was involved. In Fairfield, Coster, backed by his doctor, begged off from further questioning on the ground of ill health, and the S.E.C. investigators established that both Coster and George Dietrich had recently removed quantities of records from their office files.

In Montreal, investigators for the Attorney General and the S.E.C. separately confirmed the already strong suspicions that the Canadian warehouses that had been thought to be crammed with crude drugs simply did not exist. And the Montreal headquarters of Manning & Co. was found to be two small rooms in an office building at 1396 St. Catherine Street West, occupied by a single employee, named Violet Quesnot. Miss Quesnot, a small, middle-aged, and highly emotional French-Canadian brunette, reluctantly said that she had been hired in 1930 by Vernard, who told her that her only job would be to forward all correspondence she might receive to his Hanson Place address in Brooklyn, to place Canadian stamps on and mail all letters he might send her in a covering envelope from Brooklyn, and to follow whatever other instructions he might telephone to her from time to time. In response to calls from him, she had set up several mailing addresses in Montreal, Ottawa, and Toronto, using the names of companies he supplied, and had arranged with public stenographers and personal friends to forward to her whatever mail was received at them; Vernard had instructed her to pay these part-time agents from five to seven dollars a month, by money order. Miss Quesnot, who herself was paid twenty-seven dollars a week, said that all the mail she received from her colleagues was sent along unopened to Vernard. Presently, however, Vernard had told her to have her agents forward everything to him direct. Thereafter, Miss Quesnot declared, she had again found herself with a great deal of time on her hands as she kept her lonely vigil. "I just sit here waiting for a letter to come so I can send it on to someone else," she said, referring to periodic requests for accounting information from Price, Waterhouse, or from McGloon, the McKesson & Robbins comptroller; in such instances, Miss Quesnot would forward the letter to Vernard, who would have his secretary type out the reply and send it back to Miss Quesnot, for remailing with a Montreal postmark. Once in a while, Miss Quesnot added, Vernard broke the monotony of her business hours by paying her a visit, but since he did little while in Montreal except get drunk and telephone to friends in a place called Jack's Bar, in Brooklyn, she was always rather relieved when he went home and left her in solitude. A few blocks from the Manning office was the office of W. W. Smith & Co., Ltd., which Miss Quesnot had opened in 1934 at Vernard's direction, and where the current secretary, whom she had hired, was Betty Whyte, a pretty, eighteen-year-old blonde. The vigil of Miss Whyte, who received only seven dollars a week, was even duller than Miss Quesnot's. She relieved Miss Quesnot every day for an hour at lunchtime but otherwise had nothing to do except forward about two letters a month to Vernard. Miss Quesnot said that on December 2nd she had received a call from Vernard ordering her to burn all the records in both the Manning and the Smith offices; she and Miss Whyte had pitched in and spent the whole weekend at the task, lugging the contents of their files to a building across the street from the Manning office, where Miss Quesnot had got permission from the superintendent to use the furnace.

In Fairfield, the New York S.E.C. investigators were joined by one sent up from Washington—Frederic Curran, who spent a good deal of time questioning Coster's chauffeur, Frank Virelli. The chauffeur told Curran that he had frequently driven Robert Dietrich back and forth between Fairfield and a bank building

in Stamford, in which, he understood, McKesson &
Robbins had an office. Curran and Galpeer found the office, but it had been vacated and its files stripped of
their contents. In the bottom of a wastebasket, however,
were a few torn scraps of paper, which, when fitted
together, turned out to have been the wrapper of a
package sent by a printer named Solfleisch, at 124
White Street, Manhattan, to Vernard, at his Hanson
Place address. On being questioned, Solfleisch said he
had unsuspectingly printed many different letterheads,
bill forms, and invoice blanks for Vernard, all bearing
the names of Canadian companies, Manning and Smith
among them, and he produced several samples of the
letterheads that he still had in his shop, some of them
on fine English paper. In time, it was brought to light
that the Stamford office had played an important part in
Coster's maneuverings during the past few years. He
had opened it as a sort of communications center
around 1937, after Vernard's increasingly heavy drinking made him unreliable, and had installed a lone secretary—Rose Otting—to staff it. Miss Otting had at
her disposal five sets of letterheads and various business
forms, each for a different Canadian warehouse, as well
as a set for Manning and a set for Smith; she also had
seven typewriters, each with its own distinctive type. At
Robert Dietrich's direction, Miss Otting—using the appropriate letterhead or form and the corresponding
typewriter—typed out all the purchase and sales orders
for McKesson & Robbins crude drugs, as well as all
the firm's correspondence from Manning and Smith.
These documents were not sent up to Canada to be
remailed but were merely carried by Robert Dietrich to
his brother George, who sent them on through the routine channels of the McKesson & Robbins bookkeeping department. It never occurred to Miss Otting to
wonder about the seven typewriters; she simply accepted them as part of the incomprehensible abracadab-
ra of big business. When she was asked what significance she had attached to the seven letterheads, she

replied, "I thought they were all holding companies, or something."

Poring over some of the company's records that Coster and Dietrich had not got around to removing from the Fairfield office, the S.E.C. men were astonished at the brazenly slipshod way in which several of the lists of inventory had been compiled. "We figured that if they'd really had everything on hand that they claimed they had, they'd have needed a couple of buildings as big as the Empire State to hold it all," Galpeer said. Anyone with a knowledge of the available sources of crude drugs would have realized instantly that the inventories were spurious. For example, at one time McKesson & Robbins claimed to have on hand a supply of ketone musk, which is a perfume fixative derived from a gland of the Himalayan musk deer, that was greater than could have been obtained by annihilating the musk-deer population of Asia, and there was the same sort of reckless exaggeration in its listed stocks of castor-fibre paste, which is another fixative, derived from a gland of the beaver. The files also revealed some careless ways of addressing supposed shipments, such as "Ceylon, Asia," "Bavaria, Germany," and "Tasmania, Australia."

On the night of Sunday, December 11th, Henry Unterweiser, a veteran investigator for the Attorney General of New York State, was lying in bed in his Bronx apartment reading, as was his custom, the early, pink edition of the *Daily News*. Although Unterweiser hadn't been assigned to the McKessson & Robbins case, he was fascinated by it, and at this moment he was particularly fascinated by a picture of Coster, one of the first that had been printed. "Here I was looking at this picture," Unterweiser has recalled. "And then pretty soon I looked over at my wife, Mary—we have twin beds—and I said to her, 'This Coster looks like a guy I know, Mary.' 'You're crazy,' she said. You know how women are. But I kept looking at him, especially at those shrewd, piercing eyes, wonderful eyes—you could never forget them—and then I said to Mary, 'It looks like Phil Musica to me.' "

When Unterweiser arrived at work the next morning, he got in touch with Max Furman, the senior securities accountant of the Attorney General's office, who was working on the case, and told him he thought Coster was Musica.

"Who the hell is Musica?" Furman asked.

"He was once one of the biggest thieves in the country, and after that he used to work right here in this department," Unterweiser replied. "About twenty years ago."

"What was a thief doing working here?" Furman asked.

Unterweiser started to explain that Musica, after spending nearly three years in the Tombs on a swindling charge, and serving as a very useful stool pigeon during that time, had been hired by the Attorney General's office as a special investigator, but before he could get very far with his story, Furman had to dash off to one of the McKesson & Robbins hearings.

On Tuesday morning, a man telephoned the New York office of the S.E.C. and, without disclosing his name, said he was a Brooklyn attorney who had represented Coster in a case many years before. "I can tell you who he really is," he said, and gave the address of the office that he was calling from. An agent hurried over to have a talk with the lawyer. Covering a legal document on his desk with his hand, the lawyer asked, "If I give you this, what's in it for me?" "Nothing," replied the agent, but from where he sat he was able to read, at the bottom of the page, below the lawyer's palm, a typewritten name—Philip Musica. Later that day, the local S.E.C. called the Federal Bureau of Investigation in Washington and asked if there were any fingerprints or other records of a man named Philip Musica. There were none.

Meanwhile, Unterweiser had confided his hunch that Coster was Musica to other colleagues of his in

the State Attorney General's office, and they had dug
up a murky set Musica's fingerprints, together with
an old photograph of him and a record showing that he
had worked for the office as an investigator from 1916
to 1919, using the name of William Johnson. But
there seemed to be no immediate way of determining
whether Unterweiser was right or wrong in believing
Coster to be Musica, because the Attorney General of
New York had no legal right to fingerprint a suspect
in Connecticut. The atmosphere was becoming tense,
however, and during the afternoon of Wednesday, the
fourteenth, reporters covering the State Attorney Gen-
ral's hearings were told confidentially that there was
reason to believe Coster was Musica.

That same day, at around noon, federal warrants
were issued for the arrest of Coster, George Dietrich,
and Vernard, on charges of conspiring to file false information with the New York Stock Exchange. Vernard was arraigned in New York and set free on five
thousand dollars' bail. Coster insisted he was still too
ill to travel, so Irving R. Kaufman, then a young Assistant United States Attorney and now a Federal District
Court judge, went to Fairfield with some S.E.C. men,
picked up a local United States marshal, and arraigned
both Coster and Dietrich in Coster's home, where, in
the presence of Coster's attorney, the five thousand dollars' bail set for each defendant was quickly furnished.
Coster, wearing a brown bathrobe over trousers and a
shirt, seemed tired and listless. When the marshal declared him formally arrested, he said nothing and simply put his hand over his eyes, but a moment later,
when Kaufman asked for his fingerprints, he became
agitated and withdrew with his attorney to an adjacent
room, where they stayed for twenty minutes. When they
came back, Coster gingerly allowed his prints to be
taken. "This is pesky," he murmured. Back in New
York late that afternoon, Kaufman told his superior,
Acting United States Attorney Gregory F. Noonan,

"That man has a weird look in his eye. He'll either die a natural death or kill himself before this is over."

The astounding possibility that Coster might be Musica presented the press with a ticklish problem because of the laws of libel. Only one morning newspaper, the *Herald Tribune,* even alluded to it on Thursday, December 15th, and then it stated merely that the real identity of the president of McKesson & Robbins was in doubt. The afternoon papers that day were a bit bolder; two of them ingeniously noted "a curious parallel" between the McKesson & Robbins case and a fraud case in 1913, in which a young man named Philip Musica had swindled twenty-two banks out of six hundred thousand dollars by falsifying the records of a business that was supposedly engaged in the international purchase and sale of human hair, a commodity that was much in demand at the time for ladies' coiffures. Musica, the papers said, had served an indefinite term in jail and had then disappeared.

During the afternoon, the State Attorney General's office managed to obtain a copy of the set of Coster's fingerprints that Kaufman had brought back to the United States Attorney's office and tried to match them with Musica's, but the latter were so blurred that nothing definite could be established. At around four o'clock, a detective was dispatched to Police Headquarters with both sets of prints and instructions to ask Deputy Inspector Joseph Donovan, the head of the Bureau of Criminal Identification, if he could be of any help. Donovan found that, strangely, the Musica fingerprints that must have been placed in his office files at the time of the hair-swindle scandal were not there, but he remembered that some duplicate records of old cases were kept in the Sheriff Street precinct house, and sent some of his bureau's detectives there to look through them. At ten-thirty that evening, after a five-hour search, a bundle of papers relating to the hair-fraud case was discovered, and it included a musty but clear set of Musica's prints. Donovan compared them with

Coster's. They were identical. Reporters at Police Headquarters were immediately notified, and the startling news that F. Donald Coster, president of McKesson & Robbins, was in reality Philip Musica, the son of a poor Italian immigrant and the principal figure in not one but two previous swindles (the other, dating back to 1909, involved imported cheese), became a national sensation by morning.

During that morning—Friday, the sixteenth—the United States Department of Justice decided to supersede the S.E.C. indictment with an indictment for mail fraud, and the United States Attorney's office succeeded in getting the bail of Coster, George Dietrich, and Vernard raised from five thousand dollars to a hundred thousand dollars. Samuel MacLennan, an inspector for the New York branch of the Post Office Department, which was now in charge of the case, took a noon train to Fairfield to preside over the rearraignments of Coster and George Dietrich, while New York City detectives went around to rearrest Vernard at his home at 1421 East Thirty-fourth Street, Brooklyn. They found the doors and windows bolted, and it was not until they threatened to shoot their way in that Vernard, wearing striped trousers, a morning coat, and a piped vest, came out and surrendered. At just about the same time, Vernard's secretary, Eleonora Lochner, testifying at one of the State Attorney General's hearings, expressed the belief that her employer's real name might be Musica; she told of having come across the name, used as if it were his, in an angry letter that Vernard's wife, Catherine, had written to him three years earlier, during a suit for assault she had brought against him. Miss Lochner, who was paid twenty dollars a week—mostly, it seemed, for going out to a nearby restaurant and getting hangover cures (oysters and onions) for her boss—also testified that Vernard had recently asked her to look up the name Musica in the New York telephone directory and had seemed boozily relieved when she could not find it.

It was a gloomy Friday in the Coster house in Fairfield. Mrs. Coster and her brother, Leonard Jenkins, who from time to time did confidential work for Coster and was temporarily living with the couple, were concerned about his state of mind. Although Mrs. Coster and Jenkins were unaware of it, Coster had told George and Robert Dietrich during the preceding week that in the event of the exposure of his true identity he would commit suicide. Mrs. Coster and Jenkins did know, however, that three days before—Tuesday, the thirteenth—a maid had found a capsule of poison under Coster's pillow; the discovery had prompted Mrs. Coster to ask the gardener to hide three pistols that her husband kept in the house, and the gardener had put them in a woodshed. Coster couldn't sleep, and had been up most of Thursday night, brooding and drinking. He would talk to no one. At seven o'clock Friday morning, he came downstairs and had some orange juice and coffee, and then he returned to his bedroom. At about eleven, he switched on a radio on his bedside table and heard a Manhattan news broadcaster say that federal authorities were on their way to Fairfield at that very moment to rearraign him, as Philip Musica, and raise his bail, because it was feared he might escape.

Propped up beside the radio on the bedside table was a framed Harriet Beecher Stowe aphorism: "When you get into a tight place and everything goes against you till it seems as if you just couldn't hold on a minute longer—never give up then, for that is just the place and the time when the tide will turn." Coster picked up the inscription and carried it into his wife's room, next to his, where—worn out by worrying about him most of the night—she was asleep. He quietly placed it on her dressing table, and then went downstairs to a rear room, where Ricky, the parrot, was caged. For the next ten minutes Jenkins heard him talking amiably to the bird. Then the doorbell rang. It was George Dietrich, who walked into the sunroom at the front of the house and sank into a chair. Jenkins went to Coster and told him that Dietrich had arrived. Coster showed no interest, but he stopped talking to the parrot and started back upstairs. Halfway up, he turned and told Jenkins to bring him a drink.

At some time during the preceding three days while the rest of the household was otherwise occupied, Coster had poked around in the woodshed, found two of his pistols, and concealed them in a bureau drawer. Now, up in his bedroom again, he selected a .38-calibre police revolver, took it into the bathroom, and locked the door. Downstairs, Jenkins finished mixing a rye highball. "I went up and knocked on the bathroom door," he said later. " 'Are you all right?' I asked. 'Yes, I'll be right out,' Coster said. There was a moment's silence. Then I heard the shot."

Coster had placed the pistol against his right temple while standing in front of the washbasin mirror. He may have looked out of a window to his right and seen two cars entering his driveway. In the first was his lawyer and in the second was the local United States marshal, who had been instructed to assist MacLennan with the rearraignment. As Coster pulled the trigger, his glasses fell into the washbasin and he tumbled backward into the bathtub. The revolver dropped to the tile floor. Jenkins forced the door open just as the marshal came pounding up the stairs, and the two men carried Coster down and placed him on a couch in the living room. Coster fired the shot at nine minutes after noon, when MacLennan's train was just getting under way, and died six minutes later, without regaining consciousness. He had three dollars in his pockets, and two wallets. In one were some miscellaneous papers and in the other was a card on which he had written, "I am a Catholic, please notify a priest in case of accident." Although a suicide may not receive last rites, a priest was summoned anyway, but Coster was dead by the time he arrived. When Mrs. Coster, who had not heard the shot, was roused and told that her husband had killed himself, she cried, "Oh, Daddy, Daddy, why did you do it? Why didn't you face it?" Then she fainted, and after she was revived, she kept repeating, "Mama! Mama! Somebody help me!"

At almost exactly the moment that Coster shot himself, Vernard admitted to the United States Attorney in New York that his real name was Arthur Musica and that he was Coster's brother. He also admitted that George Dietrich was his brother George Musica and that Robert Dietrich was Robert Musica, the youngest of the four Musica brothers.

Coster left a four-page suicide note, scrawled in longhand, in which he contended that he was about the only virtuous individual ever associated with McKesson & Robbins. "The alleged millions 'lost' are simply 'profits' . . . they were cash sales to create a profit that did not exist," Coster declared in his note. "Bankers, lawyers, auditors, appraisers, and incompetent high-salaried executives have bled McKesson & Robbins white. The company should have been in receivership at the time of the crash . . . and again in 1932 if its profits had not been bolstered in a frantic effort to save [it]. . . . No man has ever worked harder or received less pay to make something work out for the interests of all. . . . There are no hidden treasures anywhere. . . . It was a case of who put the company into receivership first to stop the orgy first—Wall Street lawyers on the board won. As God is my judge, I am the victim of Wall Street plunder and blackmail in a struggle for honest existence. . . . Oh, merciful God, bring the truth to light. . . ."

Coster's suicide by no means cleared up the mystery of his operations; on the contrary, since he alone knew all the ins and outs of what he had been up to, his abrupt departure actually complicated the task of setting his company's affairs in order. The job faced by Wardall, the trustee, was a staggering one. A former investment banker, he had been winding up another reorganization proceeding when, on December 8th, he received a midmorning call from a judge in the United States District Court asking if he would take over as trustee of McKesson & Robbins. He at once set about clearing up his other obligations, and a few hours later, knowing nothing about the drug business, he was sitting at Coster's desk in the East Forty-fourth Street office and running the largest drug-distributing company in the United States, a job he was to hold down for the next two and a half years. Wardall quickly decided to try to keep McKesson & Robbins going, rather than throw it into bankruptcy, because he could see at a glance that three-fourths of the firm's business came from its wholesale distribution of some fifty thousand products to some thirty thousand domestic outlets, and that this was in no way affected by Coster's supposed foreign manipulations; from the outset, the trustee's big problem was to save a successful company whose reputation seemed about to be destroyed by a fraud that actually involved only about a quarter of the firm's total listed assets. It was up to Wardall to convince the public of the firm's essential soundness, deal with seven thousand creditors, and pacify several groups of stockholders and bondholders; altogether, claims totalling thirty-five million dollars were entered against the company. It was also necessary, if McKesson & Robbins was to get back on its feet, to have knowledgeable men in strategic positions, and this meant keeping key executives in their jobs. Under S.E.C. regulations, directors holding stock in the company were subject to negligence suits, based on the receipt of unwarranted dividends from securities that Coster had inflated. The S.E.C. wanted Wardall to file these suits, but he persuaded the Commission that the company's good name was the important thing, and that it would be better all around to seek restitution privately. ("I'm more interested in assets than arrests," he said at one point.) In the end, he retrieved six hundred thousand dollars in cash and stock from nine of the sixteen remaining directors. He also recovered two million dollars from other sources, including five hundred and twenty-two thousand dollars from Price, Waterhouse & Co. The firm stoutly insisted that it had done its job properly under the "prevailing" system of accounting, and described as "unbridled hindsight" an S.E.C. declaration that it had "failed to employ that degree of vigilance, inquisitiveness, and analysis" that was called for in auditing the inventories and accounts receivable of McKesson & Robbins' crude-drug division. Price, Waterhouse witnesses referred to Coster's "ceaseless experimentation with the limitations of accountancy" and one of them noted that shortly before Coster killed himself, he had been reading Morrill Goddard's "What Interests People and Why" and had underlined the sentence "The truth, which the public has never been told, is that no practical system has ever been devised by which the complicated finances of a large institution can be thoroughly checked so that every transaction is verified, except at prohibitive time and cost."

In the course of Wardall's campaign to convince the public of the basic soundness of McKesson & Robbins, he bought advertising space in newspapers in sixty-seven cities to point out that "the sensational criminal charges" brought against it had not deterred suppliers, retailers, and consumers from continuing to do business with the firm. (He also persuaded three motion-picture companies that it was not a propitious time to make a film based on the life of Philip Musica.) His methods produced results. In spite of the early adverse publicity, McKesson & Robbins sales for December, 1938, were only 3.9 per cent less than the sales for the previous December; by the end of the second quarter of 1939, sales exceeded the mark set during the corresponding period of 1938. The company's net profits for 1939, before interest payments and federal taxes, reached $4,879,306, and in 1940 they were $5,733,281—even more than the fictitious previous high that Coster had established in 1937 on the basis of his crude-drug paper earnings. Trading in McKesson &

Robbins stock was resumed on the New York Stock Exchange on July 15, 1941, after a reorganization plan submitted by Wardall had been approved by stockholder groups, the S.E.C., and the courts, and the company was returned to private ownership. New debentures and preferred issues offered in connection with the reorganization sold out rapidly. McKesson & Robbins has prospered ever since.

Before Wardall quit work on his first day as trustee, he had hired S. D. Leidesdorf & Co. as his accountants and Winthrop, Stimson, Putnam & Roberts as his legal counsel. It was months before the investigators felt that they had a fair understanding of the mechanics of the swindle, and more months before they could assess the damage done—both in dollars embezzled and in injury to the name of McKesson & Robbins. The money spent in straightening things out—not only by Wardall but by federal, state, and local agencies—came to around three million dollars, or almost as much as it was finally decided Coster stole. The amount he apparently stole was arrived at only after three hundred Leidesdorf accountants had worked a total of a hundred and forty-six thousand manhours tracking down ninety-one bank accounts, fifty-seven brokerage accounts, and ten loan accounts that Coster and his associates had used in the course of the twelve years he was president of McKesson & Robbins. It was ultimately ascertained that during that time Coster sluiced a total of $135,000,000 in cash and checks through these hundred and fifty-eight accounts. This staggering figure, however, is more indicative of the man's genius at juggling figures than of the extent of his larceny, for the amount of money he actually withdrew from the company's treasury to support his fictitious purchases of drugs was only $25,-000,000, and of this sum he returned 21,800,000, which was entered on the books as profits. The difference between these two figures—$3,200,000—was the amount, the accountants decided, that Coster must have stolen. Their findings were far from conclusive even on this point, though. They could not prove that he had put any specific sum in his own pocket; the $3,200,000 was simply money that could not be tracked down. As a matter of fact, it was generally believed that after 1931, when the company's cash balance reached a precariously low point, Coster cut down drastically on his stealing, and that after 1935 the only money he siphoned off from McKesson & Robbins and did not return was the $150,000 or so paid annually as "commissions" to W. W. Smith & Co. for supposedly handling his foreign purchases and sales of drugs, and the $12,000 paid annually to Manning & Co. for its part in taking care of the financial aspects of the negotiations. While it is true that he continued, and even stepped up, his imaginary buying and selling of crude drugs, it was thought that he did so principally in an effort—a commendable one, he appears to have come to consider it—to give the public a rosy picture of his firm's financial health and thus boost the value of McKesson & Robbins stock.

As to where the unaccounted-for $3,200,000 went, one can only guess. Coster and his brothers may have lived on a scale in excess of their legitimate incomes, but certainly not to a spectacular degree. Coster is known to have lost at least a million dollars in the stock-market crash of 1929 (on one black October afternoon of that year, he gave his brokers three checks for a hundred and fifty thousand dollars each, to meet their demands for more margin), and it is known that he had stolen a like sum by that time. But that still leaves more than two million dollars that vanished somewhere. For Coster, by the standards of men in his elevated position in the business world, died broke; his estate—apart from two hundred and fifty thousand dollars in life-insurance policies, some of which the trustee appropriated for the benefit of creditors—came to a mere thirty-six thousand two hundred dollars, and of that the valuation placed on the Carolita accounted for thirty-five thousand. (The yacht was later sold to a Chicago man for fifteen thousand dollars.) The ten per cent of the McKesson & Robbins common stock that Coster was thought to own was never traced to any of his various identities or dummy accounts. Probably the best explanation of what became of the money he stole is that it went for blackmail. Although the extent to which Coster was victimized in this fashion is impossible to determine, it was definitely established after his death that an old associate of his Musica days, Benjamin Simon, regularly served as his go-between in dealing with blackmailers, paying them off in cash. Among Coster's more persistent tormentors were Giuseppe Brandino and his sister, whom he had double-crossed while the three of them were partners in a bootlegging business in Brooklyn back in 1920. Occasionally, while Coster was sitting at his desk in his office on the second floor of the Fairfield plant, he would look out the window and see Brandino pacing back and forth in the street below—an unwelcome sign that it was time for another payment. Then the president of McKesson & Robbins would send for Simon, who was on the company's payroll under at least three different names, and tell him to go downstairs and haggle with Brandino, and pay him off as cheaply as possible.

Simon, a stooped, hook-nosed, bespectacled little man with a syrupy voice, performed other important tasks for Coster. In 1935, he arranged with a midwife to sign and file false birth certificates for Coster and his brothers. At about the same time, he completed an even stranger mission. He went to New Orleans, from which Coster—then Musica—and five members of his family had attempted to leave the country in 1913, following the exposure of the human-hair fraud, and there he filed a petition in bankruptcy for Philip Musica. His reasons for doing this are obscure, but the most generally accepted theory is that Coster had blackmailers in New Orleans who dealt with him only through Simon and still knew him only as Musica. Perhaps Simon's most dramatic known exploit on Coster's behalf was to act as his agent when, later in his career, Coster undertook to become an international gun trader, presumably in a desperate attempt to turn a quick profit with which to liquidate the crude-drug department. Just how deeply involved Coster became in this project is not clear, but there is no doubt that on more than one occasion he did attempt to sell American-made arms abroad. Early in 1937, either directly or through Simon, he made at least one offer to sell guns to Mexico, according to a representative of the Mexican government, and in May and June of 1938, according to a contract produced by one of his former lawyers at a hearing before the New York State Attorney General, he tried to arrange for the sale of a hundred thousand .30 calibre rifles (made for the United States Army in 1917), each with a bayonet and a thousand rounds of ammunition, to "a friendly, non-belligerent consignee." The contract was drawn up between McKesson & Robbins and a British concern called the Standard Oil Company of England, which proved to be non-existent; the friendly, non-belligerent consignee was reputedly China. At least two other witnesses testified at government hearings after Coster's death that Simon had approached them in connection with gun deals, and a Bridgeport banker testified that Simon had tried to get him to help finance a shipment of arms. But Coster had apparently lost his wizard's touch as a promoter for, as far as is known, he never made a cent selling weapons.

From the standpoint of criminal prosecution, the results of the many investigations were anticlimactic, although, in expenditure of time and effort, the case was the biggest that has ever confronted the Post Office Department; it dragged on for two years and involved the scrutiny of more than a million pieces of correspondence. Eventually, the three remaining Musica brothers—George, Arthur, and Robert—were indicted, and pleaded guilty to conspiracy and fraud; George was sentenced to two and a half years in prison, Arthur to three, and Robert to one and a half. Mrs. Coster's two brothers, Leonard and John Jenkins, pleaded guilty to conspiracy charges; John was sentenced to a year and a day, and Leonard received a suspended sentence. Coster's old sidekick, Simon, also pleaded guilty, and was sentenced to three years. Only one man of the three whose cases went to trial was found guilty. That was McGloon, the company comptroller; after a three-month trial, a jury decided that he should have become sufficiently leery of Coster's accounting methods to alert the S.E.C., and he was sentenced to a year and a day and fined five thousand dollars. The two other defendants—Merwin, the president of the Bridgeport-City Trust Company, and Rowley W. Phillips, an officer of the Waterbury investment firm, were acquitted.

The principals in the case and most of their relatives soon drifted out of sight. The three surviving Musica brothers served their prison terms and were released. Arthur and Robert, both of whom worked in defense plants during the war, were separated from their wives, and after their periods of probation were up, they disappeared. George continued to operate his real-estate business in Fairfield until he died, in 1947. The Musicas' mother, Assunta, who served as her son Philip's agent in Naples at the time he perpetrated his human-hair fraud, died in 1941, at the age of eighty, while her three less celebrated sons were still in jail. She had been living for years with two of her four daughters—Marie and Evelyn—in a twelve-room Italian-style house called Meadowbrook, three miles from Westbury, Long Island, where Coster visited her frequently and telephoned her every day. (He often sent a McKesson & Robbins truck to Long Island to deliver medicine for a heart ailment she suffered from.) The two sisters achieved quite a local reputation as eccentrics. They dressed in Victorian clothes, and were known for their generosity in distributing free drugs (also courtesy of McKesson & Robbins) to the poor.

(Another sister, Lucy Grace, died in 1920, and the fourth, Louise, married the chief gardener of a Hudson River estate and pretty much withdrew from the clan.) Marie Musica died six or seven years ago, and afterward Evelyn sold the Westbury house and moved to Queens; she, too, has since disappeared. Mrs. Coster remarried in 1947. With her third husband, she still lives on the Fairfield estate, part of which she recently sold to a hospital. After Coster's death, she continued to raise chows in the rear of the garden, and to keep a parrot, as he did. Her neighbors in Fairfield say that she has always maintained that Coster was a great and wronged man.

The Fertilizer Tanks that Weren't

3

More often than contemporary economic historians care to admit, something happens to the clear-eyed, firm-jawed, broad-browed American business hotshot. His whole aspect—his face, his behavior and even his temperament—becomes distorted. A bizarre streak works an imbalance on the regular features of his personality and, quite abruptly, he is different.

The streak is corruption.

Judging by the precociousness and promise of his youth, Billie Sol Estes should have developed into one of the bigger-than-life Texan heroes and become one of the country's greatest contemporary businessmen. The son of a Texas farmer and lay preacher, Billie Sol was only 13 years old when his father gave him a ewe lamb. Two years later, the youth had a flock of 100 sheep for which he collected $3,000.

While still in high school, he built such a reputation that he was able to borrow $3,500 from a local bank on his own signature. With it, he bought government surplus grain—it later became one of his specialties—and sold it at a nice profit. And when he was 28, his fortune and reputation had reached a point which compelled the U. S. Junior Chamber of Commerce to name him one of the year's ten outstanding young men.

But in the next five years, his successful methods took a different tangent, helped by a chemical company to whom he was so deeply in hock that it unwittingly staked him to a series of exploits that raised a national odor. Wheeling-dealing via a parlay of both actual and nonexistent assets and properties, he erected in a nine-year period the largest and most fragile financial house-of-cards in years. When it finally collapsed, the dust drifted from Texas up through the Southern tier of states and northward to Washington, where it besmirched the reputations of Congressmen, forced the resignations of bureaucrats and even managed to creep under the White House door.

Perhaps it was simply that the zest with which Billie Sol legitimately became a millionaire before he was 30 ran wild in the later exploits that produced a nationwide scandal. In his frenetically imaginative mind, it seemed, was there was so much of a difference between buying a cotton farm when gins everywhere were closing because business was so bad and expanding his grain operations in order to get more federal money to pay for the great amounts of fertilizer that he sold at a loss?

Oddly enough, he might have got away with his shenanigans a good deal longer, with fraud, payoffs, antitrust violations, but for one totally unexpected complication. During the height of his activities, he lost a race in Pecos for a seat, of all things, on the local school board, mainly because a twice-weekly newspaper, the *Independent,* opposed him. To get even, he set up a rival newspaper. The *Independent*'s editor retaliated by printing the first exposure of how Billie Sol sold mortgages on nonexistent fertilizer tanks. The *Independent* won the Pulitzer Prize—and Billie Sol went to prison.

He served six years and was paroled in April 1971. By then, he had lost his entire fortune and was precluded from engaging in any self-employment or promotional activity without first obtaining prior approval from the Board of Parole. The May 1962 article in *Time* succinctly tells the whole incredible story.

The Decline and Fall of Billie Sol Estes

Agriculture Secretary Orville Freeman was on the grill. What were his associations with Billie Sol Estes? Freeman shrugged, hopelessly and helplessly. He had, he told newsmen, met Estes once, briefly, when Estes was paying one of many visits to Agriculture Department headquarters in Washington. Said Freeman: "I might recognize him in pictures." Then he mustered up a bit of bitter humor: "I'm sure I'll never forget the name." The newsmen laughed.

But the Billie Sol Estes case was no laughing matter —to Freeman or anyone else. It was the case of a welfare-state Ponzi. It was a scandal that had already brought about the resignation or dismissal of four Kennedy Administration officials. It had politicians and bureaucrats of all degrees and of both parties shaking in their boots. It had set off investigations galore. It had called into question the whole administration of the mighty U. S. Department of Agriculture.

[The] official line from the White House was that the worst was already over, that further investigations would not disclose any more facts that might embarrass the Administration. In fact, the worst might be still to come. Important documents in the Estes case were carefully hidden from outside gaze. The hefty Agriculture Department file on Estes was being guarded as if it contained plans for an anti-missile missile. Down in Pecos, Texas, Federal Receiver Harry Moore, presiding over the ruins of the Estes empire, refused to let newsmen even peek at the "financial journal" in which Billie Sol had recorded his receipts and expenditures over the years. Until the full record was open to scrutiny, the Estes scandal was the hottest thing around.

According to President Kennedy, 76 FBI agents were working on the case. Receiver Moore's office in Pecos was jammed with feds poring over Billie Sol's papers. "I have working in this office at the moment," said Moore, "six Senate investigators, five men from the FBI, and four auditors—and twelve more are on the way." In Washington, the Senate Permanent Subcommittee on Investigations unanimously voted to hold a full-scale investigation of the Estes case, with public hearings to begin as soon as Chairman John McClellan [saw] fit. . . . In addition, a House Government Operations Subcommittee, newly supplied with a special $400,000 appropriation voted by the House, was undertaking its own investigation of Estes' involvements in federal farm programs. Under way in Texas were federal and state grand jury investigations, plus an inquiry by State Attorney General Will Wilson.

Arkansas' tough John McClellan promised that the Senate investigation would be "full, thorough and complete." A veteran of many messy investigations, including 1957–58's marathon inquiry into the Teamsters Union, McClellan ominously summed up the Estes case as "the darnedest mess I've ever seen."

The man who made the mess is a bundle of contradictions and paradoxes who makes Dr. Jekyll seem almost wholesome. Billie Sol (pronounced "soul" in West Texas) never smoked or drank. He considered dancing immoral, often delivered sermons as a Church of Christ lay preacher. But he ruthlessly ruined business competitors, practiced fraud and deceit on a massive scale, and even victimized Church of Christ schools that he was supposed to be helping as a fund raiser or financial adviser. He pursued money relentlessly but, despite energy, ingenuity, cunning and a dazzling gift of salesmanship, ended up not only broke but hopelessly in the red—by $12 million according to his own figures, by $20 million according to Texas' Attorney General Wilson. "The sad part of it," says a Pecos bank president, "is that he could have been an honest millionaire instead of a broke crook."

Billie Sol grew up in an environment of a sort that is supposed to produce not crooks but plain, solid, honest people—the kind often referred to as the salt of the earth. One of six children, he was raised on a prairie farm near Clyde, Texas. His sturdy, sunburned parents worked hard and went to Church of Christ services every Sunday. "We've never had any trouble in this family," [said] his father. "Why, I've never even gotten a parking ticket in my whole life." The father still [refused] to believe that Billie Sol really did anything wrong: "The Constitution says a man ain't guilty until they prove it, and they ain't proved anything on Billie yet."

The family was so poor that Billie Sol's mother sold home-churned butter from door to door to help meet the mortgage and insurance payments. Billie Sol made up his mind early in life that he was going to be rich. While other West Texas farm boys were thinking about shooting crows or catching fish after the chores were done, Billie Sol was precociously thinking up deals. His father fondly remembers an event that took place when Billie was about twelve: "I was plowing behind a team of horses, and he came out there to talk to me. I remember he was barefoot. He said he'd been thinking about a tractor and said he thought he could get one in a trade for a barn of oats we had. I told him to go ahead and try. He went off and came back with a tractor."

Billie Sol started out in farming, and he prospered at it. By the time he was 28 he was doing so well as a cotton farmer that the U.S. Junior Chamber of Commerce named him one of the U.S.' ten outstanding young men of 1953. Billie Sol traveled to Seattle to receive the award at a Jaycee dinner. While in Seattle he uttered some prophetic lines: To be successful, he said, "you have to walk out on a limb to the far end—for that's where the fruit is. If it breaks, you learn how far to go next time."

Another top-ten award winner that year was Tennessee's Frank Clement, then the youngest state Governor in the U.S., later famous in a way for his florid keynote speech ("How long, O how long?") at the 1956 Democratic Convention. With many similarities of temperament and style, Clement and Estes became fast friends. Clement made Estes an honorary "colonel" on his staff ("One of your caliber adds distinction to my staff," he wrote to Estes), and Estes cut Clement, his father and his brother-in-law in on some of his deals.

One Estes venture into which Clement and his kinsmen put some money involved buying up surplus barracks at the Air Force base near Blytheville, Ark., having the buildings chain-sawed into sections, and, after a bit of nailing here and there, selling the segments as one-family dwellings. They were mere shacks, small enough to be transported on a truck. But there was a serious housing shortage around the airbase in those days, and people bought Estes' wares for lack of anything else. Today many of the shacks are decrepit and abandoned.

Estes made other friends in Nashville, including the aged president of Nashville Christian Institute, a Negro school sponsored by the Church of Christ and endowed by a Nashville insurance magnate. Estes persuaded the institute's trustees to turn $100,000 of the endowment funds over to him in exchange for mortgages on his converted-barracks homes.

From cotton and cheap housing, Estes rapidly branched out into many other businesses—selling fertilizer and farm implements, digging wells, lining irrigation ditches, providing other agricultural services. He even founded a funeral parlor, thereby fulfilling a prophecy in the 1943 Clyde High School yearbook that he would become an undertaker. In the Estes manner, it was a grandiose establishment, far too fancy for Pecos, and it lost money.

Estes was frank about telling people what his ambition was: he wanted to get as rich as the Murchisons, the most famous of Texas' big-rich clans. He had some theories about how to get Murchison-rich. One of his basic concepts was that he could profit by handing out presents—a car, a suit of clothes, a thousand dollars in cash—since the recipient would be under an obligation to do him future favors. Another notion was that when a debt gets big enough, the creditor acquires an interest in the survival and prosperity of the debtor. "If you get into anybody far enough," he often said, "you've got yourself a partner."*

Estes got far enough into Commercial Solvents, a New York chemical manufacturer, which did become a sort of partner. It was this partnership that enabled Estes to get into big-time wheeling and dealing.

In the mid-1950s, Estes had gone into business as a distributor of anhydrous ammonia, a cheap, efficient nitrogen fertilizer widely used in large-scale farming. Indeed, the stuff has become as necessary as water to the farm economy of West Texas. Estes got way behind in his anhydrous ammonia bills from Commercial Solvents, and by 1958 he owed the firm some $550,000. He went to New York and sold officers of the firm on a complex deal: under the agreement, Commercial Solvents not only deferred payment of the $550,000 debt but agreed to lend Estes an additional $350,000—a credit of $125,000 for future purchases of anhydrous ammonia, plus $225,000 to enable Estes to get started in the grain-storage business. Estes, now into Commercial Solvents for $900,000, promised to pay off the debt in installments over a five-year span. As part of the overall deal, Estes agreed to assign to Commercial Solvents 100% of the fees he got for storing grain. And Commercial Solvents in effect agreed to ship him all the anhydrous ammonia he wanted—as long as the grain-storage money kept rolling in.

*The Murchisons are also great believers in the virtue of borrowing money to make money. Only half-jokingly, Clint Murchison once laid down a maxim that "a man is worth twice what he owes."

With his entry into grain storage, Estes acquired another partner—the U.S. Government. Grain storage is an appendage of federal price-support programs. A farmer who gets a Government price-support "loan" on a crop of grain deposits the grain in a certified warehouse or silo as collateral. He then has a period of time to decide on one of two alternatives. He can sign the stored grain over to the Government, keep the loan and leave the taxpayers stuck with some more surplus grain. Or, if he finds that he can sell the grain in the open market at a higher price, he can repay the support loan and reclaim his grain. Either way, the Agriculture Department pays the storage operator a fee, so much per bushel, for storing the grain. If the operator can keep his facilities filled to a high percentage of capacity, grain storage can be a highly profitable business.

With Commercial Solvents and the U.S. Government as his partners, Estes envisioned a scandalous cycle: he would keep using the proceeds from ammonia sales to buy or build grain-storage facilities; the federal grain-storage fees would keep flowing to Commercial Solvents; Commercial Solvents would keep shipping him anhydrous ammonia. The more ammonia he sold, the more warehouses he could control, and the more grain he stored, the more ammonia he could get, and so on in an unending spiral.

One of the flaws in this perpetual-motion machine was that other companies also manufactured anhydrous ammonia, and a lot of distributors were selling the stuff to West Texas farmers in competition with Estes. But Estes had an answer to that difficulty: smash the competitors. Estes used a characteristic gesture to illustrate a point in his business philosophy: he would hold out his left hand, doubled into a loose fist, and slap it sharply with the palm of his right hand. "If you shatter an industry," he would say, "you can pick up all the pieces for yourself."

The wholesale price of anhydrous ammonia was

$90 a ton, and a local distributor had to charge more than $100 a ton to break even. So it stirred up some commotion when Estes, shortly after setting up his deal with Commercial Solvents, started selling the stuff for $60 a ton. In some intense price battles, he slashed his price down to $40 and even $20. One after another, he drove rival dealers out of business, sometimes picking up the pieces for himself by buying up the failed or failing firm's assets cheap. In a few years, Estes became the biggest anhydrous-ammonia dealer in West Texas, and one of the biggest in the U.S. He lost millions of dollars in the process. But for Estes the losses seemed only a temporary inconvenience on the way to a grand and profitable future.

If Estes failed to make money out of his ammonia dealings, so did Commercial Solvents. In 1959–61 some $7,000,000 in grain-storage fees flowed from the U.S. Government to Commercial Solvents by way of Estes' bank accounts, but anhydrous ammonia flowed to Estes even faster. By the time of his downfall, Estes was into Commercial Solvents for something like $5,700,000. Despite the unprofitability of a joint venture, Texas Attorney General Wilson . . . brought an anti-trust suit against Estes and Commercial Solvents on the ground that they had conspired to monopolize the West Texas market for anhydrous ammonia. "Commercial Solvents is named in the suit," said Wilson, "because in our judgment they made possible the whole thing and knew what they were doing."

To raise capital to expand his grain-storage domain even faster, Estes dreamed up a scheme for raising money on nonexistent anhydrous-ammonia-storage tanks. The ammonia is a gas under normal atmospheric conditions; it must be stored in tanks to keep it liquid. Working with Superior Manufacturing Co., a Texas firm that made ammonia tanks, Estes persuaded a lot of West Texas farmers to go through the motions of purchasing tanks from Superior on credit, taking out mortgages on them, and leasing them back to Estes.

Estes conveniently made the lease payments equal to the mortgage payments, so the farmer would not have to pay out any money. Estes explained to the farmers that he needed the tanks for his operations, but was short of working capital and simply wanted to use the farmer's credit to obtain the tanks. In return, he offered the farmer a fee of 10% of the price—in effect, something for nothing.

In this implausible way, Estes collected more than $30 million in mortgages on imaginary tanks. He used the bogus mortages as collateral to borrow roughly $22 million from commercial finance companies in New York, Chicago and other cities. To get the finance companies to accept the mortgages, Estes and his henchmen had to fake a lot of documents relating to the farmers' personal finances. One Estes secretary later admitted to typing five phony documents on five typewriters.

Estes' grain-storage kingdom grew fast—the amount of grain in storage soared from 2.3 million bushels in March 1959 to 54 million in February 1962. But there was an oversupply of grain-storage facilities in West Texas, and Estes could not keep his warehouses full enough to reap really massive profits. After the collapse, amid mounting evidence that Estes had been doing favors for Agriculture Department officials, the department put out these figures as proof of its virtue; early [in 1962] Estes' facilities were 43.4% filled with federal grain as against a Texas state-wide average of 48.6%; later on, Estes' figure rose to 58.3%, but the state average also went up, to 62.9%. Said a White House staffer: "If Estes was spending a lot of money at Agriculture, he sure wasn't getting much for it."

All the while that Estes' assets were growing, his liabilities were mounting even faster. In 1960 he ventured on another desperate scheme for making big money. Estes had found cotton-farming profitable. The only obstacle to growing more cotton and making more profits was that the U.S. Government, in exchange for its generous price supports on cotton, imposes strict acreage controls. Each cotton farmer has an acreage allotment, which cannot be sold or otherwise transferred; it remains attached to the parcel of land.

But the Government makes a special exception for farmers whose land is taken over under the right of eminent domain—to make way for a new highway, perhaps. In such a case, if the displaced farmer buys another farm within three years, he has the right to transfer his old cotton allotment to his new land.

Schemer Estes saw a way to get hold of allotments so he could increase his cotton plantings and profits. He and his agents persuaded numerous farmers in Texas, Oklahoma, Georgia and Alabama, who had been dispossessed by eminent domain, to buy Texas farm land from him, transfer their allotments to the new land, and lease the land-plus-allotments back to him for $50 an acre. Each farmer agreed to pay for the land in four equal installments, with the understanding that if he defaulted on the first installment, the land (with the allotment still attached) would revert to Estes. It was expected that the farmer would default when the first installment came due. When he did, Estes had the land and the allotment; the farmer had the first year's $50-per-acre lease payments (Estes, as part of the deal, made the lease payments in advance). The net result of this devious and complicated deal was that the farmer had sold his cotton allotment to Estes for $50 an acre.

These deals, by which Estes obtained more than 3,000 acres of cotton allotments in the course of two years, were legal only if the sale of the land was a bona fide sale, and if the default was a bona fide default. Since Estes' deals with the farmers were set up in the expectation that they would default, the deals were obviously suspect. After long delays, the Agriculture Department finally decided . . . that the deals were faked, and fined Estes for growing cotton under the illegally obtained allotments.

Estes' rickety empire was doomed to collapse sooner or later under the weight of its accumulating deficits. But while it lasted, his rapidly burning candle at least gave off a bit of dazzle. With his wife and five children, Estes lived in the most lavish house in town. Out in the backyard, he had a swimming pool and Texas-sized barbecue facilities. The Amarillo *Daily News* called him "probably the biggest wheeler and dealer in all of West Texas." He conveyed an impression that he wielded a lot of political influence beyond the boundaries of Pecos, and even beyond Texas. He liked to flash a card indicating that he had donated $100,000 to the Democratic Party during the 1960 campaign. He displayed on the walls of his office photos, some fondly signed, of President Kennedy, Vice President Johnson, Harry Truman, Adlai Stevenson, John McClellan and other Democratic political notables. He boasted of his friendships with politicians, including Texas' Democratic Senator Ralph Yarborough.

But for all his aura of wealth and power, Billie Sol remained a somewhat ridiculous figure; the inner bumpkin kept showing through. One acquaintance recalls him as "the kind of man whose lapels always seem a little too wide." He sported a diamond stickpin that seemed garish even in Texas. He was constantly bumbling into grotesque situations. Invited to Governor Clement's second inaugural in 1955, he was the only guest to show up in the ornate regalia of a Tennessee colonel. In 1956 he made a fool of himself by trying to persuade the president of a Pecos bank to help finance a wacky scheme to help Adlai Stevenson win the election. Under the Estes plan, large schools of parakeets, trained to say "I like Adlai" in unison, would fly over U.S. cities. When the banker tried to tell Estes that parakeets could not be trained to say "I like Adlai," much less say it in unison, Estes got purple-angry, accused the banker of being anti-Stevenson and stomped out.

Estes was widely feared in Pecos because of his

seeming wealth and power. But he was not widely liked. When he ran for a place on the local school board . . . he lost to a write-in candidate. That humiliating defeat led to Estes' downfall. The local paper, the twice-weekly *Independent,* had opposed him for the school board post. To get revenge, Estes set up a rival paper. Upshot: the *Independent* investigated and printed the first exposure of Billie Sol's tank-mortgage fraud. The alarmed finance companies sent in swarms of investigators, and Billie Sol's empire came crashing down with a thud that reverberated all the way to Washington. On March 29, the FBI arrested Estes on charges of transporting the bogus mortgages across state lines. Estes [was released] on bail . . . under both a federal indictment for fraud and a state indictment for theft.

Several days after the FBI arrived in Pecos, Texas Attorney General Wilson set off on his own investigation, and his first revelations made the front pages. Employees of Dallas' Neiman-Marcus luxury store testified that Estes had bought—or gone through convincing motions of buying—expensive clothing for three officials of the U.S. Agriculture Department. In September 1961, the testimony ran, Estes went into the men's wear department of Neiman-Marcus with Assistant Secretary (for Agricultural Stabilization) James T. Ralph and Ralph's assistant, William E. Morris; Ralph and Morris selected more than $1,000 worth of clothing, which was billed to Estes. In October, Estes came in again, this time with Emery E. Jacobs, deputy administrator of the Commodity Stabilization Service. After Jacobs had selected $1,433.20 worth of clothing, including a $245 suit and a $195 sports coat, Estes went into the fitting room with him. When they came out, Jacobs proceeded to pay the entire bill himself—with cash.

One by one, Ralph, Morris and Jacobs . . . all departed from the Agriculture Department [after] the Neiman-Marcus revelations. Morris proved to have other links with Billie Sol. His wife had been on Billie

Sol's payroll as "Washington columnist" for the paper in Pecos, and in Estes' files were some very friendly letters that Morris had written to him. When Morris failed to appear for departmental questioning about his relations with Estes, Secretary Freeman fired him outright.

Jacobs denied that Billie Sol bought any clothing for him. The only gifts he ever accepted from Estes, he said, were two rides in Estes' private plane, several meals, a box of cigars and a five-lb. bag of pecans. Yes, Billie Sol did go into Neiman-Marcus with him, Jacobs admitted, but "I had my own money." Jacobs resigned his post anyway. Maybe he knew it would be hard for people to believe that a $16,500-a-year Government official would be carrying around $1,433.20 in cash to spend for clothing.

Ralph was the last to go and the most vehement in his denials. He actually went to Texas to submit to questioning by Wilson. But while he kept insisting that he never received any clothing, he did admit, under hard questioning, that a salesman had come up with a chalk and tape measure and worked on a suit that Ralph was trying on. Since Ralph persisted in denying that he got any clothing, his case remained hanging until . . . further investigation showed that he had used an Estes credit card to pay for personal telephone calls. Freeman fired him.

Besides the Agriculture men, one other Administration official has lost his job because of ties to Billie Sol: Assistant Secretary of Labor Jerry Holleman, former president of the Texas A.F.L.-C.I.O., who got to know Estes well in the liberal faction of the Texas Democratic Party. Holleman's name first broke into the Estes scandal when it got out that Holleman had asked Estes and other Texans to ante up for a big dinner party given by Labor Secretary Arthur Goldberg . . . for Lyndon Johnson. Holleman admitted it, but said that he had not consulted Goldberg in advance. Goldberg offered to produce canceled checks to prove that

he had paid the bills himself, and the tremor passed
away.

But hardly was it gone when another hunk of Estes
debris fell on Holleman: evidence that he had accepted
a check for $1,000 from Billie Sol. Holleman admitted
that he took the money—and his explanation was a telling commentary on life in official Washington. Holleman said that he needed the $1,000 to help meet his
"living expenses." His $20,000-a-year salary, he said,
was inadequate to meet the social demands that his position placed upon him. Holleman said the $1,000 gift
was "personal," and had "no connection with any of
Mr. Estes' interests," but he resigned anyway. Said he
when he got back to Texas: "The only place you eat
free in Washington is at an embassy."

On Capitol Hill, one of the men most seriously tarnished by the Estes case [was] Minnesota's Republican
Congressman H. Carl Andersen. Early [in 1962],
William Morris, one of Estes' Neiman-Marcus trio,
wrote Estes a letter suggesting that Andersen, a member of the House subcommittee on agricultural appro-
priations, would be a "good Republican contact" in
Congress, and that it might be a "good investment" to
help him out of a financial pinch. Shortly afterward,
Morris took Andersen down to Pecos to talk to Estes.
Then, and again on another occasion in Washington,
Estes gave Andersen money—totaling $4,000 or $5,000
or $5,500 according to various versions—for stock in
an Andersen-owned coal mine. After this transaction
came to light, Andersen insisted that Estes was only
making a business investment in the mine. But that
seemed unconvincing, since Estes never even bothered
to get any stock certificates from Andersen.

Also spattered by the Estes case was Texas' liberal
Democratic Senator Yarborough. He admitted that he
had received some $7,500 from Estes as political con-
tributions, including $1,700 to help defray the cost of
broadcasts he had made in Texas. These contributions
did not seem extraordinary—but what did seem strange

was the evidence that Yarborough had used lots of influence to help Estes out of his difficulties with the Agriculture Department.

In Estes' financial records in Pecos, investigators came across ominous-looking entries totaling $235,000 for something listed as "Washington Project." But this proved to be a housing venture in the state of Washington rather than payoffs in the District of Columbia. Still not adequately explained are three checks totaling $145,015.14 that Estes drew on a bank account in Pecos [in January 1962] and then cashed in Austin just before taking off on a trip to Washington, D.C.

Among the most sinister aspects of the Estes case were the bizarre and mysterious deaths of two Texans. . . . When Estes was already in trouble about his cotton allotments, Henry M. Marshall, the Agriculture Department agent in charge of cotton allotments in Texas, was found dead in a lonely pasture. He had been shot in the abdomen five times with his own .22-cal., bolt-action rifle, which lay nearby. The local sheriff ruled it a suicide. Apart from the awkwardness of firing the rifle while holding the muzzle against his abdomen, Marshall would have had to pull the bolt back after each shot. Strange, too, was the death of George Krutilek, an accountant who had kept books for the farmers who signed bogus tank mortgages. A few days after the Estes scandal broke, Krutilek was found dead in his car with the windows up and a rubber hose leading from the exhaust to the interior of the car. But an autopsy revealed no trace of carbon monoxide in his lungs, and local authorities ruled that he had died of a heart attack.

Secretary Freeman said that the Estes affair had been "ballooned out of all proportion." There was "no evidence," he insisted, that Estes had received special favors from the Agriculture Department.

On the contrary, there was evidence aplenty. Items:

Grain-storage operators are required to post a bond

as a prerequisite to getting federal storage. The amount of the bond is based on the capacity of the storage facilities, and other factors, including the operator's financial status. The better the risk, the lower the bond. Estes' bond was set at $700,000 back in 1960, and it remained at that level, although both the amount of grain he had in storage and his capital deficit increased enormously. A passing gesture toward upping the bond was made after the New Frontier took over the Agriculture Department, but Estes protested, and the bond remained at $700,000. Freeman explained the department's generosity to Estes by saying that he had filed a financial statement showing a net worth of $12 million to prove that he was a good risk. But that financial statement was grossly inflated, and could not have passed a reasonably careful scrutiny. Furthermore, a routine check with Internal Revenue would have shown that for 1959, 1960 and 1961 Estes reported no taxable income at all—just a steady stream of losses.

Freeman confirmed Estes' appointment to the National Cotton Advisory Committee in November 1961, two months after the department had already fined him $42,000 for planting cotton under illegally obtained acreage allotments. Freeman's explanation: Estes had originally been appointed to the board in July 1961, and in November the department had merely "reconstituted" the old board. Furthermore, said Freeman, the issue of the legality of the allotments was a "lawyers' quarrel." Shortly after Freeman offered this explanation, the department belatedly got around to fining Estes $554,162 for additional cotton-allotment violations that had been under investigation since mid-1961.

The pace of the department's handling of Estes' cotton-allotment case was glacial even by bureaucratic standards. On January 6, two weeks before Kennedy's inauguration, at a time when it appeared that a decision adverse to Estes might be imminent, Senator Yarborough and J. T. Rutherford, the Democratic Congressmen from Estes' home district, went to the

Agriculture Department and interceded for Billie Sol at a meeting with department officials. They succeeded in getting a postponement of the final ruling. "This was more than favoritism," charged South Dakota's Republican Senator Karl E. Mundt. . . . "This was complete capitulation to a guy out on the make."

A lower-rung Agriculture Department official named Battle Hales openly charged . . . that the department had shown "favoritism" toward Estes. Hales also dropped hints that he had been shunted to another job in the department, and denied access to the Estes files, because he knew too much about the case Hales' transfer led to one of the unseemliest scenes ever enacted in the somber corridors of the Agriculture Department. Miss Mary Jones, a nervous spinster of 51, who had been Hales' secretary for eleven years, was upset about the prospect of being transferred to a new boss. After being out sick for two days, she came back and went to Hales' old office to get her leave record signed. What happened next is obscured by confusion and controversy. But apparently an official ordered her to leave the office. When she refused, he called in a departmental doctor, who decided that the distraught Miss Jones should be taken away for observation. Result: Miss Jones was dragged off to a mental hospital and held for 13 days until a judge ordered her released to the custody of her sister and her own doctor. Says Miss Jones: "It was all a horrible nightmare."

Republican leaders charged that Freeman and his department had mishandled everything connected with the Estes case, from the grain-storage bond to Miss Mary Jones. At his press conference, President Kennedy came to Freeman's defense but on rather odd grounds—not that Freeman had been doing a good job but that he played football in college, made Phi Beta Kappa, "had most of his jaw shot off in Bougainville," and served three terms as Governor of Minnesota. These points are true enough, but irrelevant. All Kennedy said about Freeman as Secretary was that the job had been "challenging."

Having made a weak defense, Kennedy followed up with a weak counterattack. The substance of his argument: it was his Administration that pounced on Estes by arresting and indicting him, so there was nothing to holler about. But the President was claiming undue credit. Estes was first exposed by the Pecos *Independent*. Then the finance-company investigators moved in. Only after that did the FBI—which [was] under Bobby Kennedy's jurisdiction—put Estes under arrest. Moreover, the revelations about Estes' involvements with the Administration came out not through federal channels but through the Wilson investigation in Texas.

. . . The Estes case [was not] a Teapot Dome, but it [was] certainly far more than what the President and his Agriculture Secretary claimed it to be—merely a teapot tempest. The most important villain in the Estes case is the vast tangle of the farm price-support system, with its accompanying systems of production controls and surplus storage. Price-support programs provide scant help for the neediest farmers; the most bountiful benefits flow to prosperous farmers, who could get along with no Government aid at all. Laxly administered, too vast and complex to be effectively policed, the price-support programs provide a constant invitation to dishonesty.

Billie Sol was largely financed by cotton-price supports and grain-storage fees paid for by the taxpayers. If there had been no price-support programs, there would have been no inviting storage business for him to get into, no cotton allotments to obtain by fraud.

In its sheer gaudiness, the Estes mess dramatizes the farm scandal more vividly than ever before. If that dramatization were to result in something really being done about the farm fiasco, who knows but that the U.S. might even owe a vote of thanks to none other than Billie Sol Estes.

4

Vegetable oil, used for sardines, salad dressings and margarine, is patently an innocuous product. But what can you say about guilelessness on the part of stockbrokers, investment bankers, banks and trading companies? Put them together and you have the great soybean scandal of the mid-Sixties which involved a $150-million swindle by a former butcher who became a major entrepreneur in the New Jersey oil vats. The only problem was that those vats were largely empty.

The fiasco in 1963 forced Ira Haupt & Co., a respected brokerage, out of business, caused another to merge, stuck 20 banks with bad loans, embarrassed trading companies and brought still other concerns to the brink.

One can't help being reminded of the similarity between Tino DeAngelis and Billie Sol Estes. Coming from widely different ethnic and geographical backgrounds, both dealt in vast claims, in inventories that largely didn't exist, but both felt certain that their swindle would remain uncovered. When did that self-deception, the fantasy, begin? There can be little doubt that it exploded the moment Tino and Billie Sol figured that they were 100 percent successes and that they ought to capitalize on it.

Tino served nearly seven years of a 20-year sentence he received because of his swindle. He was granted a parole in spring of 1972. Before that, however, reflecting his own kind behavior while he was engaged in his mind-boggling exploits, Tino proved to be a humanitarian in jail. While there, he helped organize a branch of the NAACP and contributed $126 of the $500 the prisoners presented to the new black group. The article that follows was published on December 8, 1963 in the *New York Herald Tribune*.

The Great Soybean Scandal

Anthony DeAngelis is a roly-poly little man who was a hog-dresser 25 years ago. His taste runs to plain off-the-rack gray suits and he lives on Edson Ave. in the Bronx. He appears a most unlikely man to be in the middle of a multimillion-dollar international scandal.

But Mr. DeAngelis, primarily using vegetable oils more commonly considered food for man and beast, secondarily as a base for paints and plastics, built an empire.

[In December, 1963, it began] falling apart with a rumble said to be worth at least $100 million. The debris touched:

The New York Stock Exchange, which decided to put up as much as $12 million to pay customers of an old-line brokerage house that had lent millions of dollars to Allied Crude Vegetable Oil Refining Corp. This was the main company in what investigators found to be an intricate structure of DeAngelis-controlled firms.

At least 30 exporters, food companies, warehouse firms, including a subsidiary of American Express, which started a frantic search through a spaghetti-like maze of pipes and tanks in Bayonne, N. J., for millions of gallons of vegetable oil pledged as security on loans. (In a matter of days after the news broke, American Express stock slumped $23 to about $39 a share.)

At least 30 insurance companies with claims already totaling $41 million against just one firm that rented tanks from Allied. This outfit, Harbor Tank Storage Co., is insured for $7.5 million. Allied's other Bayonne tenant, American Express Warehousing Ltd., [was] also said to be insured, although there have been no details. Allied itself places its insurance with four companies.

Institutions like Bank of America, Chase Manhattan, First National City, Marine Midland, Manufacturers Hanover and other titans on both sides of the Atlantic which found themselves holding millions of dollars in notes backed by the same elusive oil, which some people said did not exist.

Commodity markets, where people buy and sell contracts for future delivery of basic products. Mr. DeAngelis, in a spectacular year of buying and borrowing, had become owner of 90 percent of the available contracts to buy cottonseed oil, a holding of 600 million pounds, or 10,000 railroad tank cars, enough, had he gone through with the purchase, to swallow one-third of American production for a year.

It was a time of rumor and intense speculation on the commodity exchanges because the Soviet Union had indicated it wanted to buy huge amounts of wheat. Maybe it wanted to buy other things, too. Maybe, some dealers thought, Mr. DeAngelis would be able to sell soybean and cottonseed oil to Russia.

Discounting the prevailing hysteria, it was not a wholly improbable guess. Allied was the nation's largest supplier of vegetable oil for export, and Mr. DeAngelis had been active in foreign trade for years. As a matter of fact, it was a foreign flop—a $1 million sale of lard to Italy back around the Korean War days—that first put his name in headlines.

That was a complex case, too; he made the sale in one corporate role, then merged his firm with the buyer, a meat packer called Adolf Gobel, Inc. Eventually Italy and a collection of other creditors sued Gobel, which by now was controlled by Mr. DeAngelis. By July, 1953, the firm was bankrupt.

The rules say a registered commodity dealer needs little money to trade in commodity futures. He can buy them on a miniscule margin, as low as 5 cents on each dollar pledged. (To buy stock, by contrast, you now must put up at least 70 cents of every dollar.) Allied built heavy debts with two brokerage firms, most with Ira Haupt & Co., some with J. R. Williston & Beane.

Allied also took physical delivery of huge amounts of vegetable oils, which were shipped to a "tank farm" at the Bayonne waterfront and pumped into custody of storage firms like American Express Warehousing and Harbor. Then, using warehouse receipts for the stuff, Allied went to banks, factories, all sorts of firms in the lending business, and borrowed to buy more oil. It had not yet paid for some of the oil it was using as collateral.

Its collapse was touched off by the slide in commodity prices that began when it seemed in mid-November the Russian wheat deal—and thus a possible oil deal — might not go through. The price decline meant the contracts that brokers held for Mr. DeAngelis were losing value, and he was told to put up enough money to cover the difference between the shrunken value and the price he had agreed to pay. This totaled about $19 million. Mr. DeAngelis couldn't raise it. Allied, which did a $100-million-a-year business, filed for bankruptcy.

That was on November 18.

A day later, in an unprecedented step, the Produce Exchange called off all trading in cottonseed oil futures, while arrangements were made to cancel all contracts to buy and sell at a compromise price.

Haupt & Co. and Williston & Beane, which had borrowed to buy commodity futures for Allied, reported to the Stock Exchange that their net capital had fallen below the minimum requirements. Both were told to stop business. The accounts of their customers were frozen.

Williston & Beane was able to borrow enough to pay its debts, but it was absorbed by another firm. Haupt was too far behind. It went out of business, and the Stock Exchange did something it had never done before —it agreed to make up to $12 million available to repay Haupt customers for cash and securities they had in account with Haupt.

This set a Wall Street precedent; the Exchange had agreed three years earlier to protect customers against a member firm's fraud; now it agreed to protect them against its business failure as well. (The Exchange says 17 million Americans are stockholders; of these, about 20,000 were Haupt customers.)

While the Exchange was assuring the world that this was strictly "a one-shot deal" and not setting a precedent, those directly interested in the oil itself—an item almost overlooked in the paper dealing about future contracts—got worried.

Six surveying firms, hired by those who lent money against receipted warehouse bills saying that the oil was in Mr. De Angelis' possession, were sent to Bayonne to check the tanks. One of the firms, Bunge Corp., was pained to discover only 7 million pounds of oil where it had receipts for 161 million.

One of the problems was that while Allied rented much of the Bayonne storage space, it also leased out some space—and some of the spaces were interconnected. . . . Another problem was that Allied was officially ruled bankrupt following a Federal Court hearing in Newark at which Mr. DeAngelis gave his name once and took the Fifth Amendment 50 times.

A Jersey City lawyer, Daniel De Lear, Allied's court-appointed receiver, was trying to sort out the firm's affairs.

There were inquiries by the FBI, the Hudson County, N.J., prosecutor's office, the SEC, the Agriculture Department, perhaps others (some said Scotland Yard was looking into overseas aspects).

In Chicago, another DeAngelis satellite, Chicago Refining Corp., filed for bankruptcy and said one of its big creditors was Allied. The name of Mr. DeAngelis was linked with a company that had been denied a rendering license because Chicago police said one of its stockholders consorted with at least three known hoodlums.

No one had made any definite charges, but it was already clear that for sheer size and complexity, it was one of the most fascinating business intrigues in years. . . .

The last big Wall Street scandal involved the brokerage firm of Homsey. The president of that firm was accused in 1960 of appropriating customers' securities. The New York Stock Exchange ousted him. . . . The case caused the Exchange to set up new fraud insurance [and] a backup fund for itself. . . .

It was clear, too, that regulatory gaps had been disclosed. The Agriculture Department's Commodity Exchange Authority said it knew that the big DeAngelis holdings of futures had no power to curb his huge hold on the market. The Produce Exchange said it lacked any legal powers to prosecute him. The Stock Exchange conceded that the rules provided no bars to a member firm's overextension in commodities trading. . . .

Little needs to be said to preface the Great Modern Antisuccess Story, the 1957–1959 debacle of Ford's Edsel car. Unbelievable as it seems, the powerful Ford Motor Company gave its new car the heaviest advertising barrage in years and then backed it the first year with a ridiculously high number of faultily performing models. Even before that, though, there was a big name-game, in which the advertising agency bravely cut down the list of 18,000 to a mere 6,000. And then on E-Day (Edsel Day) Minus One, there was the wild, circuslike press introduction in Detroit, culminating in 71 of the 250 reporters happily cooperating by personally delivering as many Edsels to the showrooms of their own local dealers.

Hard to believe? What, there's more, much more. John Brooks's tale, tantalizing and utterly satisfying in its detail and élan, awaits you. It is a toothsome chapter from his 1969 book.

The Fate of the Edsel

By John Brooks

In the calendar of American economic life, 1955 was the Year of the Automobile. That year, American automobile makers sold over seven million passenger cars, or over a million more than they had sold in any previous year. That year, General Motors easily sold the public $325 million worth of new common stock, and the stock market as a whole, led by the motors, gyrated upward so frantically that Congress investigated it. And that year, too, the Ford Motor Company decided to produce a new automobile in what was quaintly called the medium-price range—roughly, from $2,400 to $4,000—and went ahead and designed it more or less in conformity with the fashion of the day, which was for cars that were long, wide, low, lavishly decorated with chrome, liberally supplied with gadgets, and equipped with engines of a power just barely insufficient to send them into orbit. Two years later, in September, 1957, the Ford Company put its new car, the Edsel, on the market, to the accompaniment of more fanfare than had attended the arrival of any other new car since the same company's Model A, brought out thirty years earlier. The total amount spent on the Edsel before the first specimen went on sale was announced as a quarter of a billion dollars; its launching—as *Business Week* declared and nobody cared to deny—was more costly than that of any other consumer product in history. As a starter toward getting its investment back, Ford counted on selling at least 200,000 Edsels the first year.

There may be an aborigine somewhere in a remote rain forest who hasn't yet heard that things failed to turn out that way. To be precise, two years, two months and fifteen days later Ford had sold only 109,466 Edsels, and, beyond a doubt, many hundreds, if not several thousands, of those were bought by Ford executives, dealers, salesmen, advertising men, assembly-line workers, and others who had a personal interest in seeing the car succeed. The 109,466 amounted to considerably less than one per cent of the passenger cars sold in the United States during that period, and on November 19, 1959, having lost, according to some outside estimates, around $350 million on the Edsel, the Ford Company permanently discontinued its production.

How could this have happened? How could a company so mightily endowed with money, experience, and, presumably, brains have been guilty of such a monumental mistake? Even before the Edsel was dropped, some of the more articulate members of the car-minded public had come forward with an answer —an answer so simple and so seemingly reasonable that, though it was not the only one advanced, it became widely accepted as the truth. The Edsel, these people argued, was designed, named, advertised, and promoted with a slavish adherence to the results of public-opinion polls and of their younger cousin, motivational research, and they concluded that when the public is wooed in an excessively calculated manner, it tends to turn away in favor of some gruffer but more spontaneously attentive suitor. Several years ago, in the face of an understandable reticence on the part of the Ford Motor Company, which enjoys documenting its boners no more than anyone else, I set out to learn what I could about the Edsel debacle, and my investigations have led me to believe that what we have here is less than the whole truth.

For, although the Edsel was *supposed* to be advertised, and otherwise promoted, strictly on the basis of preferences expressed in polls, some old-fashioned snake-oil-selling methods, intuitive rather than scientific, crept in. Although it was *supposed* to have been named in much the same way, science was curtly discarded at the last minute and the Edsel was named for the father of the company's president, like a nineteenth-century brand of cough drops or saddle soap. As for the design, it was arrived at without even a pretense of consulting the polls, and by the method that has been standard for years in the designing of automobiles— that of simply pooling the hunches of sundry company committees. The common explanation of the Edsel's downfall, then, under scrutiny, turns out to be largely a myth, in the colloquial sense of that term. But the facts of the case may live to become a myth of a symbolic sort—a modern American antisuccess story.

The origins of the Edsel go back to the fall of 1948, seven years before the year of decision, when Henry Ford II, who had been president and undisputed boss of the company since the death of his grandfather, the original Henry, a year earlier, proposed to the company's executive committee, which included Ernest R. Breech, the executive vice-president, that studies be undertaken concerning the wisdom of putting on the market a new and wholly different medium-priced car. The studies were undertaken. There appeared to be a good reason for them. It was a well-known practice at the time for low-income owners of Fords, Plymouths, and Chevrolets to turn in their symbols of inferior caste as soon as their earnings rose above five thousand dollars a year, and "trade up" to a medium-priced car. From Ford's point of view, this would have been all well and good except that, for some reason, Ford owners usually traded up not to Mercury, the company's only medium-priced car, but to one or another of the medium-priced cars put out by its big rivals—Oldsmobile, Buick, and Pontiac, among the General Motors products, and, to a lesser extent, Dodge and De Soto, the Chrysler candidates. Lewis D. Crusoe, than a vice-president of the Ford Motor Company, was not overstating the case when he said, "We have been growing customers for General Motors."

The outbreak of the Korean War, in 1950, meant that Ford had no choice but to go on growing customers for its competitors, since introducing a new car at such a time was out of the question. The company's executive committee put aside the studies proposed by President Ford, and there matters rested for two years. Late in 1952, however, the end of the war appeared sufficiently imminent for the company to pick up where it had left off, and the studies were energetically resumed by a group called the Forward Product Planning Committee, which turned over much of the detailed work to the Lincoln-Mercury Division, under the direction of Richard Krafve (pronounced Kraffy), the division's assistant general manager. Krafve, a forceful, rather saturnine man with a habitually puzzled look, was then in his middle forties. The son of a printer on a small farm journal in Minnesota, he had been a sales engineer and management consultant before joining Ford, in 1947, and although he could not have known it in 1952, he was to have reason to look puzzled. As the man directly responsible for the Edsel and its fortunes, enjoying its brief glory and attending it in its mortal agonies, he had a rendezvous with destiny.

In December, 1954, after two years' work, the Forward Product Planning Committee submitted to the executive committee a six-volume blockbuster of a report summarizing its findings. Supported by copious statistics, the report predicted the arrival of the American millennium, or something a lot like it, in 1965. By that time, the Forward Product Planning Committee estimated, the gross national product would be $535 billion a year—up more than $135 billion in a decade. (As a matter of fact, this part of the millennium arrived much sooner than the Forward Planners estimated. The G.N.P. passed $535 billion in 1962, and for 1965 was $681 billion.) The number of cars in operation would be seventy million—up twenty million. More than half the families in the nation would have incomes of over five thousand dollars a year, and more than forty percent of all the cars sold would be in the medium-price range or better. The report's picture of America in 1965, presented in crushing detail, was of a country after Detroit's own heart—its banks oozing money, its streets and highways choked with huge, dazzling medium-priced cars, its newly rich, "upwardly mobile" citizens racked with longings for more of them. The moral was clear. If by that time Ford had not come out with a second medium-priced car—not just a new model, but a new make—and made it a favorite in its field, the company would miss out on its share of the national boodle.

On the other hand, the Ford bosses were well aware of the enormous risks connected with putting a new car on the market. They knew, for example, that of the 2,900 American makes that had been introduced since the beginning of the Automobile Age—the Black Crow (1905), the Averageman's Car (1906), the Bugmobile (1907), the Dan Patch (1911), and the Lone Star (1920) among them—only about twenty were still around. They knew all about the automotive casualties that had followed the Second World War— among them Crosley, which had given up altogether, and Kaiser Motors, which, though still alive in 1954, was breathing its last. (The members of the Forward Product Planning Committee must have glanced at each other uneasily when, a year later, Henry J. Kaiser wrote, in a valediction to his car business, "We expected to toss fifty million dollars into the automobile pond, but we didn't expect it to disappear without a ripple.") The Ford men also knew that neither of the other members of the industry's powerful and well-heeled Big Three—General Motors and Chrysler—had ventured to bring out a new standard-size make since the former's La Salle in 1927, and the latter's Plymouth in 1928, and that Ford itself had not attempted to turn the trick since 1938, when it launched the Mercury.

Nevertheless, the Ford men felt bullish—so remarkably bullish that they resolved to toss into the automobile pond five times the sum that Kaiser had. In April, 1955, Henry Ford II, Breech, and the other members of the executive committee officially approved the Forward Product Planning Committee's findings, and, to implement them, set up another agency, called the Special Products Division, with the star-crossed Krafve as its head. Thus the company gave its formal sanction to the efforts of its designers, who, having divined the trend of events, had already been doodling for several months on plans for a new car. Since neither they nor the newly organized Krafve outfit, when it took over, had an inkling of what the thing on their drawing boards might be called, it became known to everybody at Ford, and even in the company's press releases, as the E-Car—the "E," it was explained, standing for "experimental."

The man directly in charge of the E-Car's design—or, to use the gruesome trade word, "styling"—was a Canadian, then not yet forty, named Roy A. Brown, who, before taking on the E-Car (and after studying industrial design at the Detroit Art Academy), had had a hand in the designing of radios, motor cruisers, colored-glass products, Cadillacs, Oldsmobiles, and Lincolns.* Brown recently recalled his aspirations as he went to work on the new project. "Our goal was to create a vehicle which would be unique in the sense that it would be readily recognizable in styling theme from the nineteen other makes of cars on the road at that time," he wrote from England, where at the time of his writing he was employed as chief stylist for the Ford Motor Company, Ltd., manufacturers of trucks, tractors, and small cars. "We went to the extent of making photographic studies from some distance of all nineteen of these cars, and it became obvious that at a distance of a few hundred feet the similarity was so great that it was practically impossible to distinguish one make from the others. . . . They were all 'peas in a pod.' We

*The word "styling" is a weed deeply embedded in the garden of automobilia. In its preferred sense, the verb "to style" means to name; thus the Special Products Division's epic efforts to choose a name for the E-Car, which will be chronicled presently, were really the styling program, and what Brown and his associates were up to was something else again. In its second sense, says Webster, "to style" means "to fashion in . . . the accepted style"; this was just what Brown, who hoped to achieve originality, was trying not to do, so Brown's must have been the antistyling program.

decided to select [a style that] would be 'new' in the sense that it was unique, and yet at the same time be familiar."

While the E-Car was on the drawing boards in Ford's styling studio—situated, like its administrative offices, in the company's barony of Dearborn, just outside Detroit—work on it progressed under the conditions of melodramatic, if ineffectual, secrecy that invariably attend such operations in the automobile business: locks on the studio doors that could be changed in fifteen minutes if a key should fall into enemy hands; a security force standing round-the-clock guard over the establishment; and a telescope to be trained at intervals on nearby high points of the terrain where peekers might be roosting. (All such precautions, however inspired, are doomed to fail, because none of them provide a defense against Detroit's version of the Trojan horse—the job-jumping stylist, whose cheerful treachery makes it relatively easy for the rival companies to keep tabs on what the competition is up to. No one, of course, is better aware of this than the rivals themselves, but the cloak-and-dagger stuff is thought to pay for itself in publicity value.) Twice a week or so, Krafve—head down, and sticking to low ground—made the journey to the styling studio, where he would confer with Brown, check up on the work as it proceeded, and offer advice and encouragement. Krafve was not the kind of man to envision his objective in a single revelatory flash; instead, he anatomized the styling of the E-Car into a series of laboriously minute decisions—how to shape the fenders, what pattern to use with the chrome, what kind of door handles to put on, and so on and on. If Michelangelo ever added the number of decisions that went into the execution of, say, his "David," he kept it to himself, but Krafve, an orderly-minded man in an era of orderly-functioning computers, later calculated that in styling the E-Car he and his associates had to make up their minds on no fewer than four thousand occasions. He reasoned at the time that if they arrived at the right yes-or-no choice on every one of those occasions, they ought, in the end, to come up with a stylistically perfect car—or at least a car that would be unique and at the same time familiar. But Krafve concedes today that he found it difficult thus to bend the creative process to the yoke of system, principally because many of the four thousand decisions he made wouldn't stay put. "Once you get a general theme, you begin narrowing down," he says. "You keep modifying, and then modifying your modifications. Finally, you *have* to settle on something, because there isn't any more time. If it weren't for the deadline you'd probably go on modifying indefinitely."

Except for later, minor modifications of the modified modifications, the E-Car had been fully styled by midsummer of 1955. As the world was to learn two years later, its most striking aspect was a novel, horse-collar-shaped radiator grille, set vertically in the center of a conventionally low, wide front end—a blend of the unique and the familiar that was there for all to see, though certainly not for all to admire. In two prominent respects, however, Brown or Krafve, or both, lost sight entirely of the familiar, specifying a unique rear end, marked by widespread horizontal wings that were in bold contrast to the huge longitudinal tail fins then captivating the market, and a unique cluster of automatic-transmission push buttons on the hub of the steering wheel. In a speech to the public delivered a while before the public had its first look at the car, Krafve let fall a hint or two about its styling, which, he said, made it so "distinctive" that, externally, it was "immediately recognizable from front, side, and rear," and, internally, it was "the epitome of the push-button era without wild-blue-yonder Buck Rogers concepts." At last came the day when the men in the highest stratum of the Ford Hierarchy were given their first glimpse of the car. It produced an effect that was little short of apocalyptic. On August 15 1955, in the ceremonial secrecy of the styling center, while Krafve, Brown, and their aides stood by smiling nervously and washing their hands in air, the members of the Forward Product Planning Committee, including Henry Ford II and Breech, watched critically as a curtain was lifted to reveal the first full-size model of the E-Car—a clay one, with tinfoil simulating aluminum and chrome. According to eye-witnesses, the audience sat in utter silence for what seemed like a full minute, and then, as one man, burst into a round of applause. Nothing of the kind had ever happened at an intracompany first showing at Ford since 1896, when old Henry had bolted together his first horseless carriage.

One of the most persuasive and most frequently cited explanations of the Edsel's failure is that it was a victim of the time lag between the decision to produce it and the act of putting it on the market. It was easy to see a few years later, when smaller and less powerful cars, euphemistically called "compacts," had become so popular as to turn the old autmobile status-ladder upside down, that the Edsel was a giant step in the wrong direction, but it was far from easy to see that in fat, tail-finny 1955. American ingenuity—which has produced the electric light, the flying machine, the tin Lizzie, the atomic bomb, and even a tax system that permits a man, under certain circumstances, to clear a profit by making a charitable donation—has not yet found a way of getting an automobile on the market within a reasonable time after it comes off the drawing board; the making of steel dies, the alerting of retail dealers, the preparation of advertising and promotion campaigns, the gaining of executive approval for each successive move, and the various other gavotte-like routines that are considered as vital as breathing in Detroit and its environs usually consume about two years. Guessing future tastes is hard enough for those charged with planning the customary annual changes in models of established makes; it is far harder to bring out an altogether new creation, like the E-Car, for which several intricate new steps must be worked into the dance pattern, such as endowing the product with a personality and selecting a suitable name for it, to say nothing of consulting various oracles in an effort to determine whether, by the time of the unveiling, the state of the national economy will make bringing out *any* new car seem like a good idea.

Faithfully executing the prescribed routine, the Special Products Division called upon its director of planning for market research, David Wallace, to see what he could do about imparting a personality to the E-Car and giving it a name. Wallace, a lean, craggy-jawed pipe puffer with a soft, slow, thoughtful way of speaking, gave the impression of being the Platonic idea of the college professor—the very steel die from which the breed is cut—although, in point of fact, his background was not strongly academic. Before going to Ford, in 1955, he had worked his way through Westminster College, in Pennsylvania, ridden out the depression as a construction laborer in New York City, and then spent ten years in market research at *Time*. Still, impressions are what count, and Wallace has admitted that during his tenure with Ford he consciously stressed his professorial air for the sake of the advantage it gave him in dealing with the bluff, practical men of Dearborn. "Our department came to be regarded as a semi-Brain Trust," he says, with a certain satisfaction. He insisted, typically, on living in Ann Arbor, where he could bask in the scholarly aura of the University of Michigan, rather than in Dearborn or Detroit, both of which he declared were intolerable after business hours. Whatever the degree of his success in projecting the image of the E-Car, he seems, by his small eccentricities, to have done splendidly at projecting the image of Wallace. "I don't think Dave's motivation for being at Ford was basically economic," his old boss, Krafve, says. "Dave is the scholarly type, and I think he considered the job an interesting challenge." One could scarcely ask for better evidence of image projection than that.

Wallace clearly recalls the reasoning—candid enough —that guided him and his assistants as they sought just the right personality for E-Car. "We said to ourselves, 'Let's face it—there is no great difference in basic mechanism between a two-thousand-dollar Chevrolet and a six-thousand-dollar Cadillac,'" he says. "'Forget about all the ballyhoo,' we said, 'and you'll see that they are really pretty much the same thing. Nevertheless, there's something—there's *got* to be something —in the makeup of a certain number of people that gives them a yen for a Cadillac, in spite of its high price, or maybe because of it.' We concluded that cars are the means to a sort of dream fulfillment. There's some irrational factor in people that makes them want one kind of car rather than another—something that has nothing to do with the mechanism at all but with the car's personality, as the customer imagines it. What we wanted to do, naturally, was to give the E-Car the personality that would make the greatest number of people want it. We figured we had a big advantage over the other manufacturers of medium-priced cars, because we didn't have to worry about changing a pre-existent, perhaps somewhat obnoxious personality. All we had to do was create the exact one we wanted— from scratch."

As the first step in determining what the E-Car's exact personality should be, Wallace decided to assess the personalities of the medium-priced cars already on the market, and those of the so-called low-priced cars as well, since the cost of some of the cheap cars' 1955 models had risen well up into the medium-price range. To this end, he engaged the Columbia University Bureau of Applied Social Research to interview eight hundred recent car buyers in Peoria, Illinois, and another eight hundred in San Bernardino, California, on the mental images they had of the various automobile makes concerned. (In undertaking this commercial en-

terprise, Columbia maintained its academic indepen-
dence by reserving the right to publish its findings.)
"Our idea was to get the reaction in cities, among
clusters of people," Wallace says. "We didn't want a
cross section. What we wanted was something that
would show interpersonal factors. We picked Peoria as
a place that is Midwestern, stereotyped, and not loaded
with extraneous factors—like a General Motors glass
plant, say. We picked San Bernardino because the West
Coast is very important in the automobile business, and
because the market there is quite different—people tend
to buy flashier cars."

The questions that the Columbia researchers fared
forth to ask in Peoria and San Bernardino dealt ex-
haustively with practically everything having to do with
automobiles except such matters as how much they
cost, how safe they were, and whether they ran. In particular, Wallace wanted to know the respondents' impressions of each of the existing makes. Who, in their
opinion, would naturally own a Chevrolet or a Buick
or whatever? People of what age? Of which Sex? Of
what social status? From the answers, Wallace found it
easy to put together a personality portrait of each
make. The image of the Ford came into focus as that
of a very fast, strongly masculine car, of no particular
social pretensions, that might characteristically be
driven by a rancher or an automobile mechanic. In
contrast, Chevrolet emerged as older, wiser, slower, a
bit less rampantly masculine, and slightly more distin-
gué—a clergyman's car. Buick jelled into a middle-aged
lady—or, at least, more of a lady than Ford, sex in
cars having proved to be relative—with a bit of the
devil still in her, whose most felicitous mate would be a
lawyer, a doctor, or a dance-band leader. As for the
Mercury, it came out as virtually a hot rod, best suited
to a young-buck racing driver; thus, despite its higher
price tag, it was associated with persons having incomes
no higher than the average Ford owner's, so no wonder
Ford owners had not been trading up to it. This odd

discrepancy between image and fact, coupled with the circumstance that, in sober truth, all four makes looked very much alike and had almost the same horsepower under their hoods, only served to bear out Wallace's premise that the automobile fancier, like a young man in love, is incapable of sizing up the object of his affections in anything resembling a rational manner.

By the time the researchers closed the books on Peoria and San Bernardino, they had elicited replies not only to these questions but to others, several of which, it would appear, only the most abstruse sociological thinker could relate to medium-priced cars. "Frankly, we dabbled," Wallace says. "It was a dragnet operation." Among the odds and ends that the dragnet dredged up were some that, when pieced together, led the researchers to report:

> By looking at those respondents whose annual incomes range from $4,000 to $11,000, we can make an . . . observation. A considerable percentage of these respondents [to a question about their ability to mix cocktails] are in the "somewhat" category on ability to mix cocktails. . . . Evidently, they do not have much confidence in their cocktail-mixing ability. We may infer that these respondents are aware of the face that they are in the learning process. They may be able to mix Martinis or Manhattans, but beyond these popular drinks they don't have much of a repertoire.

Wallace, dreaming of an ideally loveable E-Car, was delighted as returns like these came pouring into his Dearborn office. But when the time for a final decision drew near, it became clear to him that he must put aside peripheral issues like cocktail-mixing prowess and address himself once more to the old problem of the image. And here, it seemed to him, the greatest pitfall was the temptation to aim, in accordance with what he took to be the trend of the times, for extremes of masculinity, youthfulness, and speed; indeed, the following passage from one of the Columbia reports, as he interpreted it, contained a specific warning against such folly.

> Offhand we might conjecture that women who drive cars probably work, and are more mobile than non-owners, and get gratifications out of mastering a traditionally male role. But . . . there is no doubt that whatever gratifications women get out of their cars, and whatever social imagery they attach to their automobiles, they do want to appear as women. Perhaps more worldly women, but women.

Early in 1956, Wallace set about summing up all of his department's findings in a report to his superiors in the Special Products Division. Entitled "The Market and Personality Objectives of the E-Car" and weighty with facts and statistics—though generously interspersed with terse sections in italics or capitals from which a hard-pressed executive could get the gist of the thing in a matter of seconds—the report first indulged in some airy, skippable philosophizing and then got down to conclusions:

> What happens when an owner sees his make as a car which a *woman* might buy, but is himself a *man?* Does this apparent inconsistency of car image and the buyer's own characteristics affect his trading plans? The answer quite definitely is *Yes.* When there is a conflict between owner characteristics and make image, there is greater planning to switch to another make. In other words, when the buyer is a different kind of person from the person he thinks would own his make, he wants to change to a make in which he, inwardly, will be more comfortable.
> It should be noted that "conflict," as used here, can be of two kinds. Should a make have a strong and well-defined image, it is obvious that an owner with strong opposing characteristics would be in conflict. But conflict also can occur when the make image is diffuse or weakly defined. In this case, the owner is

in an equally frustrating position of not being able
to get a satisfactory identification from his make.

The question, then, was how to steer between the
Scylla of a too definite car personality and the
Charybdis of a too weak personality. To this the report replied, "Capitalize on imagery weakness of competition," and went on to urge that in the matter of age
the E-Car should take an imagery position neither too
young nor too old but right alongside that of the mid-
dling Oldsmobile; that in the matter of social class, not
to mince matters, "the E-Car might well take a status
position just below Buick and Oldsmobile"; and that
in the delicate matter of sex it should try to straddle
the fence, again along with the protean Olds. In sum
(and in Wallace typography):

> The most advantageous personality for the E-Car
> might well be THE SMART CAR FOR THE YOUNGER
> EXECUTIVE OR PROFESSIONAL FAMILY ON ITS WAY UP.
>   Smart car: recognition by others of the owner's
> good style and taste.
>   Younger: appealing to spirited but responsible ad-
> venturers.
>   Executive or professional: millions pretend to this
> status, whether they can attain it or not.
>   Family: not exclusively masculine; a wholesome
> "good" role.
>   On Its Way Up: "The E-Car has faith in you, son;
> we'll help you make it!"

Before spirited but responsible adventurers could
have faith in the E-Car, however, it had to have a
name. Very early in its history, Krafve had suggested
to members of the Ford family that the new car be
named for Edsel Ford, who was the only son of old
Henry; the president of the Ford Motor Company from
1918 until his death, in 1943; and the father of the
new generation of Fords—Henry II, Benson, and William Clay. The three brothers had let Krafve know that

their father might not have cared to have his name
spinning on a million hubcaps, and they had consequently suggested that the Special Products Division
start looking around for a substitute. This it did, with
a zeal no less emphatic than it displayed in the personality crusade. In the late summer and early fall of
1955, Wallace hired the services of several research
outfits, which sent interviewers, armed with a list of two
thousand possible names, to canvass sidewalk crowds in
New York, Chicago, Willow Run, and Ann Arbor.
The interviewers did not ask simply what the respon-
dent thought of some such name as Mars, Jupiter,
Rover, Ariel, Arrow, Dart, or Ovation. They asked what
free associations each name brought to mind, and having got an answer to this one, they asked what word or
words was considered the opposite of each name, on
the theory that, subliminally speaking, the opposite is
as much a part of a name as the tail is of a penny. The
results of all this, the Special Products Division eventually decided, were inconclusive. Meanwhile, Krafve
and his men held repeated sessions in a darkened room,
staring, with the aid of a spotlight, at a series of card-
board signs, each bearing a name, as, one after another,
they were flipped over for their consideration. One of
the men thus engaged spoke up for the name Phoenix,
because of its connotations of ascendancy, and another
favored Altair, on the ground that it would lead practically all alphabetical lists of cars and thus enjoy an
advantage analogous to that enjoyed in the animal
kingdom by the aardvark. At a certain drowsy point in
one session, somebody suddenly called a halt to the
card-flipping and asked in an incredulous tone, "Didn't
I see 'Buick' go by two or three cards back?" Everybody looked at Wallace, the impresario of the sessions.
He puffed on his pipe, smiled an academic smile, and
nodded.

The card-flipping sessions proved to be as fruitless as
the sidewalk interviews, and it was at this stage of the

game that Wallace, resolving to try and wring from genius what the common mind had failed to yield, entered into the celebrated car-naming correspondence with the poet Marianne Moore, which was later published in *The New Yorker* and still later, in book form, by the Morgan Library. "We should like this name . . . to convey, through association or other conjuration, some visceral feeling of elegance, fleetness, advanced features and design," Wallace wrote to Miss Moore, achieving a certain feeling of elegance himself. If it is asked who among the gods of Dearborn had the inspired and inspiriting idea of enlisting Miss Moore's services in this cause, the answer, according to Wallace, is that it was no god but the wife of one of his junior assistants—a young lady who had recently graduated from Mount Holyoke, where she had heard Miss Moore lecture. Had her husband's superiors gone a step further and actually adopted one of Miss Moore's many suggestions —Intelligent Bullet, for instance, or Utopian Turtletop, or Bullet Cloisonné, or Pastelogram, or Mongoose Civique, or Andante con Moto ("Description of a good motor?" Miss Moore queried in regard to this last)— there is no telling to what heights the E-Car might have risen, but the fact is that they didn't. Dissatisfied with both the poet's ideas and their own, the executives in the Special Products Division next called in Foote, Cone & Belding, the advertising agency that had lately been signed up to handle the E-Car account. With characteristic Madison Avenue vigor, Foote, Cone & Belding organized a competition among the employees of its New York, London, and Chicago offices, offering nothing less than one of the brand-new cars as a prize to whoever thought up an acceptable name. In no time at all, Foote, Cone & Belding had eighteen thousand names in hand, including Zoom, Zip, Benson, Henry, and Drof (if in doubt, spell it backward). Suspecting that the bosses of the Special Products Division might regard this list as a trifle unwieldly, the agency got to work and cut it down to six thousand names, which it presented to them in executive session. "There you are," a Foote, Cone man said trimphantly, flopping a sheaf of papers on the table. "Six thousand names, all alphabetized and cross-referenced."

A gasp escaped Krafve. "But we don't want six thousand names," he said. "We only want one."

The situation was critical, because the making of dies for the new car was about to begin and some of them would have to bear its name. On a Thursday, Foote, Cone & Belding canceled all leaves and instituted what is called a crash program, instructing its New York and Chicago offices to set about independently cutting down the list of six thousand names to ten and to have the job done by the end of the weekend. Before the weekend was over, the two Foote, Cone offices presented their separate lists of ten to the Special Products Division, and by an almost incredible coincidence, which all hands insist *was* a coincidence, four of the names on the two lists were the same; Corsair, Citation, Pacer, and Ranger had miraculously survived the dual scrutiny. "Corsair seemed to be head and shoulders above everything else," Wallace says. "Along with other factors in its favor, it had done splendidly in the sidewalk interviews. The free associations with Corsair were rather romantic—'pirate,' 'swashbuckler,' things like that. For its opposite, we got 'princess,' or something else attractive on that order. Just what we wanted."

Corsair or no Corsair, the E-Car was named the Edsel in the early spring of 1956, though the public was not informed until the following autumn. The epochal decision was reached at a meeting of the Ford executive committee held at a time when, as it happened, all three Ford brothers were away. In President Ford's absence, the meeting was conducted by Breech, who had become chairman of the board in 1955, and his mood that day was brusque, and not one to linger long over swashbucklers and princesses. After hearing the final choices, he said, "I don't like any of them. Let's take another look at some of the others." So they took another look at the favored rejects, among them the name Edsel, which, in spite of the three Ford brothers' expressed interpretation of their father's probable wishes, had been retained as a sort of anchor to windward. Breech led his associates in a patient scrutiny of the list until they came to "Edsel." "Let's call it that," Breech said with calm finality. There were to be four main models of the E-Car, with variations on each one, and Breech soothed some of his colleagues by adding that the magic four—Corsair, Citation, Pacer, and Ranger—might be used, if anybody felt so inclined, as the subnames for the models. A telephone call was put through to Henry II, who was vacationing in Nassau. He said that if Edsel was the choice of the executive committee, he would abide by its decision, provided he could get the approval of the rest of his family. Within a few days, he got it.

As Wallace wrote to Miss Moore a while later: "We have chosen a name. . . . It fails somewhat of the resonance, gaiety, and zest we were seeking. But it has a personal dignity and meaning to many of us here. Our name, dear Miss Moore, is—Edsel. I hope you will understand."

It may be assumed that word of the naming of the E-Car spread a certain amount of despair among the Foote, Cone & Belding backers of more metaphorical names, none of whom won a free car—a despair heightened by the fact that the name "Edsel" had been ruled out of the competition from the first. But their sense of disappointment was nothing compared to the gloom that enveloped many employees of the Special Products Division. Some felt that the name of a former president of the company, who had sired its current president, bore dynastic connotations that were alien to the American temper; others, who, with Wallace, had put their trust in the quirks of the mass unconscious, believed that "Edsel" was a disastrously unfortunate combination of syllables. What were its free associations? Pretzel, diesel, hard sell. What was its opposite? It didn't seem to have any. Still, the matter was settled, and there was nothing to do but put the best possible face on it. Besides, the anguish in the Special Products Divison was by no means unanimous, and Krafve himself, of course, was among those who had no objection to the name. He still has none, declining to go along with those who contend that the decline and fall of the Edsel may be dated from the moment of its christening.

Krafve, in fact, was so well pleased with the way matters had turned out that when, at eleven o'clock on the morning of November 19, 1956, after a long summer of thoughtful silence, the Ford Company released to the world the glad tidings that the E-Car had been named the Edsel, he accompanied the announcement with a few dramatic flourishes of his own. On the very stroke of that hour on that day, the telephone operators in Krafve's domain began greeting callers with "Edsel Division" instead of "Special Products Division"; all stationery bearing the obsolete letterhead of the division vanished and was replaced by sheaves of paper headed "Edsel Division"; and outside the building a huge stainless-steel sign reading "EDSEL DIVISION" rose ceremoniously to the rooftop. Krafve himself managed to remain earthbound, though he had his own reasons for feeling buoyant; in recognition of his leadership of the E-Car project up to that point, he was given the august title of Vice-President of the Ford Motor Company and General Manager, Edsel Division.

From the administrative point of view, this off-with-the-old-on-with-the-new effect was merely harmless window dressing. In the strict secrecy of the Dearborn test track, vibrant, almost full-fledged Edsels, with their name graven on their superstructures, were already being road-tested; Brown and his fellow stylists were already well along with their designs for the *next* year's Edsel; recruits were already being signed up for an entirely new organization of retail dealers to sell the Edsel to the public; and Foote, Cone & Belding, having been relieved of the burden of staging crash programs to collect names and crash programs to get rid of them again, was already deep in schemes for advertising the Edsel, under the personal direction of a no less substantial pillar of his trade than Fairfax M. Cone, the agency's head man. In planning his campaign, Cone relied heavily on what had come to be called the "Wallace prescription"; that is, the formula for the Edsel's personality as set forth by Wallace back in the days before the big naming bee—"The smart car for the younger executive or professional family on its way up." So enthusiastic was Cone about the prescription that he accepted it with only one revision—the substitution of "middle-income" family for "younger executive," his hunch being that there were more middle-income families around than young executives, or even people who *thought* they were young executives. In an expansive mood, possibly induced by his having landed an account that was expected to bring billings of well over ten million dollars a year, Cone described to reporters on several occasions the kind of campaign he was plotting for the Edsel—quiet, self-assured, and avoiding as much as possible the use of the adjective "new," which, though it had an obvious application to the product, he considered rather lacking in cachet. Above all, the campaign was to be classic in its calmness. "We think it would be awful for the advertising to compete with the car," Cone told the press. "We hope that no one will ever ask, 'Say, did you see that Edsel ad?' in any newspaper or magazine or on television, but, instead, that hundreds of thousands of people will say, and say again, 'Man, did you read about that Edsel?' or 'Did you see that car?' This is the difference between advertising and selling." Evidently enough, Cone felt confident about the campaign and the Edsel. Like a chess master who has no doubt that he will win, he could afford to explicate the brilliance of his moves even as he made them.

Automobile men still talk, with admiration for the

virtuosity displayed and a shudder at the ultimate outcome, of the Edsel Division's drive to round up retail dealers. Ordinarily, an established manufacturer launches a new car through dealers who are already handling his other makes and who, to begin with, take on the upstart as a sort of sideline. Not so in the case of the Edsel; Krafve received authorization from on high to go all out and build up a retail-dealer organization by making raids on dealers who had contracts with other manufacturers, or even with the other Ford Company divisions—Ford and Lincoln-Mercury. (Although the Ford dealers thus corralled were not obliged to cancel their old contracts, all the emphasis was on signing up retail outlets exclusively dedicated to the selling of Edsels.) The goal set for Introduction Day—which, after a great deal of soul-searching, was finally established as September 4, 1957—was twelve hundred Edsel dealers from coast to coast. They were not to be just any dealers, either; Krafve made it clear that Edsel was interested in signing up only dealers whose records showed that they had a marked ability to sell cars without resorting to the high-pressure tricks of borderline legality that had lately been giving the automobile business a bad name. "We simply have to have quality dealers with quality service facilities," Krafve said. "A customer who gets poor service on an established brand blames the dealer. On an Edsel, he will blame the car." The goal of twelve hundred was a high one, for no dealer, quality or not, can afford to switch makes lightly. The average dealer has at least a hundred thousand dollars tied up in his agency, and in large cities the investment is much higher. He must hire salesmen, mechanics, and office help; buy his own tools, technical literature, and signs, the latter costing as much as five thousand dollars a set; and pay the factory spot cash for the cars he receives from it.

The man charged with mobilizing an Edsel sales force along these exacting lines was J. C. (Larry) Doyle, who, as general sales-and-marketing manager of the division, ranked second to Krafve himself. A veteran of forty years with the Ford Company, who had started with it as an office boy in Kansas City and had spent the intervening time mainly selling, Doyle was a maverick in his field. On the one hand, he had an air of kindness and consideration that made him the very antithesis of the glib, brash denizens of a thousand automobile rows across the continent, and, on the other, he did not trouble to conceal an old-time salesman's skepticism about such things as analyzing the sex and status of automobiles, a pursuit he characterized by saying, "When I play pool, I like to keep one foot on the floor." Still, he knew how to sell cars, and that was what the Edsel Division needed. Recalling how he and his sales staff brought off the unlikely trick of persuading substantial and reputable men who had already achieved success in one of the toughest of all businesses to tear up profitable franchises in favor of a risky new one, Doyle said not long ago, "As soon as the first few new Edsels came through, early in 1957, we put a couple of them in each of our five regional sales offices. Needless to say, we kept those offices locked and the blinds drawn. Dealers in every make for miles around wanted to see the car, if only out of curiosity, and that gave us the leverage we needed. We let it be known that we would show the car only to dealers who were really interested in coming with us, and then we sent our regional field managers out to surrounding towns to try to line up the No. 1 dealer in each to see the cars. If we couldn't get No. 1, we'd try for No. 2. Anyway, we set things up so that no one got in to see the Edsel without listening to a complete one-hour pitch on the whole situation by a member of our sales force. It worked very well." It worked so well that by midsummer, 1957, it was clear that Edsel was going to have a lot of quality dealers on Introduction Day. (In fact, it missed the goal of twelve hundred by a couple of dozen.) Indeed, some dealers in other makes were apparently so confident of the Edsel's success, or so bemused by the

Doyle staff's pitch, that they were entirely willing to sign up after hardly more than a glance at the Edsel itself. Doyle's people urged them to study the car closely, and kept reciting the litany of its virtues, but the prospective Edsel dealers would wave such protestations aside and demand a contract without further ado. In retrospect, it would seem that Doyle could have given lessons to the Pied Piper.

Now that the Edsel was no longer the exclusive concern of Dearborn, the Ford Company was irrevocably committed to going ahead. "Until Doyle went into action, the whole program could have been quietly dropped at any time at a word from top management, but once the dealers had been signed up, there was the matter of honoring your contract to put out a car," Krafve has explained. The matter was attended to with dispatch. Early in June, 1957, the company announced that of the $250 million it had set aside to defray the advance costs of the Edsel, $150 million was being spent on basic facilities, including the conversion of various Ford and Mercury plants to the needs of producing the new cars; $50 million on special Edsel tooling; and $50 million on initial advertising and promotion. In June, too, an Edsel destined to be the star of a television commercial for future release was stealthily transported in a closed van to Hollywood, where, on a locked sound stage patrolled by security guards, it was exposed to the cameras in the admiring presence of a few carefully chosen actors who had sworn that their lips would be sealed from then until Introduction Day. For this delicate photographic operation the Edsel Division cannily enlisted the services of Cascade Pictures, which also worked for the Atomic Energy Commission, and, as far as is known, there were no unintentional leaks. "We took all the same precautions we take for our A.E.C. films," a grim Cascade official has since said.

Within a few weeks, the Edsel Division had eighteen hundred salaried employees and was rapidly filling some fifteen thousand factory jobs in the newly converted plants. On July 15th, Edsels began rolling off assembly lines at Somerville, Massachusetts; Mahwah, New Jersey; Louisville, Kentucky; and San Jose, California. The same day, Doyle scored an important coup by signing up Charles Kreisler, a Manhattan dealer regarded as one of the country's foremost practitioners in his field, who had represented Oldsmobile—one of Edsel's self-designated rivals—before heeding the siren song from Dearborn. On July 22nd, the first advertisement for the Edsel appeared—in *Life*. A two-page spread in plain black-and-white, it was impeccably classic and calm, showing a car whooshing down a country highway at such high speed that it was an indistinguishable blur. "Lately, some mysterious automobiles have been seen on the roads," the accompanying text was headed. It went on to say that the blur was an Edsel being road-tested, and concluded with the assurance "The Edsel is on its way." Two weeks later, a second ad appeared in *Life,* this one showing a ghostly-looking car, covered with a white sheet, standing at the entrance to the Ford styling center. This time the headline read, "A man in your town recently made a decision that will change his life." The decision, it was explained, was to become an Edsel dealer. Whoever wrote the ad cannot have known how truly he spoke.

During the tense summer of 1957, the man of the hour at Edsel was C. Gayle Warnock, director of public relations, whose duty was not so much to generate public interest in the forthcoming product, there being an abundance of that, as to keep the interest at white heat, and readily convertible into a desire to buy one of the new cars on or after Introduction Day—or, as the company came to call it, Edsel Day. Warnock, a dapper, affable man with a tiny mustache, is a native of Converse, Indiana, who, long before Krafve drafted him from the Ford office in Chicago, did a spot of publicity work for county fairs—a background that has enabled him to spice the honeyed smoothness of the modern public-relations man with a touch of the old carnival pitchman's uninhibited spirit. Recalling his summons to Dearborn, Warnock says, "When Dick Krafve hired me, back in the fall of 1955, he told me, 'I want you to program the E-Car publicity from now to Introduction Day.' I said, 'Frankly, Dick, what do you mean by "program"?' He said he meant to sort of space it out, starting at the end and working backward. This was something new to me—I was used to taking what breaks I could get when I could get them—but I soon found out how right Dick was. It was almost too easy to get publicity for the Edsel. Early in 1956, when it was still called the E-Car, Krafve gave a little talk about it out in Portland, Oregon. We didn't try for anything more than a play in the local press, but the wire services picked the story up and it went out all over the country. Clippings came in by the bushel. Right then I realized the trouble we might be headed for. The public was getting to be hysterical to see our car, figuring it was going to be some kind of dream car—like nothing they'd ever seen. I said to Krafve, 'When they find out it's got four wheels and one engine, just like the next car, they're liable to be disappointed.' "

It was agreed that the safest way to tread the tightrope between overplaying and underplaying the Edsel would be to say nothing about the car as a whole but to reveal its individual charms a little at a time—a sort of automotive strip tease (a phrase that Warnock couldn't with proper dignity use himself but was happy to see the *New York Times* use for him). The policy was later violated now and then, purposely or inadvertently. For one thing, as the pre-Edsel Day summer wore on, reporters prevailed upon Krafve to authorize Warnock to show the Edsel to them, one at a time, on what Warnock called a "peekaboo," or "you've-seen-it-now-forget-it," basis. And, for another, Edsels loaded on vans for delivery to dealers were appearing on the highways in ever-increasing numbers, covered fore and aft with canvas flaps that, as if to whet the desire of the motoring public, were forever blowing loose. That summer, too, was a time of speechmaking by an Edsel foursome consisting of Krafve, Doyle, J. Emmet Judge, who was Edsel's director of merchandise and product planning, and Robert F. G. Copeland, its assistant general sales manager for advertising, sales promotion, and training. Ranging separately up and down and across the nation, the four orators moved around so fast and so tirelessly that Warnock, lest he lose track of them, took to indicating their whereabouts with colored pins on a map in his office. "Let's see, Krafve goes from Atlanta to New Orleans, Doyle from Council Bluffs to Salt Lake City," Warnock would muse of a morning in Dearborn, sipping his second cup of coffee and then getting up to yank the pins out and jab them in again.

Although most of Krafve's audiences consisted of bankers and representatives of finance companies who it was hoped would lend money to Edsel dealers, his speeches that summer, far from echoing the general hoopla, were almost statesmanlike in their cautious—even somber—references to the new car's prospects. And well they might have been, for developments in the general economic outlook of the nation were making more sanguine men than Krafve look puzzled. In July, 1957, the stock market went into a nose dive, marking the beginning of what is recalled as the recession of 1958. Then, early in August, a decline in the sales of medium-priced 1957 cars of all makes set in, and the general situation worsened so rapidly that, before the month was out, *Automotive News* reported that dealers in all makes were ending their season with the second-largest number of unsold new cars in history. If Krafve, on his lonely rounds, ever considered retreating to Dearborn for consolation, he was forced to put that notion out of his mind when, also in August, Mercury, Edsel's own stablemate, served notice that it was going to make things as tough as possible for the newcomer by undertaking a million-dollar, thirty-day advertising drive aimed especially at "price-conscious buyers"—a clear reference to the fact that the 1957 Mercury, which was then being sold at a discount by most dealers, cost less than the new Edsel was expected to. Meanwhile, sales of the Rambler, which was the only American-made small car then in production, were beginning to rise ominously. In the face of all these evil portents, Krafve fell into the habit of ending his speeches with a rather downbeat anecdote about the board chairman of an unsuccessful dog-food company who said to his fellow directors, "Gentlemen, let's face facts—dogs don't like our product." "As far as we're concerned," Krafve added on at least one occasion, driving home the moral with admirable clarity, "a lot will depend on whether people like our car or not."

But most of the other Edsel men were unimpressed by Krafve's misgivings. Perhaps the least impressed of all was Judge, who, while doing his bit as an itinerant speaker, specialized in community and civic groups. Undismayed by the limitations of the strip-tease policy, Judge brightened up his lectures by showing such a bewildering array of animated graphs, cartoons, charts, and pictures of parts of the car—all flashed on a Cinemascope screen—that his listeners usually got halfway home before they realized that he hadn't shown them an Edsel. He wandered restlessly around the auditorium as he spoke, shifting the kaleidoscopic images on the screen at will with the aid of an automatic slide changer—a trick made possible by a crew of electricians who laced the place in advance with a maze of wires linking the device to dozens of floor switches, which, scattered about the hall, responded when he kicked them. Each of the "Judge spectaculars," as these performances came to be known, cost the Edsel Division five thousand dollars—a sum that included the pay and expenses of the technical crew, who would arrive on the scene a day or so ahead of time to set up the electrical rig. At the last moment, Judge would descend melodramatically on the town by plane, hasten to the hall, and go into his act. "One of the greatest aspects of this whole Edsel program is the philosophy of product and merchandising behind it," Judge might start off, with a desultory kick at a switch here, a switch there. "All of us who have been a part of it are real proud of this background and we are anxiously awaiting its success when the car is introduced this fall. . . . Never again will we be associated with anything as gigantic and full of meaning as this particular program. . . . Here is a glimpse of the car which will be before the American public on September 4, 1957 [at this point, Judge would show a provocative slide of a hubcap or section of fender]. . . . It is a different car in every respect, yet it has an element of conservatism which will give it maximum appeal. . . . The distinctiveness of the frontal styling integrates with the sculptured patterns of the side treatment. . . ." And on and on Judge would rhapsodize, rolling out such awesome phrases as "sculptured sheet metal," "highlight character," and "graceful, flowing lines." At last would come the ringing peroration. "We are proud of the Edsel!" he would cry, kicking switches right and left. "When it is introduced this fall, it will take its place on the streets and highways of America, bringing new greatness to the Ford Motor Company. This is the Edsel story."

The drum-roll climax of the strip tease was a three-day press preview of the Edsel, undraped from pinched-in snout to flaring rear, that was held in Detroit and Dearborn on August 26th, 27th, and 28th, with 250 reporters from all over the country in attendance. It differed from previous automotive jamborees of its kind in that the journalists were invited to bring their wives along—and many of them did. Before it was over, it had cost the Ford Company ninety thousand dollars. Grand as it was, the conventionality of its setting was a disappointment to Warnock, who had proposed, and seen rejected, three locales that he thought would provide a more offbeat *ambiance*—a steamer on the Detroit River ("wrong symbolism"); Edsel, Kentucky ("inaccessible by road"); and Haiti ("just turned down flat"). Thus hobbled, Warnock could do no better for the reporters and their wives when they converged on the Detroit scene on Sunday evening, August 25th, than to put them up at the discouragingly named Sheraton-Cadillac Hotel and to arrange for them to spend Monday afternoon hearing and reading about the long-awaited details of the entire crop of Edsels—eighteen varieties available, in four main lines (Corsair, Citation, Pacer, and Ranger), differing mainly in their size, power, and trim. The next morning, specimens of the models themselves were revealed to the reporters in the styling center's rotunda, and Henry II offered a few words of tribute to his father. "The wives were not asked to the unveiling," a Foote, Cone man who helped plan the affair recalls. "It was too solemn and business-like an event for that. It went over fine. There was excitement even among the hardened newspapermen." (The import of the stories that most of the excited newspapermen filed was that the Edsel seemed to be a good car, though not so radical as its billing had suggested.)

In the afternoon, the reporters were whisked out to the test track to see a team of stunt drivers put the Edsel through its paces. This event, calculated to be thrilling, turned out to be hair-raising, and even, for some, a little unstringing. Enjoined not to talk too much about speed and horsepower, since only a few months previously the whole automobile industry had nobly resolved to concentrate on making cars instead of delayed-action bombs, Warnock had decided to emphasize the Edsel's liveliness through deeds rather than words, and to accomplish this he had hired a team of stunt drivers. Edsels ran over two-foot ramps on two wheels, bounced from higher ramps on all four wheels, were driven in crisscross patterns, grazing each other, at sixty or seventy miles per hour, and skidded into complete turns at fifty. For comic relief, there was a clown driver parodying the daredevil stuff. All the while, the voice of Neil L. Blume, Edsel's engineering chief, could be heard on a loudspeaker, purring about "the capabilities, the safety, the ruggedness, the maneuverability and performance of these new cars," and skirting the words "speed" and "horsepower" as delicately as a sandpiper skirts a wave. At one point, when an Edsel leaping a high ramp just missed turning over, Krafve's face took on a ghastly pallor; he later reported that he had not known the daredevil stunts were going to be so extreme, and was concerned both for the good name of the Edsel and the lives of the drivers. Warnock, noticing his boss's distress, went over and asked Krafve if he was enjoying the show. Krafve replied tersely that he would answer when it was over and all hands safe. But everyone else seemed to be having a grand time. The Foote, Cone man said, "You looked over this green Michigan hill, and there were those glorious Edsels, performing gloriously in unison. It was beautiful. It was like the Rockettes. It was exciting. Morale was high."

Warnock's high spirits had carried him to even wilder extremes of fancy. The stunt driving, like the unveiling, was considered too rich for the blood of the wives, but the resourceful Warnock was ready for them with a fashion show that he hoped they would find at least equally diverting. He need not have worried. The star of the show, who was introduced by Brown, the Edsel stylist, as a Paris *couturière,* both beautiful and talented, turned out at the final curtain to be a female impersonator—a fact of which Warnock, to heighten the verisimilitude of the act, had given Brown no advance warning. Things were never again quite the same since between Brown and Warnock, but the wives were able to give their husbands an extra paragraph or two for their stories.

That evening, there was a big gala for one and all at the styling center, which was itself styled as a night club for the occasion, complete with a fountain that danced in time with the music of Ray McKinley's band, whose emblem, the letters "GM"—a holdover from the days of its founder, the late Glenn Miller—was emblazoned, as usual, on the music stand of each musician, very nearly ruining the evening for Warnock. The next morning, at a windup press conference held by Ford officials, Breech declared of the Edsel, "It's a husky youngster, and, like most other new parents, we're proud enough to pop our buttons." Then seventy-one of the reporters took the wheels of as many Edsels and set out for home—not to drive the cars into their garages but to deliver them to the showrooms of their local Edsel dealers. Let Warnock describe the highlights of this final flourish: "There were several unfortunate occurrences. One guy simply miscalculated and cracked up his car running into something. No fault of the Edsel *there*. One car lost its oil pan, so naturally the motor froze. It can happen to the best of cars. Fortunately, at the time of this malfunction the driver was going through a beautiful-sounding town—Paradise, Kansas, I think it was—and that gave the news reports about it a nice little positive touch. The nearest dealer gave the reporter a new Edsel, and he drove on home, climbing Pikes Peak on the way. Then one car crashed through a tollgate when the brakes failed. That was bad. It's funny, but the thing we were most worried about—other drivers being so eager to get a look at the Edsels that they'd crowd our cars off the road—happened only once. That was on the Pennsylvania Turnpike. One of our reporters was tooling along—no problems—when a Plymouth driver pulled up alongside to rubberneck, and edged so close that the Edsel got sideswiped. Minor damage."

Late in 1959, immediately after the demise of the Edsel, *Business Week* stated that the big press preview a Ford executive had said to a reporter, "If the company weren't in so deep, we never would have brought it out now." However, since *Business Week* neglected to publish this patently sensational statement for over two years, and since to this day all the former ranking Edsel executives (Krafve included, notwithstanding his preoccupation with the luckless dog-food company) firmly maintained that right up to Edsel Day and even for a short time thereafter they expected the Edsel to succeed, it would seem that the quotation should be regarded as a highly suspect archaeological find. Indeed, during the period between the press preview and Edsel Day the spirit of everybody associated with the venture seems to have been one of wild optimism. "Oldsmobile, Goodbye!" ran the headline on an ad, in the Detroit *Free Press,* for an agency that was switching from Olds to Edsel. A dealer in Portland, Oregon, reported that he had already sold two Edsels, sight unseen. Warnock dug up a fireworks company in Japan willing to make him, at nine dollars apiece, five thousand rockets that, exploding in mid-air, would release nine-foot scale-model Edsels made of rice paper that would inflate and descend like parachutes; his head reeling with visions of filling America's skies as well as its highways with Edsels on Edsel Day, Warnock was about to dash off an order when Krafve, looking something more than puzzled, shook his head.

On September 3rd—E Day-minus-one—the prices of the various Edsel models were announced; for cars delivered to New York they ran from just under $2,800 to just over $4,100. On E Day, the Edsel arrived. In Cambridge, a band led a gleaming motorcade of the new cars up Massachusetts Avenue; flying out of Richmond, California, a helicopter hired by one of the most jubilant of the dealers lassoed by Doyle spread a giant Edsel sign above San Francisco Bay; and all over the nation, from the Louisiana bayous to the peak of Mount Rainier to the Maine woods, one needed only a radio or a television set to know that the very air, despite Warnock's setback on the rockets, was quivering with the presence of the Edsel. The tone for Edsel Day's blizzard of publicity was set by an ad, published in newspapers all over the country, in which the Edsel shared the spotlight with the Ford Company, President Ford and Chairman Breech. In the ad, Ford looked like a dignified young father, Breech like a dignified gentleman holding a full house against a possible straight, the Edsel just looked like an Edsel. The accompanying text declared that the decision to produce the car had been "based on what we knew, guessed, felt, believed, suspected—about you," and added, "YOU are the reason behind the Edsel." The tone was calm and confident. There did not seem to be much room for doubt about the reality of that full house.

Before sundown, it was estimated, 2,850,000 people had seen the new car in dealers' showrooms. Three days later, in North Philadelphia, an Edsel was stolen. It can reasonably be argued that the crime marked the highwater mark of public acceptance of the Edsel; only a few months later, any but the least fastidious of car thieves might not have bothered.

DECLINE AND FALL

The most striking physical characteristic of the Edsel was, of course, its radiator grille. This, in contrast to the wide and horizontal grilles of all nineteen other American makes of the time, was slender and vertical. Of chromium-plated steel, and shaped something like an egg, it sat in the middle of the car's front end, and was embellished by the word "EDSEL" in aluminum letters running down its length. It was intended to suggest the front end of practically any car of twenty or thirty years ago and of most contemporary European cars, and thus to look at once seasoned and sophisticated. The trouble was that whereas the front ends of the antiques and the European cars were themselves high and narrow—consisting, indeed, of little more than the radiator grilles—the front end of the Edsel was broad and low, just like the front ends of all its American competitors. Consequently, there were wide areas

on either side of the grille that had to be filled in with
something, and filled in they were—with twin panels of
entirely conventional horizontal chrome grillwork. The
effect was that of an Oldsmobile with the prow of a
Pierce-Arrow implanted in its front end, or, more
metaphorically, of the charwoman trying on the duch-
ess' necklace. The attempt at sophistication was so
transparent as to be endearing.

But if the grille of the Edsel appealed through guilelessness, the rear end was another matter. Here, too,
there was a marked departure from the conventional design of the day. Instead of the notorious tail fin, the car
had what looked to its fanciers like wings and to others,
less ethereal-minded, like eyebrows. The lines of the
trunk lid and the rear fenders, swooping upward and
outward, did somewhat resemble the wings of a gull in
flight, but the resemblance was marred by two long,
narrow tail lights, set partly in the trunk lid and partly
in the fenders, which followed those lines and created
the startling illusion, especially at night, of a slant-eyed
grin. From the front, the Edsel seemed, above all, anxious to please, even at the cost of being clownish;
from the rear it looked crafty, Oriental, smug, one-up
—maybe a little cynical and contemptuous, too. It was
as if, somewhere between grille and rear fenders, a sinister personality change had taken place.

In other respects, the exterior styling of the Edsel was
not far out of the ordinary. Its sides were festooned with
a bit less than the average amount of chrome, and
distinguished by a gouged-out bullet-shaped groove extending forward from the rear fender for about half the
length of the car. Midway along this groove, the word
"EDSEL" was displayed in chrome letters, and just below the rear window was a small grille-like decoration,
on which was spelled out—of all things—"EDSEL."
(After all, hadn't Stylist Brown declared his intention
to create a vehicle that would be "readily recognizable"?) In its interior, the Edsel strove mightily to live
up to the prediction of General Manager Krafve that

the car would be "the epitome of the push-button era."
The push-button era in medium-priced cars being what
it was, Krafve's had been a rash prophecy indeed, but
the Edsel rose to it with a devilish assemblage of gadgets such as had seldom, if ever, been seen before. On
or near the Edsel's dashboard were a push button that
popped the trunk lid open; a lever that popped the hood
open; a lever that released the parking brake; a speed-
ometer that glowed red when the driver exceeded his
chosen maximum speed; a single-dial control for both
heating and cooling; a tachometer, in the best racing-
car style; buttons to operate or regulate the lights, the
height of the radio antenna, the heater-blower, the
windshield wiper, and the cigarette lighter; and a row
of eight red lights to wink warnings that the engine was
too hot, that it wasn't hot enough, that the generator was
on the blink, that the parking brake was on, that a door
was open, that the oil pressure was low, that the oil
level was low, and that the gasoline level was low, the
last of which the skeptical driver could confirm by consulting the gas gauge, mounted a few inches away.
Epitomizing this epitome, the automatic-transmission
control box—arrestingly situated on top of the steering
post, in the center of the wheel—sprouted a galaxy of
five push buttons so light to the touch that, as Edsel
men could hardly be restrained from demonstrating,
they could be depressed with a toothpick.

Of the four lines of Edsels, both of the two larger
and more expensive ones—the Corsair and the Citation
—were 219 inches long, or two inches longer than the
biggest of the Oldsmobiles; both were eighty inches
wide, or about as wide as passenger cars ever get; and
the height of both was only fifty-seven inches, as low
as any other medium-priced car. The Ranger and the
Pacer, the smaller Edsels, were six inches shorter, an
inch narrower, and an inch lower than the Corsair and
the Citation. The Corsair and the Citation were
equipped with 345-horsepower engines, making
them more powerful than any other American car at

the time of their debut, and the Ranger and the Pacer were good for 303 horsepower, near the top in their class. At the touch of a toothpick to the "Drive" button, an idling Corsair or Citation sedan (more than two tons of car, in either case) could, if properly skippered, take off with such abruptness that in ten and three-tenths seconds it would be doing a mile a minute, and in seventeen and a half seconds it would be a quarter of a mile down the road. If anything or anybody happened to be in the way when the toothpick touched the push button, so much the worse.

When the wraps were taken off the Edsel, it received what is known in the theatrical business as a mixed press. The automotive editors of the daily newspapers stuck mostly to straight descriptions of the car, with only here and there a phrase or two of appraisal, some of it ambiguous ("The difference in style is spectacular," noted Joseph C. Ingraham in the *New York Times*) and some of it openly favorable ("A handsome and hard-punching newcomer," said Fred Olmstead, in the Detroit *Free Press*). Magazine criticism was generally more exhaustive and occasionally more severe. *Motor Trend,* the largest monthly devoted to ordinary automobiles, as distinct from hot rods, devoted eight pages of its October, 1957, issue to an analysis and critique of the Edsel by Joe H. Wherry, its Detroit editor. Wherry liked the car's appearance, its interior comfort, and its gadgets, although he did not always make it clear just why; in paying his respects to the transmission buttons on the steering post, he wrote, "You need not take your eyes off the road for an instant." He conceded that there were "untold opportunities for more . . . unique approaches," but he summed up his opinion in a sentence that fairly peppered the Edsel with honorific adverbs: "The Edsel performs fine, rides well, and handles good." Tom McCahill, of *Mechanix Illustrated,* generally admired the "bolt bag," as he affectionately called the Edsel, but he had some reservations, which, incidentally, throw some interesting light on an automobile critic's equivalent of an aisle seat. "On ribbed concrete," he reported, "every time I shot the throttle to the floor quickly, the wheels spun like a gone-wild Waring Blendor. . . . At high speeds, especially through rough corners, I found the suspension a little too horsebacky. . . . I couldn't help but wonder what this salami would really do if it had enough road adhesion."

By far the most downright—and very likely the most damaging—panning that the Edsel got during its first months appeared in the January, 1958, issue of the Consumers Union monthly, *Consumer Reports,* whose 800,000 subscribers probably included more potential Edsel buyers than have ever turned the pages of *Motor Trend* or *Mechanix Illustrated.* After having put a Corsair through a series of road tests, *Consumer Reports* declared:

> The Edsel has no important basic advantages over other brands. The car is almost entirely conventional in construction. . . . The amount of shake present in this Corsair body on rough roads—which wasn't long in making itself heard as squeaks and rattles —went well beyond any acceptable limit. . . . The Corsair's handling qualities—sluggish, over-slow steering, sway and lean on turns, and a general detached-from-the-road feel—are, to put it mildly, without distinction. As a matter of simple fact, combined with the car's tendency to shake like jelly, Edsel handling represents retrogression rather than progress. . . . Stepping on the gas in traffic, or in passing cars, or just to feel the pleasurable surge of power, will cause those big cylinders really to lap up fuel. . . . The center of the steering wheel is not, in CU's opinion, a good pushbutton location. . . . To look at the Edsel buttons pulls the driver's eyes clear down off the road. [*Pace* Mr. Wherry.] The "luxury-loaded" Edsel—as one magazine cover described it—will certainly please anyone who confuses gadgetry with true luxury.

Three months later, in a roundup of all the 1958-model cars, *Consumer Reports* went at the Edsel again, calling it "more uselessly overpowered . . . more gadget bedecked, more hung with expensive accessories than any car in its price class," and giving the Corsair and the Citation the bottom position in its competitive ratings. Like Krafve, *Consumer Reports* considered the Edsel an epitome; unlike Krafve, the magazine concluded that the car seemed to "epitomize the many excesses" with which Detroit manufacturers were "repulsing more and more potential car buyers."

And yet, in a way, the Edsel wasn't so bad. It embodied much of the spirit of its time—or at least of the time when it was designed, early in 1955. It was clumsy, powerful, dowdy, gauche, well-meaning—a de Kooning woman. Few people, apart from employees of Foote, Cone & Belding, who were paid to do so, have adequately hymned its ability, at its best, to coax and jolly the harried owner into a sense of well-being. Furthermore, the designers of several rival makes, including Chevrolet, Buick, and Ford, Edsel's own stablemate, later flattered Brown's styling by imitating at least one feature of the car's much reviled lines—the rear-end wing theme. The Edsel was obviously jinxed, but to say that it was jinxed by its design alone would be an oversimplification, as it would be to say that it was jinxed by an excess of motivational research. The fact is that in the short, unhappy life of the Edsel a number of other factors contributed to its commercial downfall. One of these was the scarcely believable circumstance that many of the very first Edsels—those obviously destined for the most glaring public limelight—were dramatically imperfect. By its preliminary program of promotion and advertising, the Ford Company had built up an overwhelming head of public interest in the Edsel, causing its arrival to be anticipated and the car itself to be gawked at with more eagerness than had ever greeted any automobile before it. After all that, it seemed, the car didn't quite work. Within a few weeks after the Edsel was introduced, its pratfalls were the talk of the land. Edsels were delivered with oil leaks, sticking hoods, trunks that wouldn't open, and push buttons that, far from yielding to a toothpick, couldn't be budged with a hammer. An obviously distraught man staggered into a bar up the Hudson River, demanding a double shot without delay and exclaiming that the dashboard of his new Edsel had just burst into flame. *Automotive News* reported that in general the earliest Edsels suffered from poor paint, inferior sheet metal, and faulty accessories, and quoted the lament of a dealer about one of the first Edsel convertibles he received: "The top was badly set, doors cockeyed, the header bar trimmed at the wrong angle, and the front springs sagged." The Ford Company had the particular bad luck to sell to Consumers Union—which buys its test cars in the open market, as a precaution against being favored with specially doctored samples—an Edsel in which the axle ratio was wrong, an expansion plug in the cooling system blew out, the power-steering pump leaked, the rear-axle gears were noisy, and the heater emitted blasts of hot air when it was turned off. A former executive of the Edsel Division has estimated that only about half of the first Edsels really performed properly.

A layman cannot help wondering how the Ford Company, in all its power and glory, could have been guilty of such a Mack Sennett routine of buildup and anticlimax. The wan, hard-working Krafve explains gamely that when a company brings out a new model of any make—even an old and tested one—the first cars often have bugs in them. A more startling theory—though only a theory—is that there may have been sabotage in some of the four plants that assembled the Edsel, all but one of which had previously been, and currently also were, assembling Fords or Mercurys. In marketing the Edsel, the Ford Company took a leaf out of the

book of General Motors, which for years had successfully been permitting, and even encouraging, the
makers and sellers of its Oldsmobiles, Buicks, Pontiacs,
and the higher-priced models of its Chevrolet to fight
for customers with no quarter given; faced with the
same sort of intramural competition, some members of
the Ford and Lincoln-Mercury Divisions of the Ford
Company openly hoped from the start for the Edsel's
downfall. (Krafve, realizing what might happen, had
asked that the Edsel be assembled in plants of its own,
but his superiors turned him down.) However, Doyle,
speaking with the authority of a veteran of the automobile business as well as with that of Krafve's secondin-command, pooh-poohs the notion that the Edsel was
the victim of dirty work at the plants. "Of course the
Ford and Lincoln-Mercury Divisions didn't want to see
another Ford Company car in the field," he says, "but
as far as I know, anything they did at the executive
and plant levels was in competitive good taste. On the
other hand, at the distribution and dealer level, you got
some rough infighting in terms of whispering and propaganda. If I'd been in one of the other divisions, I'd
have done the same thing." No proud defeated general
of the old school ever spoke more nobly.

It is a tribute of sorts to the men who gave the
Edsel its big buildup that although cars tending to rattle, balk, and fall apart into shiny heaps of junk kept
coming off the assembly lines, things didn't go badly at
first. Doyle says that on Edsel Day more than 6,500
Edsels were either ordered by or actually delivered to
customers. That was a good showing, but there were
isolated signs of resistance. For instance, a New England dealer selling Edsels in one showroom and
Buicks in another reported that two prospects walked
into the Edsel showroom, took a look at the Edsel, and
placed orders for Buicks on the spot.

In the next few days, sales dropped sharply, but that
was to be expected once the bloom was off. Automobile
deliveries to dealers—one of the important indicators

in the trade—are customarily measured in ten-day periods, and during the first ten days of September, on only six of which the Edsel was on sale, it racked up 4,095; this was lower than Doyle's first-day figure because many of the initial purchases were of models and color combinations not in stock, which had to be factory-assembled to order. The delivery total for the second ten-day period was off slightly, and that for the third was down to just under 3,600. For the first ten days of October, nine of which were business days, there were only 2,751 deliveries—an average of just over three hundred cars a day. In order to sell the 200,000 cars per year that would make the Edsel operation profitable the Ford Company would have to move an average of between six and seven hundred each business day—a good many more than three hundred a day. On the night of Sunday, October 13th, Ford put on a mammoth television spectacular for Edsel, pre-empting the time ordinarily allotted to the Ed Sullivan show, but though the program cost $400,000 and starred Bing Crosby and Frank Sinatra, it failed to cause any sharp spurt in sales. Now it was obvious that things were not going at all well.

Among the former executives of the Edsel Division, opinions differ as to the exact moment when the portents of doom became unmistakable. Krafve feels that the moment did not arrive until sometime late in October. Wallace, in his capacity as Edsel's pipe-smoking semi-Brain Truster, goes a step further by pinning the start of the disaster to a specific date—October 4th, the day the first Soviet sputnik went into orbit, shattering the myth of American technical pre-eminence and precipitating a public revulsion against Detroit's fancier baubles. Public Relations Director Warnock maintains that his barometric sensitivity to the public temper enabled him to call the turn as early as mid-September; contrariwise, Doyle says he maintained his optimism until mid-November, by which time he was about the only man in the division who had not concluded it would take a miracle to save the Edsel. "In November," says Wallace, sociologically, "There was panic, and its concomitant—mob action." The mob action took the form of a concerted tendency to blame the design of the car for the whole debacle; Edsel men who had previously had nothing but lavish praise for the radiator grille and rear end now went around muttering that any fool could see they were ludicrous. The obvious sacrificial victim was Brown, whose stock had gone through the roof at the time of the regally accoladed debut of his design, in August, 1955. Now, without having done anything further, for either better or worse, the poor fellow became the company scapegoat. "Beginning in November, nobody talked to Roy," Wallace says. On November 27th, as if things weren't bad enough, Charles Kreisler, who as the only Edsel dealer in Manhattan provided its prize showcase, announced that he was turning in his franchise because of poor sales, and it was rumored that he added, "The Ford Motor Company has laid an egg." He thereupon signed up with American Motors to sell its Rambler, which, as the only domestic small car then on the market, was already the possessor of a zooming sales curve. Doyle grimly commented that the Edsel Division was "not concerned" about Kreisler's defection.

By December, the panic at Edsel had abated to the point where its sponsors could pull themselves together and begin casting about for ways to get sales moving again. Henry Ford II, manifesting himself to Edsel dealers on closed-circuit television, urged them to remain calm, promised that the company would back them to the limit, and said flatly, "The Edsel is here to stay." A million and a half letters went out over Krafve's signature to owners of medium-priced cars, asking them to drop around at their local dealers and test-ride the Edsel; everyone doing so, Krafve promised, would be given an eight-inch plastic scale model of the car, whether he bought a full-size one or not. The Edsel

Division picked up the check for the scale models—a symptom of desperation indeed, for under normal circumstances no automobile manufacturer would make even a move to outfumble its dealers for such a tab. (Up to that time, the dealers had paid for everything, as is customary.) The division also began offering its dealers what it called "Sales bonuses," which meant that the dealers could knock anything from one hundred to three hundred dollars off the price of each car without reducing their profit margin. Krafve told a reporter that sales up to then were about what he had expected them to be, although not what he had hoped they would be; in his zeal not to seem unpleasantly surprised, he appeared to be saying that he had expected the Edsel to fail. The Edsel's advertising campaign, which had started with studied dignity, began to sound a note of stridency. "Everyone who has seen it knows—with us—that the Edsel is a success," a magazine ad declared, and in a later ad this phrase was twice repeated, like an incantation: "The Edsel is a success. It is a new idea—a YOU idea—on the American Road. . . . The Edsel is a success." Soon the even less high-toned but more dependable advertising themes of price and social status began to intrude, in such sentences as "They'll know you've *arrived* when you drive up in an Edsel" and "The one that's really new is the lowest-priced, too!" In the more rarefied sectors of Madison Avenue, a resort to rhymed slogans is usually regarded as an indication of artistic depravity induced by commercial necessity.

From the frantic and costly measures the Edsel Division took in December, it garnered one tiny crumb: for the first ten-day period of 1958, it was able to report, sales were up 18.6 per cent over those of the last ten days of 1957. The catch, as the *Wall Street Journal* alertly noted, was that the latter period embraced one more selling day than the earlier one, so, for practical purposes, there had scarcely been a gain at all. In any case, that early-January word of meretricious cheer turned out to be the Edsel Division's last gesture. On January 14, 1958, the Ford Motor Company announced that it was consolidating the Edsel Division with the Lincoln-Mercury Division to form a Mercury-Edsel-Lincoln Division, under the management of James J. Nance, who had been running Lincoln-Mercury. It was the first time that one of the major automobile companies had lumped three divisions into one since General Motors' merger of Buick, Oldsmobile, and Pontiac back in the depression, and to the people of the expunged Edsel Division the meaning of the administrative move was all too clear. "With that much competition in a division, the Edsel wasn't going anywhere," Doyle says. "It became a stepchild."

For the last year and ten months of its existence, the Edsel was very much a stepchild—generally neglected, little advertised, and kept alive only to avoid publicizing a boner any more than necessary and in the forlorn hope that it *might* go somewhere after all. What advertising it did get strove quixotically to assure the automobile trade that everything was dandy; in mid-February an ad in *Automotive News* had Nance saying,

> Since the formation of the new M-E-L Division at Ford Motor Company, we have analyzed with keen interest the sales progress of the Edsel. We think it is quite significant that during the five months since the Edsel was introduced, Edsel sales have been greater than the first five months' sales for any other new make of car ever introduced on the American Road. . . . Edsel's steady progress can be a source of satisfaction and a great incentive to all of us.

Nance's comparison, however, was almost meaningless, no new make ever having been introduced anything like so grandiosely, and the note of confidence could not help ringing hollow.

It is quite possible that Nance's attention was never called to an article by S. I. Hayakawa, the semanticist, that was published in the spring of 1958 in *ETC: A Review of General Semantics,* a quarterly magazine, under the title, "Why the Edsel Laid an Egg." Hayakawa, who was both the founder and the editor of *ETC,* explained in an introductory note that he considered the subject within the purview of general semantics because automobiles, like words, are "important . . . symbols in American culture," and went on to argue that the Edsel's flop could be attributed to Ford Company executives who had been "listening too long to the motivation-research people" and who, in their efforts to turn out a car that would satisfy customers' sexual fantasies and the like, had failed to supply reasonable and practical transportation, thereby neglecting "the reality principle." "What the motivation researchers failed to tell their clients . . . is that *only* the psychotic and the gravely neurotic *act out* their irrationalities and their compensatory fantasies," Hayakawa admonished Detroit briskly, and added, "The trouble with selling symbolic gratification via such expensive items as . . . the Edsel Hermaphrodite . . . is the competition offered by much cheaper forms of symbolic gratification, such as *Playboy* (fifteen cents a copy), *Astounding Science Fiction* (thirty-five cents a copy), and television (free)."

Notwithstanding the competition from *Playboy,* or possibly because the symbol-motivated public included people who could afford both, the Edsel kept rolling— but just barely. The car moved, as salesmen say, though hardly at the touch of a toothpick. In fact, as a stepchild it sold about as well as it had sold as a favorite son, suggesting that all the hoopla, whether about symbolic gratification or mere horsepower, had had little effect one way or the other. The new Edsels that were registered with the motor-vehicle bureaus of the various states during 1958 numbered 34,481— considerably fewer than new cars of any competing make, and less than one-fifth of the 200,000 a year necessary if the Edsel was to show a profit, but still representing an investment by motorists of over a hundred million dollars. The picture actually brightened in November, 1958, with the advent of the Edsel's second-year models. Shorter by up to eight inches, lighter by up to five hundred pounds, and with engines less potent by as much as 158 horsepower, they had a price range running from five hundred to eight hundred dollars less than that of their predecessors. The vertical grille and the slant-eyed rear end were still there, but the modest power and proportions persuaded *Consumer Reports* to relent and say, "The Ford Motor Company, after giving last year's initial Edsel model a black eye, has made a respectable and even likable automobile of it." Quite a number of motorists seemed to agree; about two thousand more Edsels were sold in the first half of 1959 than had been sold in the first half of 1958, and by the early summer of 1959 the car was moving at the rate of around four thousand a month. Here, at last, was progress; sales were at almost a quarter of the minimum profitable rate, instead of a mere fifth.

On July 1, 1959, there were 83,849 Edsels on the country's roads. The largest number (8,344) were in California, which is perennially beset with far and away the largest number of cars of practically all makes, and the smallest number were in Alaska, Vermont, and Hawaii (122, 119, and 110, respectively). All in all, the Edsel seemed to have found a niche for itself as an amusingly eccentric curiosity. Although the Ford Company, with its stockholders' money still disappearing week after week into the Edsel, and with small cars now clearly the order of the day, could scarcely affect a sentimental approach to the subject, it nonetheless took an outside chance and, in mid-October of 1959, brought out a third series of annual models. The 1960 Edsel appeared a little more than a month after the Falcon, Ford's first—and instantly successful—venture into the small-car field, and was scarcely an Edsel at all; gone were both the vertical grille and the horizontal rear end, and what remained looked like a cross between a Ford Fairlane and a Pontiac. Its initial sales were abysmal; by the middle of November only one plant—in Louisville, Kentucky—was still turning out Edsels, and it was turning out only about twenty a day. On November 19th, the Ford Foundation, which was planning to sell a block of its vast holdings of stock in the Ford Motor Company, issued the prospectus that is required by law under such circumstances, and stated therein, in a footnote to a section describing the company's products, that the Edsel had been "introduced in September 1957 and discontinued in November 1959." The same day, this mumbled admission was confirmed and amplified by a Ford Company spokesman, who did some mumbling of his own. "If we knew the reason people aren't buying the Edsel, we'd probably have done something about it," he said.

The final quantitative box score shows that from the beginning right up to November 19th, 110,810 Edsels were produced and 109,466 were sold. (The remaining 1,344, almost all of them 1960 models, were disposed of in short order with the help of drastic price cuts.) All told, only 2,846 of the 1960 Edsels were ever produced, making models of that year a potential collector's item. To be sure, it will be generations before 1960 Edsels are as scarce as the Type 41 Bugatti, of which no more than eleven specimens were made, back in the late twenties, to be sold only to bona-fide kings, and the 1960 Edsel's reasons for being a rarity are not exactly as acceptable, socially or commercially as the Type 41 Bugatti's. Still, a 1960-Edsel Owners' Club may yet appear.

The final fiscal box score on the Edsel fiasco will probably never be known, because the Ford Motor Company's public reports do not include breakdowns of gains and losses within the individual divisions. Financial buffs estimate, however, that the company lost something like $200 million on the Edsel after it appeared; add to this the officially announced expenditure of $250 million before it appeared, subtract about a hundred million invested in plant and equipment that were salvageable for other uses, and the net loss is $350 million. If these estimates are right, every Edsel the company manufactured cost it in lost money about $3,200, or the price of another one. In other, harsher words, the company would have saved itself money if, back in 1955, it had decided not to produce the Edsel at all but simply to give away 110,810 specimens of its comparably priced car, the Mercury.

The end of the Edsel set off an orgy of hindsight in the press. *Time* declared, "The Edsel was a classic case of the wrong car for the wrong market at the wrong time. It was also a prime example of the limitations of market research, with its 'depth interviews' and 'motivational' mumbo-jumbo." *Business Week,* which shortly before the Edsel made its bow had described it with patent solemnity and apparent approval, now pronounced it "a nightmare" and appended a few pointedly critical remarks about Wallace's research, which was rapidly achieving a scapegoat status equal to that of Brown's design. (Jumping up and down on motivational research was, and is, splendid sport, but, of course, the implication that it dictated, or even influenced, the Edsel's design is entirely false, since the research, being intended only to provide a theme for advertising and promotion, was not undertaken until after Brown had completed his design.) The *Wall Street Journal's* obituary of the Edsel made a point that was probably sounder, and certainly more original.

Large corporations are often accused of rigging markets, administering prices, and otherwise dictating to the consumer [it observed]. And yesterday Ford Motor Company announced its two-year experiment with the medium-priced Edsel has come to an end . . . for want of buyers. All this is quite a ways from auto makers being able to rig markets or force consumers to take what they want them to take. . . . And the reason, simply, is that there is no accounting for tastes. . . . When it comes to dictating, the consumer is the dictator without peer.

The tone of the piece was friendly and sympathetic; the Ford Company, it seemed, had endeared itself to the *Journal* by playing the great American situation-comedy role of Daddy the Bungler.

As for the post-mortem explanations of the debacle that have been offered by former Edsel executives, they are notable for their reflective tone—something like that of a knocked-out prize fighter opening his eyes to find an announcer's microphone pushed into his face. In fact, Krafve, like many a flattened pugilist, blames his own bad timing; he contends that if he had been able to thwart the apparently immutable mechanics and economics of Detroit, and had somehow been able to bring out the Edsel in 1955, or even 1956, when the stock market and the medium-priced-car market were riding high, the car would have done well and would still be doing well. That is to say, if he had seen the punch coming, he would have ducked. Krafve refuses to go along with a sizable group of laymen who tend to attribute the collapse to the company's decision to call the car the Edsel instead of giving it a brisker, more singable name, reducible to a nickname other than "Ed" or "Eddie," and not freighted with dynastic connotations. As far as he can seen Krafve still says, the Edsel's name did not affect its fortunes one way or the other.

Brown agrees with Krafve that bad timing was the chief mistake. "I frankly feel that the styling of the automobile had very little, if anything, to do with its failure," he said later, and his frankness may pretty safely be left unchallenged. "The Edsel program, like any other project planned for future markets, was based on the best information available at the time in which decisions were made. The road to Hell is paved with good intentions!"

Doyle, with the born salesman's intensely personal feeling about his customers, talks like a man betrayed by a friend—the American public. "It was a buyers' strike," he says. "People weren't in the mood for the Edsel. Why not is a mystery to me. What they'd been buying for several years encouraged the industry to build exactly this kind of car. We gave it to them, and they wouldn't take it. Well, they shouldn't have acted like that. You can't just wake up somebody one day and say, 'That's enough, you've been running in the wrong direction.' Anyway, *why* did they do it? Golly, how the industry worked and worked over the years— getting rid of gear-shifting, providing interior comfort, providing plus performance for use in emergencies! And now the public wants these little beetles. I don't get it!"

Wallace's sputnik theory provides an answer to Doyle's question about why people weren't in the mood, and, furthermore, it is sufficiently cosmic to befit a semi-Brain Truster. It also leaves Wallace free to defend the validity of his motivational-research studies as of the time when they were conducted. "I don't think we yet know the depths of the psychological effect that that first orbiting had on us all," he says. "Somebody had beaten us to an important gain in technology, and immediately people started writing articles about how crummy Detroit products were, particularly the heavily ornamented and status-symbolic medium-priced cars. In 1958, when none of the small cars were out except the Rambler, Chevy almost ran away with the market, because it had the simplest car. The American people had put themselves on a self-imposed austerity program. Not buying Edsels was their hair shirt."

To any relics of the sink-or-swim nineteenth-century days of American industry, it must seem strange that

Wallace can afford to puff on his pipe and analyze the holocaust so amiably. The obvious point of the Edsel's story is the defeat of a giant motor company, but what is just as surprising is that the giant did not come apart, or even get seriously hurt in the fall, and neither did the majority of the people who went down with him. Owing largely to the success of four of its other cars—the Ford, the Thunderbird, and, later on the small Falcon and Comet and then the Mustang— the Ford Company, as an investment, survived gloriously. True, it had a bad time of it in 1958, when, partly because of the Edsel, net income per share of its stock fell from $5.40 to $2.12, dividends per share from $2.40 to $2.00, and the market price of its stock from a 1957 high of about $60 to a 1958 low of under $40. But all these losses were more than recouped in 1959, when net income per share was $8.24, dividends per share were $2.80, and the price of the stock reached a high of around $90. In 1960 and 1961, things went even better. So the 280,000 Ford stockholders listed on the books in 1957 had had little to complain about unless they had sold at the height of the panic. On the other hand, six thousand white-collar workers were squeezed out of their jobs as a result of the Mercury-Edsel-Lincoln consolidation, and the average number of Ford employees fell from 191,759 in 1957 to 142,076 the following year, climbing back to only 159,541 in 1959. And, of course, dealers who gave up profitable franchises in other makes and then went broke trying to sell Edsels weren't likely to be very cheerful about the experience. Under the terms of the consolidation of the Lincoln-Mercury and Edsel Divisions, most of the agencies for the three makes were consolidated, too. In the consolidation, some Edsel dealers were squeezed out, and it can have been small comfort to those of them who went bankrupt to learn later that when the Ford Company finally discontinued making the car, it agreed to pay those of their former colleagues who had weathered the crisis one-half of the original cost of their Edsel signs, and was granting them substantial rebates on all Edsels in stock at the time of discontinuance. Still, automobile dealers, some of whom work on credit margins as slim as those of Miami hotel operators, occasionally go broke with even the most popular cars. And among those who earn their living in the rough-and-tumble world of automobile salesrooms, where Detroit is not always spoken of with affection, many will concede that the Ford Company, once it had found itself stuck with a lemon, did as much as it reasonably could to bolster dealers who had cast their lot with Edsel. A spokesman for the National Automobile Dealers Association has since stated, "So far as we know, the Edsel dealers were generally satisfied with the way they were treated."

Foote, Cone & Belding also ended up losing money on the Edsel account, since its advertising commissions did not entirely compensate for the extraordinary expense it had gone to of hiring sixty new people and opening up a posh office in Detroit. But its losses were hardly irreparable; the minute there were no more Edsels to advertise, it was hired to advertise Lincolns, and although that arrangement did not last very long, the firm has happily survived to sing the praises of such clients as General Foods, Lever Brothers, and Trans World Airways. A rather touching symbol of the loyalty that the agency's employees have for its former client is the fact that for several years after 1959, on every workday its private parking lot in Chicago was still dotted with Edsels. These faithful drivers, incidentally, are not unique. If Edsel owners have not found the means to a dream fulfillment, and if some of them for a while had to put up with harrowing mechanical disorders, many of them more than a decade later cherish their cars as if they were Confederate bills, and on Used Car Row the Edsel is a high-premium item, with few cars being offered.

By and large, the former Edsel executives did not

just land on their feet, they landed in clover. Certainly no one can accuse the Ford Company of giving vent to its chagrin in the old-fashioned way, by vulgarly causing heads to roll. Krafve was assigned to assist Robert S. McNamara, at that time a Ford divisional vice-president (and later, of course, Secretary of Defense), for a couple of months, and then he moved to a staff job in company headquarters, stayed there for about a year, and left to become a vice-president of the Raytheon Company, of Waltham, Massachusetts, a leading electronics firm. In April, 1960, he was made its president. In the middle sixties he left to become a high-priced management consultant on the West Coast. Doyle, too, was offered a staff job with Ford, but after taking a trip abroad to think it over he decided to retire. "It was a question of my relationship to my dealers," he explains. "I had assured them that the company was fully behind the Edsel for keeps, and I didn't feel that I was the fellow to tell them now that it wasn't." After his retirement, Doyle remained about as busy as ever, keeping an eye on various businesses in which he has set up various friends and relatives, and conducting a consulting business of his own in Detroit. About a month before Edsel's consolidation with Mercury and Lincoln, Warnock, the publicity man, left the division to become director of news services for the International Telephone & Telegraph Corp., in New York—a position he left in June, 1960, to become vice-president of Communications Counselors, the public-relations arm of McCann-Erickson. From there he went back to Ford, as Eastern promotion chief for Lincoln-Mercury—a case of a head that had not rolled but had instead been anointed. Brown, the embattled stylist, stayed on in Detroit for a while as chief stylist of Ford commercial vehicles and then went with the Ford Motor Company, Ltd., of England, where, again as chief stylist, he was assigned to direct the design of Consuls, Anglias, trucks, and tractors. He insisted that this post didn't represent the Ford version of Siberia. "I have found it to be a most satisfying experience, and one of the best steps I have ever taken in my . . . career," he stated firmly in a letter from England. "We are building a styling office and a styling team second to none in Europe." Wallace, the semi-Brain Truster, was asked to continue semi-Brain Trusting for Ford, and, since he still didn't like living in Detroit, or near it, was permitted to move to New York and to spend only two days a week at headquarters. ("They didn't seem to care any more where I operated from," he says modestly.) At the end of 1958, he left Ford, and he has since finally achieved his heart's desire—to become a full-time scholar and teacher. He set about getting a doctorate in sociology at Columbia, writing his thesis on social change in Westport, Connecticut, which he investigated by busily quizzing its inhabitants; meanwhile, he taught a course on "The Dynamics of Social Behavior" at the New School for Social Research, in Greenwich Village. "I'm through with industry," he was heard to declare one day, with evident satisfaction, as he boarded a train for Westport, a bundle of questionnaires under his arm. Early in 1962, he became Dr. Wallace.

The subsequent euphoria of these former Edsel men did not stem entirely from the fact of their economic survival; they appear to have been enriched spiritually. They are inclined to speak of their Edsel experience —except for those still with Ford, who are inclined to speak of it as little as possible—with the verve and garrulity of old comrades-in-arms hashing over their most thrilling campaign. Doyle is perhaps the most passionate reminiscer in the group. "It was more fun than I've ever had before or since," he told a caller in 1960. "I suppose that's because I worked the hardest ever. We all did. It was a good crew. The people who came with Edsel knew they were taking a chance, and I like people who'll take chances. Yes, it was a wonderful experience, in spite of the unfortunate thing that happened. And we were on the right track, too!

When I went to Europe just before retiring, I saw how it is there—nothing but compact cars, yet they've still got traffic jams over there, they've still got parking problems, they've still got accidents. Just try getting in and out of those low taxicabs without hitting your head, or try not to get clipped while you're walking around the Arc de Triomphe. This small-car thing won't last forever. I can't see American drivers being satisfied for long with manual gear-shifting and limited performance. The pendulum will swing back."

Warnock, like many a public-relations man before him, claims that his job gave him an ulcer—his second. "But I got over it," he says. "That great Edsel team— I'd just like to see what it could have done if it had had the right product at the right time. It could have made millions, that's what! The whole thing was two years out of my life that I'll never forget. It was history in the making. Doesn't it all tell you something about America in the fifties—high hopes, and less than complete fulfillment of them?"

Krafve, the boss of the great team *manqué*, is entirely prepared to testify that there is more to his former subordinates' talk than just the romantic vaporings of old soldiers. "It was a wonderful group to work with," he said not long ago. "They really put their hearts and guts into the job. I'm interested in a crew that's strongly motivated, and that one was. When things went bad, the Edsel boys could have cried about how they'd given up wonderful opportunities to come with us, but if anybody did, I never heard about it. I'm not surprised that they've mostly come out all right. In industry, you take a bump now and then, but you bounce back as long as you don't get defeated inside. I like to get together with somebody once in a while—Gayle Warnock or one of the others—and go over the humorous incidents, the tragic incidents. . . ."

Whether the nostalgia of the Edsel boys for the Edsel runs to the humorous or to the tragic, it is a thought-provoking phenomenon. Maybe it means merely that they miss the limelight they first basked in and later squirmed in, or maybe it means that a time has come when—as in Elizabethan drama but seldom before in American business—failure can have a certain grandeur that success never knows.

Mr. Real Estate
Takes a Fall, for a While

Three years after his giant real-estate empire, Webb & Knapp, Inc., was compelled to go into bankruptcy, William Zeckendorf still had his bone-grating handshake, an unquenchable zest and a bunch of schemes for new projects. "I did not," he said, "put my brain in bankruptcy."

Before Webb & Knapp went down the drain in 1965 to the tune of $84 million in debt claims and losses of $70 million in the prior six years, Zeckendorf had created the biggest real-estate firm in the country and probably in the world. At one point he owned 8,000 hotel rooms, and his accomplishments ran from being responsible for the coming of the United Nations to New York to owning some of New York's and Chicago's principal hotels. He was involved in urban-renewal projects in half a dozen cities and several of the country's biggest superregional shopping centers.

But Freedomland, the spectacular amusement park in the Bronx which became a spectacular failure, was the pivotal rock which, once jarred loose, toppled the whole mountain. Now the site of Co-Op City, a vast city cooperative housing development, Freedomland went bankrupt in 1964 after five years of operation with a $20-million loss to Webb & Knapp.

Big, bluff, a born salesman with the ability to sell

visions often of great pragmatism, Zeckendorf was a speculator who was frequently in debt. He succeeded, however, in getting others to put up money for a good many of his pet projects.

The 1968 piece from *New York* magazine which follows, unlike most of the other reprinted articles in this book, appeared three years after Zeckendorf's disaster but just about the time he filed his personal bankruptcy (liabilities of $79,076,101 vs. assets of $1,885,621). But the Zeckendorf *joie de vivre,* as writer Elliott Bernstein found, remained undiminished. Not bad, either, for a then 63-year-old man whom bankruptcy trustee Mortimer M. Caplin called "the Babe Ruth of Real Estate."

By mid-1972, after settling with both Caplin and his personal creditors, Zeckendorf was off again on another venture, a $100-million apartment project on Staten Island, New York. He was, he said, "undergoing a renaissance."

Real Estate's Humpty-Dumpty: Bill Zeckendorf After the Fall

By Elliott Bernstein

Watching Bill Zeckendorf in his office, swinging real estate deals over the phone, is a rare spectator experience. He is one of the legenday promoters, a man who changed the faces of cities with a five-minute call. And the secret of his spiel is that he passionately believes in the ideas he is selling and he wants you to believe in them, too.

Zeckendorf sells realty with Soul.

"What I'm calling about now could be a waste of time," he told an airline president recently, offering an unusual hotel lease in Florida and another hotel in New York. "Or it could be one of your more valuable opportunities." He sketched in the advantages of the Florida facility, which he said he had thought of offering to the airline's "cheaper competitor" but preferred to sell to them instead. "I can tell you that this will be a very valuable lease and will be an enormous attraction in this part of Florida, especially in the slack season. This will be a blockbuster. And I can tell you before you're five years older no airline will not be in the hotel business, both for positive and preclusive reasons."

He hung up, his broad face beaming with confidence. The airline president seemed interested. "We might have a ten-strike," he informed his son, Bill Jr., over the interoffice phone. "If they take one they could take both. We might have a ten-strike." Now that he had made the approach, it was up to Bill Jr. to follow through.

The blinking light indicated that another potential customer was on the line. It was a Mr. Smith who represented one of the wealthiest, most moss-backed families in the social resgister. "Does everyone who works for the ____s have to have a boll weevil accent?" he jested, speaking into the telephone's two-way voice box. The man with the boll weevil accent laughed weakly in the distance with a slight echo. Then Zeckendorf unreeled a series of fascinating propositions: first he offered for sale a parcel of high income commercial property on New York's Upper East Side; next he suggested a swap of the East Side property for 400 country acres the family owned on a lake down South; or, the agent might want to improve his principals' lake holdings by buying a 1,600-foot strip of shore frontage that belonged to the estate of Zeckendorf's late wife. "You get all riparian rights, of course," he added reassuringly. He described all three deals with equal enthusiasm and it was difficult to tell which one he was really most intent on making.

"Well," said Zeckendorf, wrapping things up for the speechless agent, "you can buy, swap or sell. Any way you want to go." He put down the phone, not sure he had gotten a bite, but obviously in good form and pleased with his performance.

But Holy Unsecured Promissory Notes! Or, for that matter, Great Suffering Debentures! What is William Zeckendorf doing back in the real estate business? Didn't he crash to earth three years ago when his company, Webb & Knapp, Inc, tottered into bankruptcy, and didn't that finish off his colossal career?

The answer, simply, is that his debacle was nearly total but not quite. The court deprived him of his company, which in twenty years was responsible for $3-billion worth of construction in North America, took away his freedom to dream up and execute extraordinary sales-and-leaseback deals, and took off his back the $60-million of debts and $30-million in back taxes that was balanced by only $22-million of assets.

Also snatched away with his mantle of Mr. Real Estate, which fit no one else, were his corporate jet, the customized Cadillac bearing New York license WZ–1, and his 70-acre estate in Greenwich, Connecticut, with its 24,000-bottle wine cellar. All to satisfy company obligations. Since he had co-signed many loans, it was presumed he would have to file for personal bankruptcy, too. However, he did not have to petition for it immediately—at least he had avoided doing it for three years. Nor did he forfeit the privilege of doing business, although it had to be on a considerably smaller scale.

It may come as a surprise to some of his former admirers and creditors, but Bill Zeckendorf never even vacated his old offices on the top floor of 383 Madison Avenue. Except that now the tenant and half-owner of the building was General Property Corporation, a real estate sales and management firm that engaged him as a "consultant," he said. His employers were his son, the chairman, and his son-in-law, Ronald Nicholson, the president. There were reasons why Bill Sr. could not be a principal of the new company while his affairs were still being unraveled, but whatever the legaldy-gook, the consultant's cap scarcely covered Bill's ample dome.

He worked a full schedule. "I live in New York and I go to work from my apartment at 30 Beekman Place every day. Go to work early, work very late, enjoy my life," he explained in his deep-chested voice and quick, clipped sentences. "I'm doing constructive things. We're trading, buying and selling, and financing, and building—not so much construction as the others," he corrected himself.

Work was a solace because in addition to his other troubles he had lost his wife, Marion, in an air crash earlier that year. She died in an Air France flight coming into Guadeloupe where they had planned to meet and go on vacation. Bill had arrived earlier and was waiting at the airport when her plane struck the other side of the mountain.

His wife, a petite, quiet woman from a wealthy Georgia family, was the second Mrs. Zeckendorf (his two children were from the first marriage, which ended in divorce), and they had been married 27 years.

Except for the effects of his very recent mourning, though, he was remarkably free of pessimism. He couldn't be bothered. Even nor, after losing an empire, he still talked like a winner, especially when he had something to sell. "He is an organic optimist," a former associate observed. "He is a man who cannot accept defeat."

As he sat in his leather swivel chair behind his desk, one could not help looking for cracks in his shell. Despite his many other resemblances to Humpty-Dumpty, he had none. Having just passed his 63rd birthday he looked fine, plump and rosy-cheeked. His smooth, powerfully-shaped head, which widened at the base, was attached to the 235-pound frame of a former NYU lineman ("The more unimaginative side of football").

He wore a comfortably-fitted banker's-gray suit of

expensive fabric, a handkerchief pointed out of his pocket, and in his lapel was the ribbon of the French Legion of Honor. When Bill Zeckendorf sailed down the street wearing his fedora, people turned.

A large, smoke-colored hound that was lying at his feet stood up and leaned against him heavily. It was his Weimaraner, Cheer.

"Did you ever have a dog?" he asked, petting his best friend. Cheer was his companion at the office, on midnight walks, and on country rambles. Dogs didn't read bankruptcy announcements.

Abruptly, Cheer's master returned to a business mood and spoke about the activities of the new firm. He wanted to talk only about the new things. With other parties, he said, they had assembled the site for the new Gimbels . . . built on East 86th Street. They were the developers of Robert R. Young Village, a privately financed community of artists' studios and high-rise apartments proposed for West Street, on the Hudson River. Also, they had acted as agents in the sale of the Queen Mary to the city of Long Beach, California, where it was being fitted out with shops, a hotel and—he said—"God knows what else." The unusual hotel lease he had been tempting the airline executive with earlier was on a similar floating property, the Queen Elizabeth, soon to become a tourist attraction in Fort Lauderdale, Florida.

Some of the projects had a little of the old Zeckendorf style. Most of them, however, were being handled for other people on commission, with General Property acting essentially as a middleman. Then, there were the more humdrum functions such as managing buildings, collecting rents, the daily bread of the real estate business. Zeckendorf emphasized that he took part in few of the affairs and that his son and son-in-law "carried the ball most of the time."

But there was another deal in the works—something major, he hinted—that was all his. He introduced it with an air of mystery. "Unfortunately you came a little early. I will have a big story soon, but I don't want to pull the props out of the deal. It will be a big story."

On the table, near a picture of his wife, was a signed picture of Ike, and one from LBJ. There was a raft of other memorabilia about the office: a letter of thanks from Syngman Rhee for some service rendered to South Korea fifteen years ago, a giant, chrome-plated construction bolt from a dedication, Zeckendorf's own framed note to somebody, marking the closing of a deal, a softball trophy won by the old Webb & Knapp team, and a bronze bust of Lincoln. A hanging plaque bore these words of the Emancipator: "If I tried to read, much less answer all of the criticisms made of me and all the attacks leveled against me, this office would have to be closed for other business. I do the best I know how, the very best I can; I mean to keep doing this, down to the very end."

His personal office, itself, was a kind of memorial, his celebrated office in the round. Designed by Ieoh Ming Pei—whom Zeckendorf had hired away from Harvard to head his architectural staff—the office was 20 feet in diameter, with glass skylights running all around the top rim, and it sat smack in the middle of the main reception area like a teak pillbox. Here the Great Zeckendorf had hatched his grand schemes, jollied bankers and industrialists into advancing him money, and at last overextended himself with loan sharks. Here, finally, he had been cornered, notwithstanding the design of the place.

His buildings, of course, were his real trophies. They had in common a high level of taste, a generous use of open space, and completion costs that were often more than expected. Some of the more famous, which he built alone or with others, were downtown Denver's Mile High Center, Hilton hotel, and May department store; Montreal's splendid Place Ville Marie; Washington, D.C.'s $100-million Southwest renewal; and the sprawling Century City in Los Angeles on the former 20th Century-Fox lot. In New York, he left his imprint on a legion of properties, including Chase Manhattan Plaza; the 40 Wall Street tower; Roosevelt Field shopping center (the largest one in the East); Kips Bay Plaza; and the United Nations, for which he had proposed and assembled the site. Displayed in the conference room was a 1946 letter from Nelson Rockefeller (whose father had bought and donated the land) lauding Zeckendorf, then the brash, executive vice president of conservative Webb & Knapp.

He fully appreciated the measure of achievements. "I'm not sorry for myself," he told a *Life* writer on the eve of his crash. "I've had no reverses of anything except money. My sense of accomplishment is full and the cities and the art and the architecture I have influenced will live long after I'm gone."

Then there were the office buildings that he collected like children's blocks; the Chrysler and Graybar buildings that he bought in one afternoon; and the armada of hotel flagships that he had amassed—the two Ambassadors in Chicago, the Astor, Taft, St. Regis, Commodore, Manhattan and Drake in New York, not to omit the unrealized Hotel Zeckendorf, planned on the location of the old Roxy theater.

Indeed, for a while *The New Yorker* cartoon seemed prophetic: a man standing with his son on a terrace, pointing at the city and saying, "Someday, my boy, all of this will belong to Mr. William Zeckendorf."

He was to be stopped by overextension, a form of corporate *hubris*. The entire structure was founded on debt, long term, short and intermediate, at sharply increasing rates of interest. When land values ceased rising with the velocity of the immediate postwar period, and people began to desert his old buildings and hotels for new ones, Webb & Knapp began to slide. The end was only hastened by such ill-advised ventures as Freedomland, the Bronx amusement park, where perhaps $20-million went down the drain, and the steel extraction process with which he had hoped to wring ingots from slag heaps.

Despite heroic shufflings, and infusions of borrowed capital ($43,750,000 from a British group), everything had to go. Paychecks began to bounce, the stock was delisted, and one of the banks blew the whistle. A reminder of the last days stood in the waiting area, next to the leather couches and philodendrons—the empty, glass-topped wooden stand where the Dow Jones ticker had been uprooted.

Zeckendorf came off the phone and smiled. He remembered exactly where the conversation had left off. What was the big new deal that he had been alluding to? He readily acknowledged that it was not such a mystery after all. It was the urban renewal project in Newburgh, New York, in which he had assumed a leading role, and which had been written up in the papers.

It was an ambitious project, in "a city that was forlorn," he said, shaking his head sadly, "where whole blocks were without water, sewage . . . a city that had made itself best known by racial strife, riots, civil commotion . . . a city that needed me."

Zeckendorf was donating his services free. "I decided that before I get too old I want to do one great redevelopment job and I wanted a community that could afford my services the least, because I had in mind to do whatever it was on a gratis basis, strictly *pro bono publico*." He smiled magnanimously. "I've had a lifetime of experience in all kinds of construction and urban renewal at every level, always on a private capital level, always hopefully for profit, but not necessarily so ending." He arched his dense eyebrows and cleared his throat, signifying a little joke.

"And I've gone up there and I've started something. Whether what I've started will come to fruition only the Lord knows. It will involve urban renewal of the best nature—housing, employment. The most important thing is employment. And on the employment front I conceived the idea of a great seaport, making New-burgh and New Windsor, which joins in on the south, into a superb new seaport."

He pressed the buzzer, summoning his secretary. "Now I think rather than my going into a long-winded discourse, I can give you a lot of correspondence that you can read and digest to tell you what I'm doing."

The girl appeared. "Give him all the correspondence, the complete file on Newburgh," he commanded. "The press clippings, the letter to the Defense Department, everything."

As the girl led the way out of his office, he was on the phone again, talking to a money lender. "I'm sorry we couldn't get together on that last deal," he apolo-gized, "but I'll cut you in another time—"

The file was neatly compiled, with tear sheets of newspaper stories and Xeroxed copies of letters all ready for inquiring reporters. Zeckendorf always went out of his way to be friendly with the press, although now he no longer had a vice president to attend to those details.

Included were articles from New York and New-burgh papers outlining the project and glowing with enthusiasm. Then, a letter indicating Defense Depart-ment disinterest in the seaport plan. Then, a back-and-forth series of letters and statements between Zecken-dorf and Senator Javits, adding up to an endorsement.

In spite of this minor victory, however, it was far from sure whether the $100-million in public and pri-vate funds could be obtained for the project, which would take at least five years to complete. There was little doubt, too, that Zeckendorf wanted this one very much. It would probably be his last great work be-cause when it was finished he would be nearing 70.

In his office, Zeckendorf admitted that he was being resisted on other fronts, as well. The Robert R. Young development, with its artists' studios and high-rise dwell-ings, was "meeting a lot of opposition from a West Village group, Jane Jacobs," he said. So, the architect's

tinted drawing, showing helical towers (another Zeckendorf dream) rising over cerulean water, might never
become concrete.

He and other ex-officers of Webb & Knapp were
also facing a civil suit asking $50-million in damages.
The suit was lodged by the corporation's court-appointed trustee, Mortimer Caplin, the former IRS com-
missioner; it charged mismanagement and "virtually
unequaled luxury" for limousines, airplanes and lavish
dining quarters.

At his Beekman Place home, he lived alone now,
except for the Weimaraner, a miniature pinscher that
had belonged to his wife, and a French housekeeping
couple that had been with him for years. About the
only indulgences he allowed himself, social or otherwise, were chewing Sen Sen (he had long ago for-
saken cigars for the little breath fresheners), and
fishing. He fished off Montauk, sometimes with his
grandchildren, or went trout fishing in Canada with
his old friend Lord Hardinge of Montreal.

As for his personal finances, he conceded that the
long-forestalled moment was approaching. It was quite
likely that he would have to file for personal bankruptcy in the near future. "Oh, I'm gonna have to. I'm
gonna have to. I expect to file a petition. I . . . I'd
better not say that."

He flushed and asked to withdraw his remarks about
bankruptcy. It was premature to talk about it, he said,
and insisted that no statement about it be attributed to
him or he would not let the interview continue. Events
were moving too quickly, however. A few days later,
Bill Jr. was to confirm his father's impending declaration. "The petition will be filed soon. We're pushing
for it," he said. Bill Jr. had his father's dome, and his
rumbling voice and large brown eyes but the son was
milder, more approachable. As he promised, the newspapers soon carried the announcement, sounding properly impressed; they listed personal liabilities of

$79,076,101 against assets of $1,885,621, a ratio of 40–1.

Zeckendorf began to look impatient and probably would have welcomed a phone call. Receiving none, the big man got up from his chair presently and the Weimaraner got up, too. It was almost lunch time. The sun was shining outside on the terrace.

"Do you have any more questions?" he asked. "I think you've got enough."

Striding quickly out of his office, he gave his opinions on two important New York projects, in which his company was not involved. The 110-story World Trade Center was good, he said. "I'm in favor of it. It will bring more payroll to the city."

It was clearly difficult for him to discuss other people's projects. There must have been that stab of envy whenever he read of a mammoth new development by the Tishmans, the Urises or the Lefraks. Their esthetic standards could be compared unfavorably with his, but they were still going strong, making profits, and he was playing a game with borrowed chips.

It was almost noon and Zeckendorf appeared on the terrace, walking Cheer beside the flower beds. Glad to be freed from confinement, the dog lifted his leg and proceeded to water the geraniums.

"No, no, Cheer!" said Zeckendorf crossly, and the dog obeyed as soon as it could.

But he still looked disapproving as he gazed out over the skyline. There was a time when everyone used to listen.

In the biggest ligation involving Section 1 of the Sherman Antitrust Act, a large segment of executives and an increasing number of major electrical-equipment companies were summoned in February 1961 to a federal courtroom in Philadelphia to answer charges of collusion and conspiracy. A series of tales then unfolded as each defendant, many of them cut loose by their employers, testified on how he had been sucked into the conspiracy in the belief that he was conducting himself as his company wanted him to.

Those who will remember the many stories that emanated from that Philadelphia courtroom may recall how firmly each corporation separated its own policies and actions from the behavior of the 45 men indicted. It was the corporate communications gap at its best—or worst. But the judge involved didn't go for it one bit. He admitted that the Justice Department hadn't enough evidence to convict the men in the highest echelons of the corporations indicted but would have to settle for those directly involved. But the real blame, he asserted, should be laid at the "doorstep" of the top men.

In its way, the entire matter may rank as one of the worst examples of corporate misbehavior on record. Although it involved a highly intricate set of devious circumstances, I have attempted to tell it in a simple, brief way in the piece that follows.

The Great Electrical Conspiracy

By Isadore Barmash

Judge J. Cullen Ganey, chief judge of the United States District Court in Philadelphia, fixed his blue eyes coldly on some 45 corporate executives in his court that morning but spoke first to their superiors, who were not present.

"One would be most naïve indeed to believe that these violations of the law, so long persisted in, affecting so large a segment of the industry and finally involving so many millions of dollars, were facts unknown to those responsible for the corporation and its conduct," he said.

Then, when he addressed the executives present, the irony in his voice was unmistakable. "Many of the individual defendants are torn between conscience and an approved corporate policy," he observed. Then he cited "the company man, the conformist, who goes along with his superiors and finds balm for his conscience in additional comforts and the security of his place in the corporate setup."

On a winter day in 1961, the biggest criminal case in the history of the Sherman Antitrust Act was being heard. Five of the country's largest electrical-equipment manufacturers and a large group of their top executives had been indicted the previous February on charges of price rigging and collusive bidding in sales to the federal government and private industry. Shifting with determination in his chair, Judge Ganey promised jail to the "individuals with ultimate responsibility for corporate conduct among those indicted."

The companies involved were the General Electric Company, Westinghouse Electric Corporation, Allis-

Chalmers Manufacturing Company, I-T-E Circuit Breaker Company and Federal Pacific Electric Company. Eighteen men were indicted but their numbers swelled to 45. Ultimately three other producers were also indicted. After a year-long investigation of the electrical industry, the charges were that:

The companies involved allocated among themselves the percentage that each would get of government business on specific products. For example, GE would have 42 percent, Westinghouse 38 percent, and so on. Because the government buys through sealed bids, the manufacturers reached their agreed percentage of business by conspiring to predetermine the low bid each time. Calling their allocations of the share to private ultilities and producers "the phase of the moon," the companies agreed on a formula under which each took turns in submitting the low bids.

Using code names in communicating with each other, the executives of the concerns met dozens of times in cities all around the country to arrange their bids and prices. And, on some items, the companies agreed to raise prices simultaneously.

The violation of the Sherman Act called for a maximum penalty of a fine of $50.000 and, in the case of individuals, a year in prison. But, despite the steel in his eye, Judge Ganey was moderate in his first day's sentencing. He meted out to a group of vice presidents sentences of 30 days in jail and fines ranging from $2000 to $12,500.

But some had already had their comeuppance, corporate style. In an extraordinary statement the month before the indictment was handed down, Ralph J. Cordiner, GE's chairman of the board, said that he had first learned from the Philadelphia investigation that certain of his officials had violated the company's policy of strict compliance with the antitrust laws. Although the officials' legal punishment could be "most severe," he said that the company had its own responsibility and that he had demoted the offenders and removed them from positions of responsibility in the company.

The value of the contracts on which the conspirators had rigged bids was vast, totaling $1.75 billion. The collusion had involved items from two-dollar insulators through turbine generators that cost several million dollars. The shenanigans had lasted over an eight-year period.

The backdrop to the conspiracy concept helped to explain to irate students of the corporate scene why the big guns in the electrical industry had got in so deeply. For one thing, after World War II, the industry had become marked by big companies with broad product lines. But there was little difference between the products offered, so that the area of choice was narrowed to one of price. The sealed-bid technique allowed the bidder—and the buyer—to work in a climate of secret bidding if they wished to. But the big manufacturers elected to hide their bidding only from certain competitors but not from others, the largest in the industry.

In GE, a corporate debate along strongly pragmatic lines had been waged for some years. Cordiner, an advocate of decentralization, preached that cartel-like organizations liquidated their present strength and future opportunities. Competition served GE better than, for example, entering into price restrictions with competitors. This simply put GE on a level with others that had neither the market impact nor the research facilities that it had.

But the opponents of this kind of thinking argued that getting together with competition was just a way of dealing with reality. It was simpler to rig market share than to compete freely since size entitled a firm to a commensurate share of the total pie. Of course, the point was made, this was a violation of the Sherman Act, but when everyone is committing the same violation, who, in effect, is wrong?

Cordiner, who was destined to bear some of the

stigma for the conspiracy as head of the largest company, paradoxically enough and inadvertently built some of the climate for it. Enforcing his decentralization plan after becoming chairman, he allowed the heads of the more than 100 GE units to set their own policies on marketing and thus pricing policy. Under such conditions, the collusion and summit meetings easily flourished.

How could such a practice endure for eight years? In the wake of the indictments and the sentences, the question became a frequent one. Despite considerable haggling among the conspirators, and mutual accusations that each wasn't living up to the "principles" of the arrangement, some of the executives involved explained that corporate pressure kept them at it, even though the knowledge that they were breaking the law and fighting with one another made them uncomfortable. As one said, "All we got from HQ was the command to get our share of the available business."

Before the antitrust case ended, seven executives went to jail for short periods and fines of almost two million dollars were levied against 29 corporations. The Great Electrical Conspiracy ruined the careers of most, if not all, of the executives indicted, even though most of them came out of the case without being sentenced. The bad smell, however, lasted for years and kept reemerging many times in discussions, meetings and conferences when corporate and executive ethics was the topic.

Did it spell the end of business collusion, rigging, competitive conspiracies? Hardly. Since 1961, there have been numerous cases brought to the surface by the Justice Department. One can only conclude that the electrical conspiracy, and those that have since been brought to light, may well be only the tip of the iceberg.

Telling phrases leap off the page in M. J. Rossant's 1965 story about the collapse of Atlantic Acceptance Corporation. "Investment by crony . . . an aura of respectability . . . watchdogs who failed to live up to their responsibilities . . . experts who were apparently as gullible and as greedy as the greenest investor. . . ."

The kiting of a tiny Toronto finance company into a seemingly powerful lending and investment company with wheeler-dealers on both sides of the Canadian border ultimately rocked the international financial community. By the time Canada's marathon public hearings ended 18 months after Atlantic Acceptance was forced into receivership, the inquiry had pulled in many fish. Tainted by the scandal were 35 separate groups of people who ran 286 companies in six countries.

But the big question remains why some of the most respected and largest American banks, insurance companies, mutual funds, investment advisers, tax-exempt foundations and universities were sucked in. Charges flew thick and fast, but most of the principals hid behind their counsel's warnings not to reply to even the mildest allegations. As Rossant, in his *New York Times'* piece, quotes an officer of the First National City Bank, New York, one of the victims of the fiasco:

"Atlantic proved that you must not take anything for granted."

Because of the financial collapse, Canadian accounting standards were tightened and tougher securities laws were put on the books. But Canada lost some of its reputation as a home of cautious financial practices, and for a while major United States investors who were burned buying Atlantic notes refused to buy any more Canadian finance paper.

In 1969, a Canadian Royal Commission handed down its report on the Atlantic Acceptance fiasco, recommending sweeping changes in the regulation of Canadian finance companies. It urged the appointment of an Inspector General of Finance Companies who would be responsible for administrating the much needed new legislation. The report attacked potential conflicts of interest and loose reporting of financial data and asked for considerably more disclosure and control of loans. And it placed the bulk of the blame on Atlantic's president, who had, unfortunately or perhaps fortunately for him, died early in the investigation.

Perhaps what emerges most graphically from the Rossant piece—even more than the details of the deception and shenanigans of the principals—is the naïveté and soft-headedness of the main victims, some of the best known names in the directory of American finance. But who, one might well ask, still remembers?

Atlantic Acceptance: Even the Big Ones Got Stung

By M. J. Rossant

Some of the nation's most sophisticated professional investors, respected for their prudence and their skill in handling huge amounts of other people's money, are among the victims of one of the biggest speculative crashes in history—the collapse of the Atlantic Acceptance Corporation, a $135-million Canadian enterprise now in receivership.

"Atlantic," according to one numbed casualty, "caused the slaughter of the know-it-alls."

Slaughter does not seem to be an exaggeration. The extent of the losses incurred by prestigious institutions in the United States is shrouded in secrecy and litigation, but estimates run from $50 million to $75 million, and the total could be even higher.

The intangible wounds to the reputations of allegedly astute and experienced professional portfolio managers are also great. For unlike most financial debacles in which the public takes the biggest licking, Atlantic's downfall has hit the experts, who were apparently as gullible and as greedy as the greenest investor.

Institutional investors have been hurt before, most recently in the DeAngelis food-oil scandal and in the misadventures of Billie Sol Estes. But the toll of blue-chip institutions suffering losses in funds or in prestige in the crash of Atlantic is far bigger and more varied. It includes commercial banks, investments banks, industrial corporations, insurance companies, mutual funds, investment advisers and tax-exempt foundations, churches and educational institutions. Some professional investment men have lost their jobs for speculating in Atlantic, and one international banking house with headquarters in New York has been forced out of business.

In Canada, the Atlantic crash and the downfall of the British Mortgage and Trust Company, which had been involved with it, has already caused a score of bankruptcies and threatens a rash of lawsuits against associates of the company. . . . But developments that have come to light since the collapse of the company last June [1965] and interviews with many of the participants who have been silently nursing their wounds provide the key details of Atlantic's rise and fall.

Some of these professionals ruefully confess that they

made mistakes usually made only by the rank amateur. Despite their emphasis on security analysis and the research staffs they had at their disposal, most put other people's money blindly into Atlantic. They had assumed that investing in Canada was pretty much the same as investing in the United States. They now know that Canadians play by a much looser and fuzzier set of rules.

Even more important, they have come to realize that Atlantic was never the well-managed and profitable finance company they believed it to be. A careful investigation would have revealed that its management was incompetent.

Atlantic's downfalls has been particularly embarrassing to Moody's Investors Service, one of the smaller holders of its securities. Moody's bond raters have lowered the credit rating of New York City but they failed to recognize the extremely risky status of Atlantic.

If Moody's has a red face, the United States Steel and Carnegie Pension Fund, which is reputed to be the biggest single loser, has a black eye. Its enviable reputation for astute investing is now tarnished.

But the U.S. Steel fund and Moody's are in good company. Among other prominent victims are the Morgan Guaranty Trust Company, the First National City Bank of New York, the Ford Foundation, the Connecticut General Life Insurance Company, the National Lead Company, the Chesapeake & Ohio Railway, the General Council of Congregational Christian Churches, Princeton University and the University of Pennsylvania.

On Wall Street, Kuhn, Loeb & Co., one of the nation's most reputable investment banking houses, placed more than $20 million in Atlantic securities with investment institutions and was drumming up interest in another Atlantic financing when the crash came. The New York Hanseatic Corporation and the Equitable Securities Company, two other well-established financial houses, were among the sellers of its short-term obligations. The debacle has been a catastrophe for Lambert & Co., which had been regarded on Wall Street as a smart and successful private investment house. Lambert has closed its doors, owing an estimated $15 million to Morgan Guaranty, U.S. Steel and two Canadian banks.

The whole band of investors, who once rode happily together on the Atlantic bandwagon, has had a falling out since its crash. Some of the holders of Atlantic's unsecured obligations, headed by Donald H. Tetzlaff, vice president of the National Life Insurance Company of Montpelier, Vt., are fighting holders of Atlantic's secured obligations who are eager to liquidate the company in an effort to get some of their money back.

Understandably, most investors are hunting for a scapegoat. When Atlantic first went under, they believed the prime cause was President Johnson's program of voluntary restraint on outflows of capital, which made American dollars scarce in Canada. Now they are lashing out at every conceivable target.

Some say they were misled by their illustrious institutional partners or by Canadian banks. Others put the blame on Atlantic's directors and auditors. In addition, there has been a great deal of criticism of C. Powell Morgan, the 56-year-old president of Atlantic, who has resigned and refused to answer questions, on the advice of his lawyers.

Many investors are convinced that they were victimized by fraud on the part of Atlantic. Fraud does not make their loss less severe but it does soothe their egos. As John E. Granger, assistant treasurer of the Ford Foundation explained, "There is no way to protect against dishonesty."

Apparently, fraudulent activities did take place. Members of the Royal Commission and of the Securities and Exchange Commission, who are working together on the case, acknowledge that they are tracking down some of the "most complicated and devious transactions" that they have ever come across.

Yet fraud is not the whole story. The evidence clearly indicates that many sophisticated institutions were distressingly complacent in investing their funds in Atlantic and incredibly naïve in accepting the information made available to them. Adopting an attitude reminiscent of other speculative outbursts in previous booms, they seemed to think they could not miss.

From all accounts, the professionals investing in Atlantic indulged in a common Wall Street failing— the practice of making investments by crony.

The original sponsor of Atlantic on Wall Street was Lambert & Co., a relatively new but highly successful private firm whose members included Jean Lambert, its founder, and Alan T. Christie, a Canadian-born investment man who had formerly worked for the Bank of New York.

Mr. Lambert, who was born and educated in France, started his firm after his marriage in 1949 to Phyllis Bronfman, daughter of Samuel Bronfman, the president of Distillers Corporation-Seagrams. Although the marriage ended in a divorce, Bronfman money remained in the firm.

The Lambert firm specialized in offering funds and guidance to small or problem companies with a big potential for profits.

Mr. Lambert, who is now in Paris, cultivated an air of elegance and mystery. He was usually introduced as a monetary authority who was a member of the French delegation to Bretton Woods and other international conferences, but a check reveals that he was employed at these meetings as a translator.

As the head of his firm, he avoided personal publicity but managed to impress many members of Wall Street's upper echelon.

One associate recalled that "Jean wanted to deal with big names in big projects," and another said that he "is not only interested in making money but in becoming known as an authority of international financial problems."

There are reports that Mr. Lambert was working on a Lambert Plan for international monetary reform with the assistance of some of his staff. A notable hypochondriac, he also kept his staff busy doing research on rare drugs and exotic diseases.

Mr. Christie took a more down-to-earth approach. In 1954, he persuaded Mr. Lambert and his other partners to put $300,000 into Atlantic, then a small financial company that Mr. Morgan, a fellow Canadian, had brought to his attention.

The Lambert firm attached two conditions to its investment. It insisted that Mr. Christie join Atlantic's board and that Mr. Morgan devote full time to Atlantic.

"Powell Morgan," said one Lambert partner, "was supposed to be our man in Atlantic."

Mr. Morgan, who had been controller of the International Silver Company in Canada, had good credentials. A big and affable man who had played professional football and was a trained accountant, he seemed admirably suited to run Atlantic's modest business of making small loans.

With Mr. Morgan on the scene and with Mr. Christie looking over his shoulder, the Lambert firm sold Atlantic to a company called Consolidated Toronto Development, which it controlled. At the same time, Lambert wanted fresh money in order to expand the activities of Consolidated Toronto and Atlantic.

According to an insider at Lambert, it was at this point that Mr. Christie called on Harvey Molé, head of the giant U.S. Steel pension fund and a former colleague at the Bank of New York.

As head of the nation's largest pension fund, with $1.66 billion in assets, Mr. Molé has an awesome reputation in Wall Street. Born in France and educated at Lawrenceville and Princeton, he is known for his devotion to research and his daring in making investments.

Mr. Molé does not follow the practice of most institutional fund managers, who buy either fixed-income obligations for a secure return or common stocks in hopes of a capital gain. Instead, he likes to combine the two, buying bonds with a "kicker" in the form of warrants to purchase common stock or investing in what Wall Street calls "mezzanine money"—securities between stocks and bonds that offer both a good yield and the promise of appreciation.

Informed sources report that the Toronto Development-Atlantic situation appealed to Mr. Molé, who reputedly became the first institutional investor to become involved.

The Ford Foundation was another early investor. Approached by the Lambert firm, it made its own investigation, checking with Atlantic's management, its competitors and Canadian banks.

Having the Ford Foundation and the U.S. Steel pension fund as investors made it easy to appeal to others. In the words of one investment adviser, "We were all sheep. What was good for Harvey Molé and Ford made you feel you had a sure thing."

The presence of major American investors also seemed to have an effect on Atlantic. Until 1960, sales volume had increased at a relatively moderate pace. Then, sales went into orbit, rocketing from $24.6 million to $45.6 million in 1961, $81 million in 1962, $113 million in 1963 and $176 million 1964.

As an expansion-minded finance company, whose main business was automobile loans and small personal loans, Atlantic was in constant need of fresh transfusions of capital.

It did not have large credit lines with banks, which is customary for American finance companies. So it had to depend on raising funds by sales of common stock and by borrowings in the money and capital markets.

Because it was received with open arms in Wall Street, it did an increasing amount of financing with American investors.

Atlantic's growth led the Lambert firm to think in

terms of expanding its own operation. In 1962, its partners came up with a plan to form a group designed to specialize in European investments.

They wrote a prospectus dwelling on the profit potential of the European Common Market and cited two deals, one involving a French pharmaceutical company and the other an international leasing company, on which they were working.

The firm discussed its plans with three prospective partners—the U.S. Steel pension fund, the Ford Foundation and the Morgan Guaranty Trust Company. It already had close ties with U.S. Steel and the Ford Foundation, and it also enjoyed a good relationship with Morgan Guaranty, which was the firm's banker and had been involved with it in some profitable mortgage transactions.

The foundation turned down the proposal, but both Morgan Guaranty and U.S. Steel were taken with the idea of an investment in the Lambert International Corporation. The U.S. Steel pension fund reportedly put up about $4 million, receiving notes and stocks and warrants for the purchase of additional stock.

Morgan Guaranty reportedly put in $2 million on behalf of its commingled pension fund, which pools the funds of some of its clients.

As for Lambert, it was required to invest $1 million for common stock, so that in all, Lambert International had a stake of about $7 million.

Clearly, Morgan Guaranty and the U.S. Steel fund held Mr. Lambert and his firm in high esteem, for they gave him what amounted to a blank check in Lambert International. They had the right to name only three independent members to Lambert International's board, while Lambert partners had six seats, giving them full control.

At one time or another, the independent directors included Emmett Hughes, former Ambassador Ellsworth Bunker, and Sir William Iliffe, a former vice president of the World Bank, but a Lambert associate recalled that "all the important decisions were made by Lambert men."

Despite its confidence in Mr. Lambert, however, Morgan Guaranty was strangely unimpressed by Atlantic. It turned down a request to lend money to Atlantic, taking the position that the company was too much of a one-man show and was engaged in too many different types of lending activity. That decision later helped to limit its losses.

These moves did not slow Atlantic or Mr. Morgan. On the contrary, the company was growing faster than ever in all directions, setting up a chain of subsidiaries to make commercial and industrial loans.

Its growth demanded still more borrowed money, which meant that Mr. Morgan was spending much of his time with prospective lenders, who were awed by Atlantic's record and the backing of U.S. Steel and the Ford Foundation.

Atlantic looked more solid than ever when Kuhn, Loeb & Co. get into the act. With most institutions, Mr. Christie of Lambert made the initial introduction of Atlantic, but Kuhn, Loeb took the initiative in inviting Mr. Morgan to call after some of its partners had heard of Atlantic's rapid growth.

Kuhn, Loeb thought enough of Mr. Morgan and his program to offer to market Atlantic's obligations. But it conducted a thorough study before proceeding. A Kuhn, Loeb spokesman explained, "We were more careful than usual because Atlantic was a Canadian company and because it had grown so fast. After visiting their operations and inspecting their books, we came away convinced that it was a sound situation."

Even so, Kuhn, Loeb did not buy Atlantic securities or attempt to market any common stock. In concentrated on private placements of senior—and junior—securities with institutions, mostly with insurance companies. Attracted by Atlantic's high yields and Kuhn, Loeb imprimatur, portfolio managers were happy to have them.

Lambert International was more interested in capital gains than in a good yield. It had set up lavish quarters and hired an expensive staff, but it did not find many promising investment opportunities in Europe. So, in early 1964 it negotiated to obtain majority control of Great Northern, which in turn had more than 50 per cent of Atlantic's common stock.

The risk increased . . . when Atlantic decided to sell more common stock to increase its borrowing base. To maintain its majority control, Lambert International was forced to take up more than 50 percent of the new issue.

Accountants for the Royal Commission are trying to determine whether Atlantic financed the Lambert International purchases of Atlantic shares. They have no doubt at all that the other portion of the shares sold by Atlantic went to a small group of individuals in an extremely complicated transaction involving Hugo Oppenheim of Berlin, a private German bank, and a private investment concern in Nassau.

Two members of the Nassau group have been identified. One is George H. Weinrott, who had once been indicted for conspiracy to defraud the United States in connection with a housing loan.

The other is Carrol M. Shanks, who resigned as head of the Prudential Life Insurance Company after it was revealed that he had been in a controversial financial deal with the Georgia-Pacific Corporation.

Mr. Weinrott, who headed the group buying Atlantic shares, is reported to be in Europe and has been unavailable for comment. Mr. Shanks, who acknowledged that he had been in the deal, said, "Like everybody else, I have lost money."

The sale of stock enabled Atlantic to increase its other borrowings, which it promptly did. Early in 1965, Kuhn, Loeb helped place $8.5 million of long-term obligations. At the same time, Atlantic increased its short-term liabilities through sales of commercial paper.

Atlantic used these funds to make more loans so it could maintain its image as a fast-growing finance company. The trouble was that it was trying to grow too fast. Increasingly, more and more of its money went into high-risk loans.

Most of the investors in Atlantic were satisfied with its rapid growth. A few, including Kuhn, Loeb and the Toronto Dominion Bank, its chief source of bank credit, suggested it slow down. But Mr. Morgan continued to increase his debt and his sales volume.

The Lambert firm, which had seen its $300,000 stake grow into $7.5 million, became uneasy after hearing rumors that Mr. Morgan was diverting his energies to other financial projects and that he had been using Atlantic to finance these activities.

It finally decided to strengthen its representation on Atlantic's board by naming another partner, Paul C. Sheeline, to join Mr. Christie, who had assumed the presidency of Great Northern. But beyond that move, it was not disposed to argue with success.

The New York Hanseatic Corporation, a big securities dealer that had sold more than $12 million of Atlantic's short-term commercial paper between 1962 and 1965, also picked up a rumor about Mr. Morgan's diversified activities.

Although its source had no information adverse to Atlantic, the concern was disturbed enough to carry out a check. On April 26, it requested information about Atlantic's credit standing from the Toronto Dominion Bank; on May 5, it received a favorable response that served to quiet its fears.

But in the months before the roof fell in, some institutions simply refused to take a chance on Atlantic. An American finance company interested in expanding in Canada took a careful look at Atlantic, then decided against making any offer.

Similarly, Morgan Guaranty, which was approached again, maintained its position that Atlantic did not justify a loan even though it had a big chunk of "mezzanine money" in the company through its position in Lambert International. At least one other New York bank also declined to do business with Atlantic.

Yet intimations of trouble were not general. Kuhn, Loeb, which had approached Morgan Guaranty to arrange a "bridge" financing—a short-term loan to tide Atlantic over while a new long-term issue was being readied for sale—made another investigation that showed the company was sound. Several other institutions that made checks of their own came away reassured.

Thus, late in May, the First National City Bank agreed to purchase a $3-million Atlantic note as a three-month "bridge." It did so despite the fact that the Mercantile Bank of Toronto, City Bank's Canadian affiliate, had always steered clear of lending to Atlantic. And at the beginning of June, the Madison Fund, a $200-million mutual fund, purchased a $1-million Atlantic note with a one-month maturity through Kuhn, Loeb.

The end came just two weeks later, when Atlantic paid out checks for $5 million due in notes that had matured. On Monday, June 14, the Toronto Dominion refused to honor Atlantic's checks, which meant that the company was officially in default.

That same Monday, it became known that some 41 New York brokerage houses received orders on the letterhead of a nonexistent Bahamian bank, along with phony certified checks, for a small number of stocks, including Commodore Business Machines and the Racan Photo-Copy Corporation, which had close connections with Atlantic.

These twin alarms finally alerted American investors, who immediately got in touch with Mr. Morgan. Kuhn, Loeb, along with many others, received assurances that he would be able to work out his money problem.

The partners of Lambert & Co. were placated with similar assurances, but one of them recalls that he had "a sinking feeling that our Canadian profits were going down the drain."

The initial reaction at Kuhn, Loeb was to see if Atlantic could be bailed out. On Wednesday, June 16, it dispatched Thomas E. Dewey, Jr., son of the former Governor and a partner of the firm, on a fact-finding mission to Toronto to determine whether Atlantic could be saved.

The same day, Mr. Lambert flew from Paris to New York at the excited request of his partners. That evening, at a hastily convened meeting at Kennedy International Airport, Mr. Christie is reported to have convinced the group, as he had other investors, that Atlantic's troubles would be solved. With Mr. Lambert's assent, he too left for Toronto.

By then it was too late. Following its first default, Atlantic failed to make good on other maturing notes. So on Thursday, June 17, before any measures could be taken to raise new money, the Montreal Trust Company, which was Atlantic's trustee, threw the company into receivership.

When the receivers took over, the word went out that the secured holders of Atlantic obligations would get back most of their money. But now, most senior debt holders would be grateful for anything above 50 percent.

A proposal to give the task of collecting Atlantic's debts to an American finance company [was] held up in the courts by some of the junior holders who [resented] being left out in the cold. And collection of Atlantic's debts [was not] aided by the remarks of J. G. Haxton, vice president of Montreal Trust, who pressed for a quick liquidation by announcing that "many customers won't make their payments if they think that the finance company is in trouble."

Mr. Haxton's comments have annoyed some Atlantic investors, who believe that he encouraged Atlantic's debtors to welch on their payments. His critics contend that Montreal Trust did not do a good job when

Atlantic was in business and has not improved since Atlantic has been closed down.

F. J. McDiarmid, vice president of the Lincoln National Life Insurance Company, has openly criticized Montreal Trust for apparently accepting "without question, and apparently without checking," Atlantic's own estimates about the value of the collateral it pledged to back up its obligations. Mr. McDiarmid also blamed Toronto Dominion for doing "precious little policing" of Atlantic.

L. C. E. Lawrence, deputy general manager of Toronto Dominion, refused to comment directly on Mr. McDiarmid's charges. He said only that Atlantic was warned that it was growing too fast and "we made clear that it would not get all of the credit it wanted from us."

Other Canadian bankers, who refused to be identified, deny that they have a responsibility for "policing" their clients. And one observed, "Those who were in Atlantic are supposed to be grown up and able to take care of themselves. We were hurt too, but you don't hear us crying about it."

The fact is that, in the United States, banks do "police" finance companies by requiring voluminous reports and by making use of a series of slide-rule yardsticks to determine their credit worthiness. This is not the practice in Canada, although some American investors assumed that it was.

In making their post-mortems, most professionals acknowledge that they should have spotted two early warning signals. One was the rich yields Atlantic offered, which were well above the prevailing levels, and the other was its rapid growth, which should have suggested it was making loans that no other finance company would make.

"We were trying to be heroes," said one subdued company treasurer, "and we just didn't think we could be such fools." But even with hindsight, American investors charge that they were misled by Atlantic's accountants. In the United States, an accounting firm is generally held responsible for auditing a company's books. But the firm of Deloitte, Plender, Haskin & Sells, which was Atlantic's chief accountant, accepted the reports of Wagman, Fruitman & Lando, which audited Atlantic's subsidiaries.

This proved fatal. The report of Atlantic's receiver makes plain that the greater part of the installment loans made by the parent company were relatively sound. But most of the loans made by its subsidiaries, amounting to more than $51 million, were definitely unsound.

It has been established that the senior partner of Wagman, Fruitman & Lando was on the board of one of the companies dealing with Atlantic and was himself the recipient of a loan from Atlantic. His concern, according to authorities, was personally selected by Mr. Morgan to audit Atlantic's subsidiaries.

Atlantic subsidiaries, which were operated mainly by Mr. Morgan, made other loans that turned out to be virtually worthless. In addition to Racan and Commodore Business Machines, subsidiaries and affiliates named Aurora Leasing, Commodore Sales Acceptance, Commodore Factors, Adelaide Acceptance and the Premier Finance Company provided money to many organizations that, an insider reports, "just did not know how to make a profit."

Atlantic's management may have been convinced that its loans were good when they were first made. But it persisted in throwing good money after bad, pressing fresh funds on businesses that could not repay their original advances or even the interest that they owed.

In making this mistake, Mr. Morgan followed the pattern of Ivar Kreuger, the Swedish match king whose empire came crashing down in the early nineteen-thirties.

Like Mr. Kreuger, Mr. Morgan kept making loans

to increase his company's growth and attract new funds from investors.

And, like Mr. Kreuger, he apparently believed it necessary to conceal his mistakes and prevent any loan defaults in order to maintain the pretense that Atlantic was in good shape.

Canadians are mindful of the Kreuger parallels and of the elastic standards that may have encouraged Mr. Morgan's, and Atlantic's, rise. While they are reluctant to accept any responsibility, American observers report that changes are being made.

In particular, the importance of full disclosure is beginning to take hold. Canadian banks and industrial companies have become aware of the need to present detailed information in line with American practices. At the same time, new and stiffer regulations for trust companies are being written, auditing practices are being tightened and there is talk of setting up a federal securities agency modeled on the S.E.C.

In the United States, Mr. Tetzlaff has accused Atlantic's senior holders of helping to scuttle the foundering ship. He thinks Atlantic could be salvaged for the benefit of all investors.

A similar sentiment has been expressed by Pierre Le Landais, a former Lambert partner who has been operating Western Heritage Properties, a land-development company in the Great Northern portfolio. He pointed out that Western Heritage was doing well and might help to offset Great Northern's losses in Atlantic. According to Mr. Le Landais, "Western Heritage has enormous potential, provided it is allowed to continue its growth."

There are sharp differences among institutions over just what is the correct course to follow now. Some think that their fiduciary responsibility calls for trying to pick up the pieces.

Others prefer to write off their losses and forget the whole affair. Still others believe that there are important lessons to be learned from the debacle.

An officer of the First National City Bank argued that the downfall of Atlantic emphasized the value of sticking to fundamentals. He said that the pressure of competition led the bank astray, adding that the "aura of respectability"—lent to Atlantic by its distinguished roster of credits—has often resulted in trouble.

"Atlantic proved that you must not take anything for granted," he said.

Mr. McDiarmid has declared that those directors, "whom at least some institutional debenture holders regarded as watchdogs," failed to "live up to their responsibilities."

The two conspicuous watchdogs were Mr. Christie and Mr. Sheeline, the Lambert partners who sat on Atlantic's board. Mr. Sheeline is in Morocco investigating private investment opportunities for the State Department. Mr. Christie refuses to answer questions "on the advice of counsel."

Because Lambert had control of Atlantic through Great Northern and started it in the United States, it has come in for a great deal of criticism. Former members of the firm acknowledge they made mistakes, especially in concentrating almost all its capital in a situation that had grown too big for it and over which, in retrospect, if failed to exercise adequate control.

But Lambert's partners are the biggest losers because they were investing their own money while others were investing funds entrusted to them.

There also are criticisms of the U.S. Steel pension fund, whose links to Atlantic were usually mentioned when Atlantic approached other institutions. A spokesman for U.S. Steel's pension fund pointed out that it could not be responsible for the actions of others, adding that "our policy is to give no publicity to any transaction made by the fund."

Both Morgan Guaranty and U.S. Steel are among those who are taking their beating in silence. Both institutions confirmed that they were caught in the crash but refused further comment. They both believe that they should be judged on their overall batting average rather than on the basis of one spectacular strike-out.

Certainly, both made their investments in good faith. Morgan Guaranty thought enough of Lambert International to place some of its investments in the deferred profit-sharing trust fund run for its own employes. And Mr. Molé, who is chairman of Princeton's finance committee, thought enough of Atlantic to recommend its securities for Princeton's portfolio.

The Conscience of Insiders—
How Much to Tell the Outsiders?

9

Whether it's a bull or a bear market, there is scarcely an investor who isn't looking for inside information. But according to the Securities Exchange Act of 1934, it is illegal for an insider (officer, employee or director) to make use of "inside" information by trading in securities based on that knowledge.

The most celebrated case involving this issue occurred in 1964 when Texas Gulf Suphur Company announced that it had made a major discovery in its mine in Ontario. But four days earlier the company had issued a press release playing down the Ontario mine, and this had deflated the company's stock.

The resulting litigation dragged on for four years until August 1968 when an appellate court overthrew a lower court's ruling and found that a group of the company's top brass, employees and directors had withheld information on the Canadian discovery while buying Texas Gulf stock, "calls" on Texas Gulf stock or partaking in stock options. But the individual investors, the "outsiders," the nine-man bench noted, might not have disposed of their stock if they had known what the insiders knew.

Another major case of a similar nature developed in 1968. It involved Merrill Lynch, Pierce, Fenner & Smith, the nation's largest brokerage house, whom the Securities and Exchange Commission charged with violating the securities laws by acting on inside financial data on Douglas Aircraft Company.

The Merrill Lynch proceeding had wide ripples, first because it struck at a common Wall Street practice and secondly because under traditional financial definitions Merrill Lynch was actually an outsider, not an insider. But the S.E.C. claimed that Merrill Lynch, by allegedly telling 15 investment-company customers of its inside knowledge, caused Douglas stock to plunge 26 points in one week.

Communications Problems at Texas Gulf Sulphur and Merrill Lynch

If the stock market is as nervous as a cat, if its daily fluctuations seem to have few relevancies to last week's and last month's, it is not because there aren't good reasons for it. One of the best is that the "insiders" are trying to keep what they know from the outsiders. Or that the "experts" are playing it very close to the vest for fear that their expertise, which can be translated as "knowledge," will filter out to the nonexperts, which can be translated as the unwashed investor.

Since 1968, when insider's charges were levied at Texas Gulf Sulphur Company and at Merrill Lynch, Pierce, Fenner & Smith, the problems of disclosure to the stockholder have occupied more and more time at the Securities and Exchange Commission and put many a wrinkle on the foreheads of corporate chief executives and their public-relations men. Since then, many a lawyers', investment-community and other meeting has been held to discuss the problem and find ways of either getting around it or solving it.

The Texas Gulf case involved an appellate-court decision handed down August 13, 1968, which ruled that a group of the company's top officers, directors and employees had committed fraud by withholding certain corporate information from the public while making transactions in their concern's stock. At the core of the problem are Section 10(b) of the Securities Exchange Act of 1934 and Rule 10b–5.

As the appellate court ruled, Texas Gulf's discovery of a body of copper, zinc and silver ore near Timmins, Ontario, in November 1963 represented a material fact that should have been disclosed to investors before any company officials bought any Texas Gulf stock or bought or accepted stock options. But Texas Gulf officials defended themselves by saying that the early indications of an ore strike did not necessarily mean that a commercial body of minerals existed. Therefore, they said, the first ore sample did not constitute material facts that needed to be disclosed.

So the burden appeared to be on "a material fact." What is a material fact?

Part of the S.E.C. Act's Rule 10b–5 stipulates that "it shall be unlawful for any person to make any untrue statement of a material fact or to omit to state a material fact necessary in order to make the statements made, in light of the circumstances under which they were made, not misleading."

Interpretation by lawyers after the appellate-court's decision took to extremes. One was that material facts include not only information that discloses the earnings and distributions of a company but also facts which affect the probable future of the company and/or those which might affect the wish of investors to buy, sell or hold the company's securities. But the reverse of this was the other contention—that the Texas Gulf Sulphur opinion made it clear that the kind of information that creates a problem is extraordinary. Most of the information a company has is not extraordinary.

But corporate reaction also was divided. Some corporate managements then and since have taken the position that the best way they could comply with the law would be to attempt to make greater disclosures than before. But others decided that their best course might be to talk less than before.

And, as if to add depth or another dimension to the problem, the S.E.C. proceeding against Merrill Lynch, 14 of its officers and salesmen and 15 investment companies charged that they had violated the securities laws through the use of inside financial information about Douglas Aircraft. In other words, in that instance, the insider was not necessarily an officer, director or employee of the company whose stock was involved but an employee of a brokerage or investment company that dealt in the stock.

The agency said that the defendants other than the investment companies had learned of an earnings decline at Douglas in 1966 through the brokerage's position as a prospective managing underwriter for a Douglas stock offering. The S.E.C. said that this information was passed along to the 15 institutional clients. These then sold Douglas shares that they already owned or sold shares of Douglas short on the New York Stock Exchange before the information of the earnings decline was released to the general public, the S.E.C. said.

In case you do not know what "short sales" are, profits are made on them when the price of a stock declines. The investor borrows the stock and sells it, waits for it to drop in value, then buys it back at the lower price and "returns" it to the lender. The profit is the amount of the price decline, minus brokerage commissions and taxes.

As the S.E.C. put the situation, Merrill Lynch was impelled to pass along the information about the drop in the Douglas earnings by the commissions it would receive from the institutional clients and by obtaining "give-ups." The latter is a device in which a large investor, such as an investment company, directs a portion of the commission on a securities transaction to be given up to a brokerage house other than the one that executed the transaction.

The agency said that Merrill Lynch's decision to

furnish the inside information to the institutional clients violated the securities statutes because it placed these clients in an advantageous position. The information was not available to other customers. The principle behind the disclosure provisions of the S.E.C. Act is that all investors should be equal in the sense that small investors should have full access to all the information that large, institutional investors have.

Both the Texas Gulf and the Merrill Lynch rulings sent shock waves through corporate and investment circles that have continued to reverberate into the Seventies. The S.E.C. has also stiffened its enforcement of the disclosure provisions of the act that empowers it and will probably intensify that enforcement in the years ahead.

Late in 1968, the agency penalized Merrill Lynch and a group of its employees as part of a settlement of the case. The sanctions included suspension of two of the brokerage's offices for several weeks, resulting in a loss of business estimated on Wall Street of about $1 million; suspension for a brief period without pay of seven executives and censure of several others.

But while the two cases created further communications problems at both Texas Gulf and Merrill Lynch, the 40 million small investors around the country gained in achieving more access to corporate information which, hopefully, would help them in their investment activities.

10

Wall Street, which loudly proclaims the opportunities it offers the unwashed American investor, has not been as conspicuously extroverted about the rise of its own wet-behind-the-ears entrepreneurs. The mid- and late Sixties were marked by the emergence of stockbrokers and investment bankers still in their twenties, but the old guard on Wall Street was not as quick as the press to hail them. One reason, perhaps, is the traumatic experience the pillars of Wall Street had in 1962 with an earlier boy wonder, Eddy Gilbert, former president of E. L. Bruce.

A high liver and devotee of the fanciest of night clubs, spas and resorts, Gilbert was one of the big losers in the 1962 stock-market decline. He lost $23 million and absconded to Brazil after being charged with embezzling $1.95 million from E. L. Bruce.

It all began with his attempt to take over control of Celotex Corporation, making large purchases of Celotex shares on margin. When the stock market plunged in spring 1962, he was forced to produce more margin or cash and began taking money from Bruce. Later, he arranged for the Ruberoid Corporation to buy both his shares and E. L. Bruce's shares in Celotex. But the deal fell through, and he quickly embarked to Brazil.

But 139 days later, he returned voluntarily to New York, unable to bear the stigma of failure and hoping he could make good on all his debts, knowingly facing prosecution. The 1962 story in the *New York Times* gets behind the man and shows that when you have a gift of selling "anybody anything," temptation beckons.

Gilbert Wanted an Empire of His Own

By McCandlish Phillips

As his friends see it, including some of those who lost money by investing at his personal entreaty, Edward M. Gilbert is the victim of an inner compulsion to compete, to drive to the very top, to win, win, win, at almost any cost of energy and time.

The ordinary pace of the world, especially the ordinary rhythms by which diligent men cultivate success, seemed to Mr. Gilbert to be a sort of agonizing slow motion. Waiting was exasperating to a man whose every instinct was to run, to leap, to plunge and to keep going until distant goals had drawn even and receded, leaving only stouter goals ahead.

Then all his goals collapsed. On June 12, [1962] Mr. Gilbert flew to Brazil after having admitted withdrawing nearly $2,000,000 of the funds of the E. L. Bruce Company without authorization.

Mr. Gilbert liked to gamble. At times he set his chips at the edges of the card tables and clicking wheels at Monte Carlo and Las Vegas.

Eddy Gilbert began picking up competitive momentum in his high school days (he got 100 on a final examination in mathematics at the Horace Mann School here, but flunked English).

He studied engineering in 1940 and 1941 at Cornell and went out for boxing, football, swimming and tennis, winning varsity letters in each sport. He was on the Cornell tennis team that included Dick Savitt, the national collegiate champion. Mr. Gilbert qualified in

1941 for the national tennis championships at Forest Hills, Queens, but he lost out in the second round.

He was wounded twice as a correspondent for Stars and Stripes and other Army newspapers in Europe and Africa in World War II, and he won the middleweight boxing championship of his Army Air Force group.

After the war he returned to Cornell but dropped out in 1946 to join the family business at 23.

His first job with the Empire Millwork Corporation —a maker of wooden doors, sashes, trim and mouldings—was unloading lumber from freight cars. His grandfather, Hyman, was chairman of the Corona, Queens, concern. The family name, Ginsberg, was changed to Gilbert.

The family had been in the news previous to the change. In January, 1937, Edward Gilbert's father, Harry Ginsberg, and his uncle, Morris Ginsberg, pleaded guilty in Federal Court in Brooklyn to a conspiracy to defraud the Government by means of short deliveries of lumber to a Works Progress Administration furniture factory in Brooklyn. Harry Ginsberg was fined $1,500. Morris Ginsberg received a sentence of sixty days in jail.

In 1947 Edward Gilbert was transferred to Harriman, Tennessee, where the company had a flooring plant. It was there that he got his first glimpse of the Bruce company of Memphis, one of the foremost producers of hardwood floors.

"It caught my imagination," he said later. He remembered that his thought at the time was "I'd like to be with that company."

So it was that at 24 he had set his sights on the Bruce concern. "I used to hang around their plant at every opportunity to see what I could learn," he said.

Two and a half years later, Empire sold its Harriman facility and returned Mr. Gilbert to New York, where he took over its local lumber sales, supplying Long Island builders. Empire's sales spurted, but his family was not yet ready to give him a raise or a seat on the company's board. He chafed at his salary of $7,500 a year, and he left.

In 1951, with a friend helping him and a telephone at his side, he invaded the Long Island market as the owner of Rhodes Hardwood Flooring Corporation, named for his wife, the former Rhoda Weintraub, whom he married in the St. Regis Hotel on October 11, 1951.

Four years later, when sales reached $250,000 a year, Mr. Gilbert persuaded Empire to buy Rhodes for 20,000 shares of stock. He borrowed $40,000 to gain 67,000 more shares and was soon an officer and a member of Empire's board of directors.

He was still, however, angling for Bruce. He had acquired several thousand shares of Bruce stock by 1955, and two years later he decided that the opportunity had come to strike in the direction of control. "I really started buying," he said.

Aided by friends and relatives, he paid up to $87 a share at times for stock whose book value was $41. The Bruce company, a family concern whose stock had had a quiet and uneventful history, began to be rocked as the ambitious young man from New York moved in.

Calling on his very considerable powers of persuasion, and using his rise at Empire as proof of the reasonableness of his plans, Mr. Gilbert got friends, acquaintances and total strangers to buy Bruce stock for him.

"This guy could sell anybody anything," said one observer of Mr. Gilbert's maneuvers. "Even those who have been hurt by losses say he's a great fellow. They can't believe he'd go to Brazil."

Mr. Gilbert, short and baldish with ice-blue eyes and a round yet rugged-looking countenance, went on a fiscal roller coaster ride that proved to be upward all the way. "Any one of twenty-five twists could have destroyed him," an observer said. Much of his stock was held on margin.

"If the stock had dropped eight percent, I would have been bankrupt," Mr. Gilbert himself observed.

In October, 1958, he acquired control of 50 percent of Bruce stock for Empire. He was blunt about his purpose: "I believe Bruce is really ready to move ahead; I want to use it as a vehicle to build an empire." Last September, he became president of Bruce.

Meanwhile, having achieved so much of his objective, he began to acquire social and personal status symbols.

With his stylishly dressed wife and two adopted daughters, Robin and Alexandra, seven and five years old, he moved into a ten-room, $1,500-a-month apartment at 817 Fifth Avenue. He then began to fill it with paintings by such artists as Fragonard, Canaletto and Monet.

The suite was less than two blocks from the Bruce company's former office on Madison Avenue, and Mr. Gilbert, after a quick breakfast of orange juice and coffee, walked to work. He refused to wear an overcoat, even on the coldest days, because he said he had a habit of losing overcoats by leaving them behind.

At the office, he spent much of his time on the telephone, drawing geometric doodles on a note pad while he spoke. During nontelephoned conversations, he was likely to jump up to illustrate a point with quick, sweeping hand gestures. To keep refreshed he took two cold showers a day.

Mr. Gilbert and his wife went out two or three nights a week. At the Metropolitan Opera, the Gilberts and friends occupied Box 10 on Monday nights, an eight-seat cubicle that stood fifth from the proscenium at the right of the house. It cost $1,920 a season.

He began to live lavishly in international society. He bought an eleven-bedroom villa at Roquebrune in southern France and held open house almost daily when there. On some days, a jazz band would play beside the pool in the afternoon and an orchestra would play at night.

Mr. Gilbert was at times snappishly demanding to waiters and others serving him, but he was also capable of waving $20 and $100 bills before headwaiters' eyes. When he did this, he did it with a flourish so that everybody could see, friends said.

He also hired a personal agent to get people with prominent names as guests at his parties, and he conferred with Elsa Maxwell for guidance at social climbing. His wife inspected $732,000 worth of diamonds and other jewels from Cartier, but she returned them when the jeweler brought suit.

Mr. Gilbert, estranged from his wife, took a suite . . . in the Waldorf Towers. He gave the suite up . . . but returnéd to another Towers suite [three months later.] He paid $550 in cash for his Varig Airlines ticket to Brazil. . . .

The Brokerage House Goes Broke

11

In a wave of problems that included shrinking volume in the stock market, continually rising costs and an uncontrollable glut of paperwork, 13 exchange-member brokerages failed in the 1969–1970 crisis that engulfed Wall Street.

McDonnell & Co., a 65-year-old member firm of the New York Stock Exchange, was the first big one to close its doors. According to T. Murray McDonnell, its chairman, the brokerage had to liquidate for a variety of reasons, not the least of which was a new computer that just failed to operate. What gave the McDonnell firm's passing some national prominence besides the fact that such a large, venerable firm should pass from the scene was the fact that Lawrence F. O'Brien, former Postmaster General, aide to two presidents and later Democratic National Chairman, had served briefly as its president.

The NYSE took punitive action against McDonnell's chairman, suspending him for two months from working as a securities salesman and barring him indefinitely from being either a Big Board member or acting in a supervisory capacity for a member firm. He had, the NYSE charged, failed to "provide adequate supervision and control," and his firm had "violated capital, bookkeeping and segregation rules."

The firm's failure compelled the exchange to beef up its Special Trust Fund which aids customers of a number of member firms that have gone under. But the passing of a famous traditional name also had a traumatic, if brief, effect on the Wall Street community. Here is the account from the March 15, 1970 issue of the *New York Times*.

Fears Fulfilled as Big Broker Fails

By Terry Robards

The disaster that Wall Street had been forecasting for more than a year finally came to pass when McDonnell & Co., a respected, old-line brokerage house, disclosed that it could no longer stay in business and was being forced to liquidate.

"The properly stringent requirements of the regulatory bodies concerning net capital have made it impossible to weather the storm any longer," said T. Murray McDonnell, chairman of the once-proud concern.

Thus did the death knell sound for one of Wall Street's major houses. Ever since the securities industry became engulfed in a flood of paperwork because of unexpectedly heavy stock-market volume in the late nineteen-sixties, the seers of doom had been saying that a big firm would go under and a crisis of public confidence would ensue.

Ironically, McDonnell's failure comes at a time when the industry apparently has worked its way out of its severest difficulties. However, the disastrous decline in the stock market, under way since 1968, has taken the place of the paperwork tie-up as Wall Street's biggest problem.

Virtually all brokerage houses invest their capital in securities, much of it in common stocks. When the market nosedives, capital melts away and suddenly financial difficulties come into the open.

So it was with Gregory & Sons . . . and Amott,

Baker & Co. . . . both of which went out of business because of the twin demons of plunging markets and back-office difficulties. But these were relatively small firms, whose collapse caused only minor ripples along the world's richest street.

With McDonnell & Co., the situation [was] different. In 1968 the concern listed net worth of nearly $15-million. Infusions of new capital were obtained . . . in desperate efforts to stem the tide of losses. An estimate of its net worth . . . was not immediately available, but it was understood that much of it had disappeared.

It is too early to say whether the confidence of investors in the Wall Street mechanism will be affected by McDonnell's failure, but seasoned observers of the street felt that the concern's efforts to cut back during the last eight months, coupled with the wide publicity given to the industry's operational crisis, would tend to soften the blow.

Moreover, the New York Stock Exchange moved into the situation quickly with a credit of up to $6-million from its special trust fund to assist McDonnell by delivering out its customer accounts. This should prevent investors from incurring losses.

In addition, the concern's liquidation will take place over a period of months and presumably will be accomplished in an orderly fashion. Its customers' accounts are to be introduced to other concerns belonging to the stock exchange. The major inconvenience to investors probably will arise from an inability to obtain funds or their securities immediately.

McDonnell is the house that was sufficiently prestigious to attract Lawrence F. O'Brien, the former Postmaster General and aide to Presidents Kennedy and Johnson, away from Government service to serve as its president.

Mr. O'Brien joined the firm in January, 1969, and resigned Aug. 11. "When I came to McDonnell & Co.," he said when he left, "it was with the understanding that the firm would be in a position to broaden its horizons in a variety of ways. It has become apparent, however, that this will not be possible and, in fact, the company is retrenching. . . ."

Mr. O'Brien, who . . . became Democratic National Chairman, apparently made a prudent decision. Since he left, McDonnell has closed most of its 26 branch offices here and abroad, has laid off employes, has sold the McDonnell Mutual Fund to another brokerage house and has cut costs in numerous other ways.

Rumors of distress surrounded the firm . . . most of them focusing on repeated efforts to raise substantial amounts of additional capital. One story had it that the firm had borrowed heavily from Ann McDonnell Ford, Henry Ford 2d's former wife and a member of the brokerage-house family. It was never confirmed.

. . . Less than two weeks before his resignation, Mr. O'Brien and T. Murray McDonnell issued a joint statement, saying: "We are most pleased to advise our customers, our employes and our associates in the financial community that McDonnell & Co., Inc., has completely resolved its temporary capital problem and is on a solid financial footing."

They continued: "We are issuing this clarification because of the rumors and press reports which have been circulated in recent days. The company has made arrangements for new capital in the minimum amount of $3-million and up to a maximum of $10-million, depending upon the needs."

That statement was in stark contrast to the sad message Mr. McDonnell issued [later] to employes and customers: "It is with deep regret that we have decided to close McDonnell & Co., Inc., after 65 years of business on Wall Street.

"The firm, started by my father, has had a long tradition of integrity and reliability and it is in that spirit that we have made our decision. Circumstances, many of them beyond human control, created problems for our firm that have turned out to be insoluble."

Among the difficulties cited by Mr. McDonnell were the sudden death of his younger brother, Sean, who had played a key management role until mid-1968, the deaths of two other senior officials, the failure of a new computer system to operate as planned, the sharply declining stock market and the subsequent drop in brokerage volume and other investment-banking activities.

After asserting that it had become impossible to go on, he concluded: "Therefore, we will terminate our business over the next few months, keeping faith with our customers, with our colleagues in Wall Street and with our loyal and devoted employes."

Kevin Thomas Duffy, New York regional administrator of the Securities and Exchange Commission, disclosed that McDonnell & Co. had been the subject of an S.E.C. investigation for months. He said certain facts had been uncovered, leading [the commission] to consider filing charges against the firm.

Mr. Duffy did not mention what charges might be filed. In past regulatory actions involving brokerage houses with financial and operating difficulties, the S.E.C. has made accusations of improper record keeping and violations of capital requirements. Sometimes the firms themselves are named in the actions and other times individual officials are cited.

McDonnell & Co., traditionally a fairly large firm on Wall Street, is not the only house with problems. The red ink splashed on the financial reports of some of the street's biggest institutions provides an indication of the situation.

Bache & Co. reported a net loss of more than $7-million, before taxes, in . . . nine months . . . and probably ran several million dollars deeper into the red during the balance of its fiscal year. Francis I. duPont & Co. disclosed a deficit of $7.7-million for 1969, and Goodbody & Co. operated at a loss of more than $800,000.

As far as Wall Street is concerned, there may be one

beneficial aspect of the McDonnell failure. It may add to the pressure on the S.E.C. to give preliminary approval to a commission-rate increase requested . . . by the exchange.

The exchange has repeatedly cited the need for a rate rise to stave off the losses being sustained by many firms on their commission business. The securities industry has not had a rate increase since 1958, while the cost of doing business has skyrocketed.

Meanwhile, the losses mount. And few of the industry's experts would be willing to say that McDonnell & Co. will be the final casualty of the profit pinch.

Miniskirted Companies Become Overexposed

12

"It's easy going into business," said a bright-eyed entrepreneur I know. "I've done it many times."

He certainly had. He was a bankruptcy con man—an expert in the art of slipping through the holes of the Federal Bankruptcy Act of 1903 and its 11 amendments. All of them had been carefully worked out so that no one could slip through their holes. He did.

Not all the approximately 10,000 businessmen who go bankrupt each year are crooks. But the estimated $1.5 billion in liabilities they chalk up in an average, routine year represents an overextension of commitments, most of which they will never have to repay. Thanks to the U.S. Constitution, which empowered Congress to set up uniform laws on the subject of bankruptcies, and to the derivative English statute signed in 1542 by Henry VIII, many a businessman has been taken off the hook. These laws mostly keep him out of jail while allowing him to settle with his creditors at a fraction on the dollar. The optimum is 100 percent but it is rarely reached.

Of course, there are sometimes mitigating circumstances which justify a bankruptcy. Three of the most recent amendments (1933, 1934, and 1935) to the Bankruptcy Act tried to help honest debtors to rehabilitate themselves. Many of these were corporations which because of the Depression were solvent but were unable to meet maturing obligations.

Bankruptcy means "reduced to a state of financial ruin . . . insolvent . . . being in a financial state declared subject to having an estate administered under the bankrupt laws for the benefit of creditors. . . ."

The big question the federally appointed bankruptcy referee has to decide in adjudicating a bankrupt business is to determine if the owners have any hidden assets that can be legally applied to pay off their debts. These hidden assets are occasionally discovered but more often not, because they either don't exist or have been exceptionally well hidden or are legally untouchable.

Two main categories of proceedings are available under the Bankruptcy Act. One is the "voluntary" petition, filed by the debtor himself under the Act's Chapter XI provisions. This petition is accompanied by schedules which list creditors and their claims, debtor's assets, exemptions claimed, etc. The "involuntary" action, known as Chapter X, is taken when three or more creditors decide to take the initiative, simply having lost patience, and file a petition in court to have their debtor declared bankrupt. The debtor in such cases has less control over his situation than in the voluntary proceedings.

In both cases, the aim usually is to gain time to continue the business while the Federal government allows the debtor to make an orderly settlement with his creditors. While there are no real statistics, credit-industry estimates are that roughly half of the bankrupts succeed in righting the course of their business, settle their debts and continue to operate.

What causes bankruptcies? Greed, avarice, irresponsibility, say the toughest critics. Overextension, inadequate controls, an economic downturn which finds the company owner hung over financially, say the kinder critics. The cases of both Dolly Madison Industries and Four Seasons Nursing Homes, covered in the

Robert Hershey article, are typical of many which offer ample documentation supporting either school of thought. What's your opinion?

Dolly Madison's management participated in the acquisition binge of the Sixties and ran into a severe case of corporate abdominal blockage. Projected on a springboard of Medicare and Medicaid for the proliferating aged segment of the American population, Four Seasons overexpanded in real-estate development aimed at building a nationwide chain of nursing homes.

One conclusion to it all is that the risks of flying in business are great, and I don't mean business trips in airplanes. The simple fact is that high-flyers make a resounding thud when they fall. For documentation read this 1970 *New York Times* story.

The Glamorous Road to Bankruptcy

By Robert D. Hershey, Jr.

When the mighty Penn Central Transportation Company was forced to its knees because it could not borrow money fast enough to pay off its debt, many in the business and financial world saw it as an inevitable outcome of the Government's policy to curb inflation by making money scarce.

While hardly a blue-chip concern, nevertheless the failure of a company of the sheer size of the Penn Central Railroad cast a pall over the nation's business scene and caused widespread predictions that numerous other companies would be brought down, too.

Sure enough, two days later a Philadelphia midiconglomerate called Dolly Madison Industries, Inc., filed for reorganization under Chapter X of the Bankruptcy Act, followed two days later by the largest of the once glamorous nursing home chains—Four Seasons Nursing Centers of America, Inc.

Was this confirmation that a year and a half of tight (and expensive) money—only recently somewhat relaxed—was cutting heavily into the soundness of the American economy, perhaps to an extent unrealized by financial policy makers?

BUSINESS FAILURES
Liabilities in millions of dollars

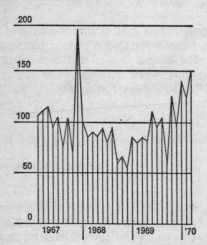

Source: Dun & Bradstreet, Inc.

Or were the failures of Dolly Madison and Four Seasons a result of circumstances that had little to do with the general business picture and nothing at all to do with Penn Central?

The answer, as best as can be determined now, seems to lie somewhere in between: the economy is not mortally wounded, according to this point of view, but there are many marginal companies that will have to scramble to remain a step ahead of increasingly watchful creditors.

Lionel D. Edie & Co., Inc., an economic consulting

concern, observes in an analysis that it is "perfectly normal" for business failures to rise whenever economic activity turns down because there is a tendency for businesses to overexpand in inflationary boom periods such as had occurred in recent years.

Then, when sales decline and profits fade such companies find money simply unavailable to them on reasonable terms—or on any terms at all—and they find

NEW INCORPORATIONS
In thousands Seasonally adjusted

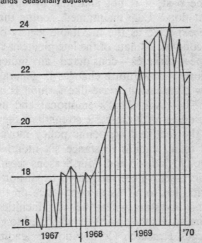

Source: Dun & Bradstreet, Inc.

that their mistakes, previously hidden by inflation, have put them in deep financial trouble.

But Edie, a division of Merrill Lynch, Pierce, Fenner & Smith, Inc., believes the dangers to the economy in general from these situations have been frequently exaggerated.

"A great deal of apprehension is being expressed about the current rate of business failures, and too much emphasis is placed on single instances, such as the Penn Central case. While the 1969–1970 failure rate has risen, it is far from alarming and must be viewed in proper perspective," Edie held.

During the first five months of 1970, according to Dun & Bradstreet, Inc., a total of 4,355 businesses —excluding banks and railroads—went under, an increase of 11 percent from the comparable 1969 period.

The liabilities of these companies, however, climbed by 47 percent to $676.5-million.

"While the present level of failure liabilities is higher than in the past, it is not alarming by any stretch of the imagination," Edie maintained, adding that failures should be expected as the inevitable legacy of the unrealistic economic climate of the late nineteen-sixties.

To expect failures—considered an indicator that tends to foreshadow future changes in general business —"to now cumulate in wave-like fashion is something else again, however. That's emotional and unrealistic. It doesn't square with the basic strength of the economy and with the fact that economic policy moved from a restrictive to an expansive stance six months ago."

Both Dolly Madison and Four Seasons seem to represent classic cases where misguided expansion during a boom period led to a loss of confidence on the part of lenders and investors when the new facilities did not produce the profits they had been expected to generate.

The Argus Research Corporation, a leading investment adviser, commented on developments of this sort in a letter, sent to clients.

"Until very recently," Argus said, "improvement in earnings per share was all the rage in the stock market and many business managements had begun to perform like dancing bears. The emphasis on showing a rising trend in earnings a share led to overexpansion and overborrowing by aggressive business managers across the country.

"Now that the 1969 money squeeze is having a delayed-action effect on the economy, the companies with miniskirted balance sheets find themselves overexposed in the eyes of an investment community that has suddenly begun to apply neo-Victorian standards of financial prudence," the Argus Research Corporation observed.

In the case of Dolly Madison, overexpansion came in fits and starts, and, as it turned out, frequently in the wrong direction. Four Seasons simply tried to push nursing homes too far too fast.

Dolly Madison was formed in 1963 from the old Minneapolis-Moline Power Implement Company whose farm tractor business was sold and whose proceeds from the sale were used to acquire a large part of the northeastern operations of Foremost Dairies, Inc.

The company then embarked on a succession of acquisitions in the food industry to add to its ice cream lines as well as acquisitions in furniture manufacturing and leasing.

Except for what it concedes was a "fiasco" in the foods division in 1967 that caused a major retrenchment, Dolly Madison grew quickly, tripling in size during the second half of 1968 alone.

Bernard T. Perry, 48, the company's soft-spoken president who came east from his native Indiana (where he had once been a part-time accounting and economics instructor) with the furniture division in 1964, once characterized Dolly Madison this way before the Indianapolis Society of Security Analysts in November, 1968.

"We believed, and we still believe, that the seventies would belong to the marketing people, not to the old-style light-bulb and string-saving manufacturer."

He added, "We now, and will in the future, manufacture what sells best. Not, as in earlier years, seek to sell what we manufacture best. The future belongs to the consumer."

When reached by telephone at his Philadelphia office, Mr. Perry said he was sorry that he did not feel free to speak about the company's problems. The self-described "country boy," however, hinted that he had learned some hard lessons.

"I'll write a book someday," he promised.

In the latest annual report Mr. Perry and Robert Rittmaster, chairman, told shareholders that 1969 was a year of bad surprises:

First, there was delay in getting approval for the sale of securities, raising financial problems, which, compounded with constantly rising interest rates, "caused us to direct more attention to working with the financial problems of the company than with operating the business properly."

There were also a decline in demand for retail furniture, problems with the stores selling on an installment basis, excessive distribution costs and the unexpected discovery that the company had been running at a substantial loss.

This situation caused subsequent decisions to be based on financial expediency rather than on operational judgments. In February, for example, Dolly Madison obtained a $5-million bank credit only after agreeing to pay interest at 14 ½ percent.

At the time the company appealed to the courts for protection from creditors it had sold off its most successful food business and had agreements—still pending—to sell the furniture manufacturing division, its most significant asset, and its Dolly Madison Ice Cream Company subsidiary.

. . . Two months before figures for fiscal 1969 . . . were disclosed, Dolly Madison was telling stockholders that it would show a profit.

When released, however, they showed a loss of $3,507,676, in sharp contrast to a profit in the preceding 12 months of $4,569,003, or $2.37 a common share.

"There's just no way you can end up halfway integrated," Mr. Perry told a magazine writer. "We were in a couple of industries which required continued capital, and the money market dried up."

The end came when . . . bank creditors demanded

payment of $7.5-million of loans that could not be paid, and the company's bank accounts were seized "thereby depriving the company of cash needed for the daily operation of its business," the petition said.

The latest balance sheet . . . showed current liabilities of $38,223,229, compared with current assets—about half in receivables and half in inventories—of $36,-626,993.

Four Seasons Nursing Centers, an Oklahoma City-based chain, was founded in 1963 by Jack L. Clark, a home-builder and former salesman of golf carts and gypsum products; Amos Bouse, a construction company owner; and Tom Gray, Mr. Clark's half-brother who had operated a nursing home in Henrietta, Texas, after a five-year stretch as proprietor of a restaurant there called the St. Elmo Coffee Shop.

The company adopted a standard X-shaped nursing home model that provided what it considered great efficiencies in both construction and operation.

"Every Four Seasons Nursing Center is a duplication of the nearly 13,000 beds we currently have in operation or under construction," Mr. Clark said recently. "Only through complete standardization can the economies of volume be applied to produce the optimum program of development and operation."

The company spurted into prominence with the help of Government programs that poured money into the health-care field, although it has always maintained that it could operate profitably without such funds, too.

Four Seasons went public in 1968 at $11, and its shares later that year traded at more than ten times that price as the public's fancy swung toward the nursing-care field.

But the shifting economic climate, with attendant tight money and soaring labor costs, was to catch up with Four Seasons, which depended . . . on construction revenues for a major part of its income.

. . . Financing became a serious problem, even as Mr. Clark was assuring Philadelphia financial analysts

. . . that "We are confident of our ability to continue to attract the investment community as we have done in the past."

It was about this time that large institutional holders of Four Seasons stock were selling their shares because of doubts about the company's projected earnings and the ability of companies such as Four Seasons to obtain long-term financing.

When the company . . . announced that it expected to report a loss for its third fiscal quarter . . ., the American Stock Exchange suspended trading in it . . . and the bubble burst.

The State of Ohio, a $4-million creditor that had been expected to lend many millions more, decided not to do so, and other potential lenders backed away.

Mr. Clark, who resigned . . . for health reasons, charged in a telephone interview that the American Exchange had triggered the crisis by "over-reacting" to the earnings announcement with the suspension and an investigation into Four Seasons' financings.

He said he was "absolutely" sure that Four Seasons could have avoided resorting to Chapter X if trading had not been suspended.

But others, many of whom believe they have good reason to doubt statements of Mr. Clark because of what they believe to have been his representations in the past—there are several stockholders' suits pending—dispute this, holding that the company was headed for a fall apart from any problems with the exchange.

Meanwhile, Mr. Clark reported that he was "not doing anything" except trying to recuperate from nine years of "extremely hard work in which I often put in 18-hour days."

He had a parting shot, though, for the investors who had soured on him and his company. In response to a question as to how he answered charges that he had deceived and misled the investment community, he insisted that "I did give the facts as they existed at that moment. I'm not a prophet—I couldn't forecast as drastic a change in the economy and the labor market in particular.

"Besides," he added, "I could say the same thing to those fund managers. Some of 'em touted me some stocks that just about busted me."

Meanwhile one of the nation's biggest funds has marked down its few remaining Four Seasons shares to $1 each. The high was 90 ¾.

RCA's Computer Cops Out

13

Can RCA be IBM?

Building computers and selling them is not like changing programming in television, RCA Corporation found out, much to its regret and a loss of $500 million.

The ill-fated computer venture represented RCA's biggest investment in its history, far more than the long push required on color TV. "We'll take it out of IBM's hide," said the RCA strategist, but with IBM it's usually the other way around and so it was. But RCA tried it by hiring an IBM man to launch "Project Intercept" (intercept IBM, what else?) and by making a wholesale exchange of veteran RCA men for IBM men. The copycat effort even involved the imitating of IBM systems in marketing practices, personnel-ranking systems and product development, as well as management development.

It was RCA's biggest fiasco, $490 million worth, and the company got a pretax write-off in that amount. All the same it represented the biggest bomb in recent American business history, even bigger than Ford's Edsel fiasco. As the March 1972 story from *Datamation* magazine points out, the computer venture was to be Robert Sarnoff's way of coming out from under the giant shadow cast by his father, David Sarnoff, who had gathered lots of profit and prestige from pioneering color TV. But for the son, computers did just the opposite.

Curtain Act at RCA

By W. David Gardner

Early in 1970, the RCA computer people who attended
the Marketing Achievement Club meeting in San Francisco realized that something was happening to them
and to their computer division—something good. They
were a part of a new era—the L. Edwin Donegan, Jr.,
era—and to just about everyone at the meeting in San
Francisco's mammoth Masonic Temple that seemed to
be a very good thing indeed.

Donegan was enjoying a meteoric rise at RCA, having
just been appointed vice president and general manager
of the division after only a year there. Here was a man
who was clearly different from the conservative, old-
shoe type of managers who had been running the computer division in recent years. Donegan's Irish good
looks and enormous vitality were in sharp contrast to
the folksy and plodding manner of the former chief of
the computer operation, James Bradburn, who, although
he didn't know it at that time, would gradually be eased
out of the computer operation by RCA corporate
management while Donegan would be eased in.

Donegan wasted no time in putting his stamp on the
division and he started with the meeting of the Marketing Achievement Club, membership in which is meant
to be a reward for sales achievement during the previous
year. Gone were the RCA homemade aspects of the
meeting and in their place was a slick and smooth
production with a stress on visuals. Under the old RCA
regime, the emphasis had been on individual recognition and communication among the sales people, while
Donegan used the meeting primarily as a motivational
vehicle. "Donegan really fired them up," said one ex-
RCA man who attended. "Particularly the young sales-

men. When they arrived at the meeting they were proud that they made the club, but when they left they left feeling they were going to do three times better."

There were, however, a few men at the meeting who had silent reservations about ex-IBMer Donegan's first Marketing Achievement Club meeting. To them, the meeting was somewhat more extravagant than they were accustomed to and this caught their eye. For instance, the consultant who worked on the meeting was paid a fee of more than $100,000, and attendance at the meeting was puffed up to about 1,000 people at an increase in cost by bringing in large numbers of non-sales types. The result was that RCA's Computer Division seemed to have grown larger very rapidly.

But more important, the atmosphere of the meeting had changed sharply. It didn't seem to be a meeting of RCA's Marketing Achievement Club at all; but rather, considering the slick production, a meeting of IBM's 100 Per Cent Club. In this regard, the San Francisco meeting would prove to be a microcosm of the problems that would help lead to disaster in September of 1971 when RCA would pull out of the computer business entirely, in disgrace. Donegan would attempt to transform RCA's Computer Division into an IBM with an almost missionary zeal. If IBM had done anything—anything at all—then the same thing was often good enough for RCA. When he was at IBM, for example, Donegan had attended a meeting of the 100 Per Cent Club at the very same Masonic Temple. Likewise, in the next two years, Donegan would pick as the sites of RCA's Marketing Achievement Club meetings locations where IBM had held its meetings for its 100 Per Cent Club—the Broadmoor in Colorado Springs and the Fountainebleau in Miami Beach.

Donegan joined RCA in January of 1969. An RCA press release announcing his appointment by the then chief of computer marketing, Edwin S. McCollister, stated that Donegan, who was just past 40, would be responsible for "all field and home office sales department functions, and will make his headquarters at the computer division's home office in Cherry Hill, N.J." RCA documents on file with the Securities and Exchange Commission indicate that Donegan received a basic annual salary of $75,000, but that figure presumably was inflated by bonuses. It is not entirely clear why McCollister hired a new marketing leader, but the best explanation seems to be that McCollister was tiring of his job after nearly a decade in RCA marketing and he hired Donegan with the idea that the latter would be his replacement. McCollister no doubt was thinking the changing of the marketing guard would take place over a period of years. However, within a year, not only would Donegan overtake McCollister, but he would take over the entire Computer Systems Division and be on his way to a corporate vice presidency. And in another year, Donegan would be under consideration for the presidency of the entire RCA Corp., which, with annual sales of more than $3 billion, ranked as one of the 25 largest corporations in the U.S.

McCollister was a steady, deliberate type, who quietly compiled an impressive marketing record—during his reign annual computer division revenues went from $14 million in 1960 to $237 million in 1969. He lacked Donegan's glamour and charisma perhaps, but he was decisive and he had a good common touch. As Donegan's star rose at RCA, McCollister was to suffer a fate similar to that met by some other old-line RCA employees. McCollister found that he became something of an unperson, moved aside by Donegan and the IBM team he was assembling. Nevertheless, McCollister fared better than some other old-line RCA men, who were simply sacked.

During the 1960s—during the era of Bradburn and McCollister and of A. L. Malcarney, the former group executive vice president—RCA had been taken virtually from the ground up in computers to the point where it had a solid base in the industry. Although RCA went full scale into the commercial electronic data processing field relatively late—in 1958—it had managed a few technological coups. The RCA 501 was the industry's first completely transistorized system, and the Spectra 70 product line was the first major commercial system to use integrated circuits. By and large, though, RCA trended to follow IBM's lead by fitting under the pricing umbrella of the Computer Colossus with relatively unexciting equipment. In spite of slight edp profits in 1964 and 1965, RCA's computer operation never settled into a profitable enterprise, largely because of the capital that was constantly plowed back into the rapidly growing business.

When Donegan arrived at RCA in January of 1969 he carried an impressive curriculum vitae with him. In 18 years at IBM he had moved rapidly up the ladder, starting at the bottom as a marketing representative in the Data Processing Division and, with several stops along the way, working his way up to vice president of the Service Bureau Corp. Bigger things were said to have been slated for Donegan at IBM, but he was impatient and ambitious and when the RCA offer came, he jumped. During his first year at RCA, an all-time high was set in the amount of business booked. True, McCollister was still heading RCA marketing, but the gains were in no small part due to Donegan, whose Irish wit, charm and vitality quickly won him supporters—and RCA orders. Donegan's supporters, and he had many from the start, began using words like charismatic and aggressive to describe him. Also, Bradburn and McCollister were very pleased with the way their new marketing man was working out. But there were indications that Donegan seemed to be uneasy about the quaint RCA way of doing things. To him, IBM's way was still the only way and in August of 1969 he began what would eventually turn into a wholesale raid on IBM: he hired Joseph W. Rooney to head up RCA's home office sales department at Cherry Hill.

While Donegan was consolidating his position at Cherry Hill, he was also rapidly making a name for himself at 30 Rockefeller Plaza, RCA's corporate headquarters. When he joined RCA, Donegan kept his home in Greenwich, Connecticut, and he made it a point to visit corporate [headquarters] often.

At 30 Rockefeller Plaza, Donegan found a valuable patron in Chase Morsey, Jr., who also lived in Greenwich. Morsey was the power behind the RCA throne, the throne being represented by chief executive officer Robert W. Sarnoff. Morsey's official title was executive vice president, operations staff, and in reality Morsey was the No. 2 man in influence at RCA while be held that post during 1969, 1970 and the first six months of 1971—the period during which the computer operation was taken from modest lift-off, to soaring promise, and, finally, to crashing fiasco. Morsey's credentials for his high position in a technology company like RCA were slightly unusual—he had worked at the Ford Motor Co. for 16 years, rising to general marketing manager of the Ford Division, and most immediately before his joining RCA, he owned and operated a Ford agency in Arizona. Like Donegan's training and background at IBM, Morsey's training and background at Ford would contribute to the thinking that led to the coming disaster in the RCA computer operation.

Morsey's rise at RCA was so rapid that it was only natural perhaps that corporate gossips quickly began referring to him as RCA's executive suite Rasputin. Robert Sarnoff and Morsey had ascended to power in the late 1960s and they brought with them all the *right* academic credentials and the hip new management buzz words and practices. They represented a departure from the old hard-nosed common sense and deliberate style of the RCA of David Sarnoff, the electronics pioneer who had propelled the company into a position of world leadership in electronics. There was something of the country club and the jet set in Robert Sarnoff and Morsey, and Donegan fit easily into their style.

On the other hand, Bradburn didn't fit. He was a Christian Scientist; he wouldn't take a drink; no one was ever known to have accused him of possessing charm. The inevitable happened: Sarnoff and Morsey forced a Donegan promotion on Bradburn, who was said to have quietly resisted. Bradburn, of course, lost. Donegan was made vice president and general manager of Computer Systems January 1, 1970, and Bradburn retained his old title, but lost a great deal of his power. The skids were greased under him. In December of 1970, Bradburn "resigned from RCA because of pressing personal requirements," according to the official company version. RCA insiders, however, say that Bradburn was fired abruptly by Sarnoff. Whatever the circumstances of his leaving, it must have been a difficult experience for Bradburn, who had done a creditable job in building up the computer operation and who enjoyed a good reputation in the industry. (It was expensive for Sarnoff to get rid of Bradburn: SEC records indicate RCA agreed to pay Bradburn about $230,000 when he left.)

In January, 1971, RCA formed a new organization called RCA Computer Systems with Donegan heading it up as corporate vice president and general manager. Donegan quickly began surrounding himself with IBMers. One exception in the group was an old-line RCA manufacturing vice president, John Lenox, but he was soon fired by Donegan.

Although the change in management took place over a few months, it nevertheless was extremely sudden for a high technology business like the computer industry. Coupled with the massive injection of new IBM blood into RCA, the suddenness of the management change would prove to be more than the RCA organism could tolerate, and both factors would contribute to the eventual loss of control of the computer operation. Part of the explanation for the sudden shift in management direction seems to be explained, at least in part, by Robert Sarnoff's background. For a decade, Sarnoff had been running RCA's broadcasting affiliate, the National Broadcasting Company, and sudden wholesale management changes in broadcasting are common occurrences.

Donegan proved to be as good a salesman at 30 Rockfeller Plaza selling his ideas on the computer operations as he was out in the field selling computers. RCA had always aspired to becoming No. 2 behind IBM in the computer industry, but during 1970 the drive to become No. 2 took on a new urgency and a new credibility as well, largely because Sarnoff and Donegan made such a public flap over the issue. In March of 1971, for instance, Robert Sarnoff would tell RCA stockholders the following:

"Our highest priorities today are the establishment of a profitable computer business and capture of the domestic industry's No. 2 position. RCA has made a greater investment in this effort than in any prior venture in its history, and we are convinced that the returns will be substantial.

"This investment has already resulted in a more rapid growth rate for RCA than for the domestic industry as a whole. . . ."

During this period Chase Morsey seems to have become particularly interested in share of market, and RCA targeted 10% of the U.S. commercial edp market as a goal. There are many at RCA who believed that Morsey's automotive background in Detroit—where there is something of a fetish overshare of market—was an important factor in RCA wanting to grow so rapidly, even at the cost of profitability. Morsey was instrumental in commissioning a $100,000 marketing report by . . . Arthur D. Little, Inc., which, in large part, advised RCA on how to go about increasing market share.

However, there can be a danger in growing too rapidly in the computer business, because so much of the equipment is leased rather than sold outright. In a leasing environment, of course, revenues are delayed, but the manufacturer must still bear the full expense of the equipment at the start. Sarnoff once put his finger on this problem: "It's a funny kind of business. You can be so successful and wait so long for a return."

But how do you become No. 2 if you only have 3 or 4% of the edp business? How do you get that critical mass of 10%? Why, you take it out of IBM's hide, that's how. Or, that's how Donegan felt. "We have two options if we want to get 10% of the market," Donegan once explained. "We can get a little out of the hide of each of the other Dwarfs, or we can get it out of IBM's hide. It's easier for us to get after IBM."

In this sense, Donegan resembled Napoleon licking his chops before Waterloo. No one, of course, takes anything out of IBM's hide; it's the other way around, and one can only wonder precisely what Donegan was doing during his 18 years at IBM that led him to think otherwise. Before long, Donegan would watch new IBM machines and pricing tactics throw the RCA computer operation from a state of self-inflicted confusion into a full-scale rout.

Still, Donegan persevered. Internally at RCA, his program became known as "Intercept," the idea being that RCA would introduce a new family of computers that would intercept IBM customers and bring them over to RCA. But where would RCA get a new line of computers? At that time, 1970, a new line was under development, internally called NTS (for New Technology Series), but wouldn't be ready for announcement until around the first of 1972. Donegan thought that was too far in the future, so he decided to take the existing Spectra machines, put new skins around them, soup up their memories, and, in effect, reintroduce the Spectra line with a great deal of fanfare and hoopla.

The "new" family was introduced in September of 1970 and consisted of four machines, which the company called the RCA Series 2, 3, 6 and 7, although its internal code name—FS (for Follow Spectra)—was a more appropriate and accurate appellation. The 2 corresponded to the Spectra 70/45, and the 3 with the Spectra 70/46. The 2 and the 3 were essentially cost-reduced versions of the 45 and 46 with new skins, new memory interfaces and other unimportant changes. The 6 corresponded to the 70/60, and the 7 to the 70/61. The 6 was basically the same machine as the 70/60 with a new skin. The 7 did replace a translation-table memory with a content-addressable memory, but, for all practical purposes, both the 6 and the 7 were just price cuts of the Spectra 70/60 and 70/61.

"The point I'd like to stress," said Joseph W. Rooney, Donegan's computer marketing chief when the new series was unveiled, "is that in just about every case, RCA's new series of computers offers, or will offer, the IBM user a very attractive alternative to upgrading his system to either a larger System/360 computer, or a System/370 series computer." That was the crux of the strategy for the RCA series.

At the same time, Donegan described a new marketing concept which he called "guaranteed conversion. The main thrust of the guaranteed conversion plan was that the customer and RCA would agree to a program for converting the customers from IBM equipment (the plan was restricted to IBM users), and if RCA failed to perform as specified, then RCA would pay a substantial monetary penalty to the user. Donegan claimed that guaranteed conversion was "one of the most significant business policy innovations in the history of the computer industry," and RCA embarked upon a massive merchandising and sales campaign to lure users to take advantage of the plan. The plan flopped; over the next several months, the guaranteed conversion plan attracted no more than four takers.

The "Intercept" strategy was planned with detailed knowledge of plans of IBM's 370 line, of which just two machines—the Model 370/155 and the 165— had been announced when the RCA Series was publicly unveiled. Since so many RCAers had come over from IBM, RCA had a good handle on the specifications and marketing strategy on the 145, the 135 and the 125. The 145 and the 135 had not been announced at the time of RCA's announcement, and the 125 still had not been announced by IBM at this writing. Donegan simply priced the RCA Series low enough to make it a more attractive customer buy than what he expected the entire 370 line would offer. He conceded that the RCA equipment couldn't compete in speed, so the key was what Donegan regarded as memory advantages and pricing that the RCA equipment had over the 370 and 360 lines.

"But what about the 145 that is rumored to be very close to announcement?" said Rooney at the unveiling of the RCA Series. "Well, we've studied the question and we have the answer." Rooney's "answer" was that RCA had already come to "certain conclusions" about the 145 and that RCA's pricing of its new machines was an alternative to customers who would consider buying a 145. One week later, IBM announced the 145, but it wasn't the same machine RCA had on its competitive analysis charts. The 145 had a larger memory and a lower price tag than RCA had anticipated.

So much, then, for RCA's competitive stance against the 145. Against the 145, sales of RCA's 6 and 7 were negligible.

RCA made a big fuss about what it termed the success of the new line, claiming that the RCA Series had quickly attracted more orders than the company had expected for the remainder of the year. At first, this was said to have been accomplished in three days, but later the time frame was changed to three weeks. This marked the start of great confusion over RCA's way of logging order bookings under the Donegan regime.

Some three weeks after the announcement of the new line, Donegan triumphantly proclaimed that "33% of the new orders represent customers coming to RCA for the first time." He didn't say so, but that also meant 67% *weren't* coming to RCA for the first time. The 67% represented existing RCA customers and that hinted at great problems, because it meant that the new machines could be chiefly impacting RCA equipment rather than IBM equipment. . . .

Many at RCA—particularly some old-line employees—had expressed fears about the RCA Series impacting the company's existing customer base. The safe way, they argued, would be to wait for the NTS Series, but Donegan would have none of that. The NTS Series consisted of five machines, possibly six, ranging in specifications from a relatively small machine with about one-half the capability of the IBM 360/50 to a big computer with a capability in the range of the IBM 195. The line was scheduled for introduction from September of 1971 to January of 1972 with deliveries slated to begin in the third and fourth quarters of 1972. Steady production runs were to begin in early 1973.

The NTS line was to have embodied several new and unique technological features, which led the RCA people working on it—there were as many as 150 engineers committed to the program at one point—to feel that the series would offer real, rather than imagined, advantages over the 360 and 370 line. . . .

The NTS program was slowed down for a number of reasons. First, Donegan moved the engineering group from the large machine—called the NTS 1000—over to work on his RCA Series. Second, Donegan moved the RCA design and engineering leaders aside to make way for a new flow of IBM people, who lost valuable time while they settled into their jobs and while they instituted IBM development practices, which tended to confuse old-line RCA people. These practices included involvement of marketing people during the design and development stage. . . .

As far as financial matters at RCA were concerned, Donegan remained true to form: he was upset that RCA's computer operation didn't do its accounting the way IBM did its accounting. (IBM uses the conservative operating method, while RCA used an accounting combination that utilized both the financing and operating methods.) When Donegan hacked his way through the computer operation's financial thicket (and there are those who believe it took him an inordinately long time to slice through), when he hacked through all the installment purchase contracts, third party sales agreements, in-house sales to RCA, when he finally came to the proverbial bottom line, he found that RCA's computer operation was not in the neat financial shape he had assumed it to be in. In addition, the IBMers who joined RCA were generally unhappy with what they regarded as the computer operation's liberal accounting methods. On the other hand, the pre-Donegan RCA financial people regarded the operation's bookkeeping as about average for the non-IBM segment of the computer industry. Whatever the situation, Donegan was unhappy about it and in late 1970 he removed David Campbell as controller. There was endless internal debate on the accounting practices of the computer unit, but this debate would become academic during late 1970 and 1971 as Donegan and his chief financial advisor, W. William Acker, would begin to lose their grip on finances.

On the corporate level, the computer operation was also taking its financial toll, and this problem, coupled with other financial pressures, was placing the RCA Corp. in an uncomfortable financial squeeze. In early 1971, the situation was this: operating earnings had been dropping, and the corporation was increasingly resorting to long-term financing. The company was stepping up short-term borrowing, and it was evident that it would soon need more long-term financing, primarily to keep the computer operation growing. In addition, common equity was dropping to about 40% of total capitalization, and pretax coverage of fixed charges had dropped in 1970 to slightly more than a troubling three times earnings. Small wonder, then, that there were nervous men in corporate finance.

In early 1971, RCA's top financial man, Howard L. Letts, executive vice president, finance, "retired" unexpectedly, but that was just one signal that all was not well in corporate finance. Many felt that Sarnoff had pushed Letts into early retirement, and not long thereafter, Sarnoff's favorite, Chase Morsey, was named to the financial post.

It should be made clear here that RCA was in sound financial condition at the time and still is. The point is that things were clearly deteriorating, and one of the biggest problems was caused by the computer operation in general and by the acceleration of leased edp equipment in particular. It is one of the great ironies of the computer industry that the better you do, the worse off you can be financially. Because the industry is largely a lease and rental business, companies that grow rapidly—and RCA was one—are required to make massive capital outlays, but since much of the equipment is leased, they must wait long periods to get their money back. During late 1970 and early 1971, a feeling began growing at RCA that massive cash inputs into the computer business—the most popular figure bandied about as the investment necessary was $500 million—could be justified if the computer operation's losses could be stemmed. In 1970 the loss was $10 million on revenues of $257 million, and there were great hopes that the computer operation was approaching break-even.

In late 1970, the computer operation put together its first business plan for 1971, and it was quickly apparent that the Donegan team anticipated 1971 would be a bumper year for the Computer Systems Division. The 1971 business plan estimated revenues of $323 million—up from $257 million in 1970—and a break-even or near break-even in the profit and loss column. Furthermore, the computer operation's long-range plan called for profits of $12 million in 1972, $25 million in 1973 and $50 million in 1974. If the plan's projections were reliable, then Donegan would turn the operation around in 1971. He would be the hero of the computer industry.

There were several management and financial fingers in the pie, including those of pre-Donegan personnel from the Bradburn era, but the first business plan was essentially the creation of Donegan and his financial staff, which was led by William Acker.

No one likes to tell the boss bad news, but there seemed to be a particularly great reluctance among the people surrounding Donegan to bear bad tidings to him and, as some of his critics maintain, he tended to surround himself with organization men who were not used to challenging the boss. Devil's advocates were not popular with Donegan. At any rate, there was bad news aplenty, and it took Donegan an unusually long time to get the unhappy message that 1971 would not be the year of the Great Turnaround. The new controller of the computer unit, Carmen Ferraioli, had the final responsibility for accepting the business plan and Ferraioli did not accept the plan, because, it was said, he felt it was overly optimistic.

The computer operation immediately set to work drawing up a new plan, but by now the Donegan team had begun to lose its grip on finance and planning. The computer operation worked without a budget from January 1 into April and until then an air of uncertainty hung over the computer operation. When the second plan was presented in April it was strikingly different from the first plan: instead of $323 million, revenues were estimated at $261 million, and instead of break-even, a loss of $36 million was predicted.

One of the purposes of efficient financial controls between corporate and various line operations, of course, is that they act as an early warning system for problems in line units. RCA had always maintained adequate efforts in financial operations. However, just as the computer operation began having serious problems, the relationship between corporate and the computer operation's financial units began breaking down; one result was that many problems in the line operation went unnoticed by corporate. That is hardly surprising, perhaps, because during the computer operation's crucial months from late 1970 to September of 1971 the computer operation had three different controllers and Acker, Donegan's top financial man, had sparse financial background, having been primarily a marketing type at IBM. (Donegan, too, never claimed much expertise for himself in the financial area.) At the corporate level, the top financial post was vacated suddenly in 1971 when Howard Letts left as vice president of finance.

"RCA is the first non-IBM computer company running under IBMers," Donegan boasted in late 1970. "We have an 18 to 19 year average in the business, the bulk with IBM. . . . We're on the way to a marketing organization as good as IBM's"

In order to build his own organization in the likeness of IBM, Donegan first had to repudiate what had been done by the RCA regime before him. To make way for the new stream of IBM people, there was a wholesale replacement of top RCA people. As soon as Bradburn was fired, one of Donegan's first official acts as chief of the computer operation was to fire Joseph Stefan as general manager of the Magnetics Products Division and N. Richard Miller as general manager of the Graphic Systems Division. H. H. Jones was removed as vice president of finance of the RCA Information Systems Group (another man lost from a key financial post) and named general manager of Magnetic Products. On and on the housecleaning went, spreading through all units of the computer operation. In the field, Donegan installed new regional managers in all of RCA's five regions and 27 new regional managers in 34 marketing districts. A whole new layer of IBMers took over product development. Manufacturing remained relatively stable, although Donegan fired the top manufacturing man, John Lenox.

"When high level people came in from IBM, we were just informed that they were coming," said one former RCA computer personnel officer. "On the lower levels, the personnel office got the message to hire IBM guys, too. Anytime we got someone from IBM, he had an advantage to begin with." The personnel man estimated that 18 of the top 25 jobs at the Marlboro head-quarters had been taken over by ex-IBMers. Besides Joseph Rooney in marketing and William Acker in finance, Donegan hired Orville Wright away from IBM to serve initially as vice president of government marketing and, later, as president of the new Systems Development Division. The IBM men hired IBM men, and those IBM men, in turn, hired more IBM men.

Along with the IBM people came IBM procedures—and heavy new expenses. From marketing practices and ranking systems on personal performance to a massive reorganization of product development, the RCA computer organization was being patterned after IBM. Employees were ranked according to ability a la IBM—1, 2, 3, 4, 5. An IBM-inspired attrition control program—aimed at determining why people left RCA—was instituted. There was a "Speak Up" program patterned after IBM's in which employees could make known their problems and complaints to high-ups in RCA. There were new task forces, and new study groups, and new management and development programs—all based on the way IBM did it. There were attempts to book orders along the line of the strict IBM way versus the looser RCA manner, and this overlap created enough confusion so that no one was ever quite certain precisely what the real number of bookings were and how solid orders were.

Orville Wright, who had done a bang-up marketing job in Washington, tripling sales in RCA's office there, was named to head up the new Systems Development Division, which, once again, was based on IBM's System Development Division. "At first, nobody complained about all the IBM people," said the personnel man. "The old-time RCAers felt the IBM people and their practices were necessary for us to move ahead. But the IBM way of doing things was shoved down our throats and people began resenting it. As time went on, as it became apparent there wasn't any real progress being made, then the RCAers began resenting the IBMers, too."

In the end, the problem was fairly simple: IBM, with annual revenues of $7.5 billion in 1970, could afford its highly structured apparatus, while RCA's computer operation, with revenues of less than $260 million, just couldn't.

No one, of course, can blame IBM for Donegan's zeal in attempting to remake RCA into a mini-IBM. But IBM presented RCA with another serious problem in the form of stiff competition, something Robert Sarnoff referred to obliquely when the final collapse came as "the severe pressures generated by a uniquely entrenched competition."

In attempting to fight IBM head-on, and stressing compatibility with IBM, RCA always made itself vulnerable to the Goliath's competitive moves. Because of confusion generated by the new way in which Donegan was booking orders, there was no accurate breakdown on bookings for the RCA Series, but a rough estimate would look like this: of some 225 systems ordered, the overwhelming majority were 2s, perhaps more than 150. There were no more than 20 orders for the 3, while the 6 picked up perhaps 25 orders, and the 7 no more than 10. Announced one week after the RCA Series, the IBM 370/145—cheaper than expected and with its larger-than-anticipated memory—virtually blocked sales of the 6 and 7 to all but existing RCA customers. When the 135 was announced, in March of 1971, new sales of the 2 dried up. But the crowning blows—the Nagasaki and Hiroshima—were IBM's peripherals price cuts in May, 1971, which put IBM on a par and often below RCA's charges for complete systems. New RCA orders dwindled to a trickle and many old orders turned to water.

The chief result, then, of the RCA Series was to impact the existing RCA equipment base and, because of this, the line was a disaster. Computer people no doubt will debate for years whether this happened primarily because of an overly aggressive IBM or a miscalculating RCA.

In June, the situation was clearly deteriorating further. It was becoming apparent within RCA that the RCA Series was impacting RCA equipment. At the same time, expenses in the computer operation were mounting and it seemed that every time there was a new budget estimate the loss was upped. The loss figure reportedly rose between April and June from $36 million to the low $40 millions.

Donegan, however, charged forward. In late June he presided over groundbreaking ceremonies for a new $16-million headquarters at Marlboro—a move that many regarded as an unnecessary extravagance in view of the tightening financial squeeze. The story that made the rounds at the time was that Anthony Conrad, who was then preparing to take over as RCA's new president, had opposed the $16-million building project, but that Donegan had obtained approval for it from Robert Sarnoff. At groundbreaking ceremonies for the $16-million building program, Donegan said: "RCA remains committed to play a major role in the computer industry in this decade."

A month later—just three days before the cost-conscious Anthony Conrad would take over as RCA's president and chief operating officer—Donegan announced the establishment of an expensive new computer operation in the United Kingdom (headed by former IBMers, naturally). RCA had been displaying sensitivity to criticism that it had no edp computer business in the booming European market and the new U.K. operation was the start of a master plan that envisioned the establishment of an RCA computer operation throughout the Continent. True, RCA had no operation of its own in Europe, but its arrangement with Siemens, RCA's German licensee, had been a highly profitable one for RCA with annual sales averaging about $40 million and profits on that of about $15 million. Furthermore, the cost for RCA to build up a European operation of its own would be astronomical and, given the tight financial status of things at home, would surely act as a drain on the computer operation for years to come.

On August 10, Anthony Conrad, RCA's new president, arrived in Marlboro with his corporate staff in tow for a full dress review of the computer operation. Conrad had developed a reputation at RCA for being a tough profit-and-loss man, but he was also respected for his fairness. His arrival at Marlboro was preceded by some minor trepidation on the part of the Marlboro people. Already, there had been some key changes made in financial operations. Carmen Ferraioli had resigned as controller of the computer operation to take another job, and Julius Koppelman had taken his place. Koppelman was taking over some duties from Donegan's top financial man, William Acker. And Chase Morsey was now—on August 10—the top financial man at the RCA Corp., having been appointed executive vice president of finance and planning just over a month before. Morsey attended the Marlboro meeting, too.

The meeting elicited a rather grim picture of the computer operation. (At that time, losses of the entire RCA Computer Systems Div. had been escalated to between $63 and $80 million for 1971. The total loss estimates also included figures from RCA's Graphic Systems, Memory Products, and Magnetic Products Divisions, which totaled some 15% of the computer business.) One man who attended the meeting quoted Conrad as saying at the conclusion: "Well, it's not a pretty picture, but at last we have the real picture." When Conrad and his staff left, the Marlboro people had the impression that Conrad felt he had gotten to the bottom of the situation, but that the situation could be handled. Donegan and his team went back to work, attempting to whip the computer operation into line, assuming that they had the full support of corporate to push ahead in the coming years.

The next significant contact between corporate and

the computer operation occurred on September 17. Early that Friday morning Donegan was summoned to 30 Rockefeller Plaza from Marlboro. Donegan is reported to have regarded it as just a routine meeting, but shortly after he arrived at corporate headquarters, he was told news he couldn't believe: RCA had decided to pull out of the computer business. Actually, the decision had been made before the board of directors' special meeting, and a press release announcing the board's unanimous approval had been prepared beforehand. Donegan did not attend the board meeting.

Several weeks later, in his only recorded public statement (other than the press handout) on the decision, to a United Press International reporter in London, Sarnoff would say: "I've been asked why I made the decision when I made it. In July we said we had no intention of getting out of the computer business and yet in September we were getting out. What had happened in between?

"Well, we had several studies under way and it became apparent as losses mounted that the industry itself was changing, including the problem of uniquely entrenched competition. Finally I came to the conclusion that in view of everything we could not afford the price of staying in. I made the final decision on Thursday afternoon and I called a board meeting for Friday. A decision like that is a little like getting married or divorced—it couldn't be made sooner, it couldn't be made later. I take full responsibility for it."

The decision was a blow to Sarnoff, both to him personally and to his image, which he values highly. Robert Sarnoff had been living in the shadow of David Sarnoff and the son had been attempting without much avail to shake the image of the boss's son ever since he took over as RCA's chief executive officer in 1968. Robert Sarnoff had intensified an aggressive RCA acquisition program during the height of the conglomerate rage, and when Wall Street soured on conglomerates some of that disillusion rubbed off on RCA, which had been transformed from an electronics-based company into a broader based quasi-conglomerate. In addition, Robert Sarnoff had hoped that computers would bring to him and RCA what color television had brought to his father and RCA—profits and prestige.

One of Robert Sarnoff's acquisitions was Coronet Industries, which is a highly successful carpeting firm. The deal which brought Coronet into RCA gave the carpeting company's head, Martin B. Seretean, nearly 1.5 million shares of RCA stock, more than 15 times the amount of stock owned by Robert Sarnoff, thus giving Seretean a certain clout on the RCA board of directors because he was the firm's largest single stockholder. Seretean has the reputation of being a hard-driving incisive businessman—a man who will not tolerate fumbling and indecision. Seretean, along with other RCA directors, Stephen M. DuBrul, Jr., of Lehman Bros. and Donald A. Petrie of Lazard Freres & Co., is said to have become a critic of the computer operation. Of the decision to pull out of the computer business, Seretean points out that the directors' decision was unanimous and says simply, "I think the decision was a sound one."

(Some observers believe that Sarnoff's decision to promote Anthony Conrad to RCA president and chief operating officer and, in fact, to downgrade his own position somewhat, was an attempt to placate his critics on the board. When Conrad was named president, incidentally, many of Donegan's supporters were stunned that their man didn't get the post. Donegan—and others—were under consideration for the RCA presidency early in 1971.)

Donegan also found that during the summer of 1971 he lost one of his most powerful supporters, Chase Morsey, who had turned against the computer operation. Sarnoff, then, was in the uncomfortable position of presiding over a computer operation that was beginning to give all the appearances of going out of control while a group on the board of directors and at corporate was demanding that he do something about it. Sarnoff did do something; he pulled the whole temple down.

The stunning thing is that RCA decided to scuttle its computer business without consulting anyone in the computer operation to see if it couldn't be saved, or at least to see if sections of it couldn't be salvaged for RCA. The rest of the story is well known. Donegan quickly teamed up with Mohawk Data Sciences Corp. in an attempt to keep the computer operation going pretty much as it had been, but RCA top management rejected the effort and sold its customer base to Univac. MDS said it offered more than Univac, and after the MDS offer was rejected by RCA, many RCA computer people complained bitterly that RCA had rejected the MDS offer because RCA management would have lost face if MDS succeeded with the computer operation where RCA had failed. RCA management, which went into a shell of silence about the computer operation after September 17, never offered a full explanation of why the MDS offer was rejected.

RCA's decision to get out of the general purpose computer business had massive consequences—as a result, nearly 8000 people (not counting those who went to Univac) lost their jobs and more than 500 customers with about $1 billion of equipment were confused about their future. In all, RCA got a $490-million pre-tax write-off, and that was about twice the size of the largest previous bust in the history of U.S. business—the $250-million write-off Ford Motor Co. got for bombing with the Edsel. On the other hand, Wall Street's reaction to the RCA decision was generally good and RCA stock rose on the news that the firm was getting out of the computer business. . . .

If RCA computer users were upset about the way RCA abruptly left the business, then they should have talked to RCA's employees. The users would have felt better if only because the employees felt worse. In Marlboro, as at other RCA locations across the country, people were laid off in large groups, and now only a small cadre is left. Now, as this is written, the Marlboro facility has an eerie atmosphere to it. The inside work areas are nearly silent and nearly empty, while outside there is manic activity on the headquarters building, which is an unhappy and constant reminder of the waste of it all. When the workmen look inside the building, now and then they see someone in the nearly deserted interior. They may even catch a glimpse of L. Edwin Donegan, who still walks the building, but not in the manner of the director of a 10,000-man-strong company, but in a quiet and slow step, like Hamlet's ghost. And though it's all over now, there are many who still insist, and, indeed, who will insist until the day they go to their graves, that corporate never gave the computer operation a fair chance.

"If you only knew how close we were to making it," says one of these. "We were so close, so close."

The Matriculation of National Student Marketing Corporation

14

Personally, as a fellow who has a predilection for eating and shows it, I have always been suspicious of a guy who invites you to lunch and then eats only two slices of melba toast and a slight scoop of cottage cheese. But there was more to 25-year-old W. Cortes Randell than his light diet to make me feel a bit queasy the three or four times I met him in the course of my daily work. He was, to indulge in a cliché, just too good to be true.

He was, he told me humbly, happy that he had made so many of his young associates millionaires while they were in their early twenties. And what he really wanted to do, he confided further, was to chuck it all and spend his time and money (then $50 million in NSMC stock) helping young people to become aware of religion.

In the meantime, in founding and building his youth-marketing and youth-service conglomerate into one of the most dramatically successful new firms of the late Sixties—and its stock into one of the most glamorous—he acquired many companies and proceeded to add to their income and sales in a premature proforma manner to his corporate figures even before the deal was consummated. Then, too, he failed to keep a rein on expenses—and that is putting it mildly.

"The $3,754,103 Footnote," which follows, is an excerpt from the 1972 book *The Funny Money Game*, written by Andrew Tobias, a brilliantly precocious 23-year-old, who became an NSMC vice president at age 21. While the excerpt doesn't tell the whole story of "Cort" Randell and his company, it is so flavorsome, so pertinent in describing the frenetic nonsense that went on among the young geniuses, that it is even more inviting than a recap of the entire sad affair.

Suffice it to say that the rise and fall of NSMC happened in the midst of all the excitement about the new "youth" consumer. Everyone of all ages was impressed by the fact that the youth on the campuses and everywhere else were taking over the marketplace. Only one fact was overlooked—youth are intensely loyal up to a point and then they become intensely disloyal.

Today, we are, of course, engaged in a somewhat different youth explosion, a deeply searching investigation of all our social values. It is certainly a more important development and will probably have a more lasting influence than the certainty only a year or two ago that clothes, cars, culture and entertainment had shifted to a young viewpoint, had "gone young."

But don't scoff at what happened to "Cort" and his crowd. NSMC is still in business but on a much smaller, more limited scale. Remember that we were all young once, with all the drive and lethargy, all the joys and pains attendant to it. Even you.

The $3,754,103 Footnote

By Andrew Tobias

In our opinion, based upon our examination and the aforementioned reports of other independent public accountants, the accompanying consolidated balance sheet and statements of earnings, retained earnings and additional paid-in capital present fairly the consolidated financial position of National Student Marketing Corporation and subsidiaries at August 31, 1969, and the results of their operations for the year then ended, in conformity with generally accepted accounting principles applied on a basis consistent with that of the preceding year in all material respects.

Peat, Marwick, Mitchell & Co.

I naturally developed a number of different subrationalizations to my Great Rationalization that accounted for my playing along with NSMC, for remaining in the overheated steamroom. Perhaps they are most easily described with reference to a particular situation—such as the second annual report.

August 31 was the last day of NSMC's 1969 fiscal year. The second annual report could easily have been mistaken for a copy of *Venture* Magazine. Inside the embossed cover were 64 pages of mostly full-color photographs describing a $67-million company going on $1 billion. The report was not saddlestitched with staples, like a magazine or pamphlet; rather, it was perfect bound, like a book. It was every bit as slick as reports of companies 10 or even 100 times NSMC's size, and really put NSMC's best foot forward. But isn't a company free to spend what it wants on its annual report, to highlight good news and bury bad news in footnotes, to radiate optimism and confidence in the midst of difficulties?

The content of the report was much like the press release quoted earlier. For example, the $20 million of mainly nonyouth-market insurance sales were described this way: "The newest division, Financial Services, at this time provides health, accident, and affiliated insurance coverage to students, young travelers and campers." The truth. Was the company required to describe the greenhouse and race-track specialities as well? The whole truth? I don't know. As usual, there was much that is misleading; hopes stated as plans, unprofitable projects about to be dropped described as ongoing, presumably successful. Nothing but the truth?

It didn't seem my place to tell our professional public-relations people just how far they could ethically go in applying make-up to the corporate physiognomy. Anyway, sophisticated investors usually consider financial statements the most important part of an annual report and disregard the trimmings just as naturally as a smart housewife notes the bones when she buys meat by the pound.

When NSMC's 1969 fiscal year ended (August 31), it was clear that the earnings projections Cort had made would again be impossible to meet without a little "creative accounting." He needed to show about $3.5 million in net earnings. Two problems were CompuJob, which you will recall lost a lot of money despite the good publicity it produced for NSMC, and the Canadian arm of NSMC. So on November 3,* 90 days after the fiscal year had ended, an agreement was made to sell CompuJob, and the Canadian operation to its managers. According to the footnote, "In the opinion of counsel in both transactions negotiations and agreements of sale were in effect consummated prior to August 31, 1969. . . ." These transactions allowed NSMC to add $369,000 in after-tax earnings, or about 10%, to its 1969 results. The $369,000 represented the "aggregate gain . . . as a result of the sale of the subsidiaries." Where did the buyers and the Canadians come up with the cash to buy back these subsidiaries? No cash. The footnote explains that payment was made with 1-year and 5-year personal notes. Even though NSMC didn't get any money in fiscal 1969, it was able to show in earnings the money that would come in over 5 years. Don't worry about the loans, by the way. The footnote says they are secured by 3,850

*This is the date I noted next to the footnote in my copy of the annual report; I can't remember whether this was the exact date, or an approximation. If an approximation, it was fairly close.

(original) shares of NSMC stock then valued at about $400,000, now valued at about $40,000.

How could something I saw everybody sweating over the night of November 29 have in effect been consummated prior to August 31? But I am not a lawyer or an accountant, and our lawyers and accountants were evidently on record saying this was okay. Moreover, the footnote was apparently sufficient notice to the public of what had happened.

I never learned what inducements persuaded the buyers to take CompuJob off NSMC's hands. Whatever they were, the sale was made with so little fanfare that, while notice was being given in the footnotes of the report, CompuJob was mentioned in the big type up front as though nothing had happened. I whistled, all right, but at the system, not for the cops. I was beginning to see why a business-school (or law-school?) education might be helpful, after all.

Meanwhile, another footnote explains a new item on the balance sheet called "deferred new product development and start-up costs." Here was $533,000 that was spent in fiscal 1969 but that would be charged against the future, on the theory that at least $533,000 of revenue was likely to be derived in the future from those invested expenditures. Had such a sum been charged against 1969, earnings per share would have decreased by 10¢ per share (unadjusted for splits), and the stock might have sold for $10 per share less (100 times 10¢ per share), which would have made it more difficult for NSMC to acquire other companies. The same kind of calculation could be run for similar footnotes to show the relationship between an accounting decision and stock price. I am not saying NSMC should not have deferred this $533,000. That is a matter of judgment. Take my salary, for example, which may be included in the $533,000. A conservative management would probably have considered my salary an administrative expense and charged it against the period in which it was paid out. A go-go management would probably have considered my salary a research-and-development expense and tried to persuade the auditors to allow them to spread it out over the next 3 to 5 years. In the long run, my salary would be charged against earnings either way. But to a glamour company, earnings now are worth far more than future earnings. I don't know how my salary was treated; but I think it illustrates some of the latitude a creative accountant enjoys.

The "unbilled receivables" are back, up to $2,800,000 from the $1,763,000 shown in 1968—only there is a twist. In the "1968" column of the 1969 annual report, which is shown for purposes of comparison, you would expect to see $1,763.000, as was reported in 1968. Instead, you see $945,000. This discrepancy is not explained in a footnote. Perhaps the missing $818,000 of 1968 assets had to be written off when it turned out they would not materialize.

You may recall also the $486,000 of "unamortized cost of prepared sales programs," which had been deferred in 1968 because these were expenses for printing up fliers and the like that would not produce revenue until 1969. Now that figure is up to $1,048.000. In other words, 1969 was charged with $486,000 that was actually spent in 1968; but 1969 was *not* charged with $1,048,000 that was actually spent in 1969. There are two ways of looking at these deferrals. If the $486,000 eventually brought in revenues of more than $486,000, and if the $1,048,000 eventually brought in more than $1,048,000—then this is an accounting method of "waiting for profits." Not counting your chickens, and all that. On the other hand, if the $486,000 eventually brought in less than $486.000 and the $1,048,000 less than $1,048,000—then this is an accounting method of "postponing losses." Borrowing from the future with no hope of repayment, and all that. Of course, it is hard to predict future revenues, so it is hard to accuse anyone of purposely trying to postpone losses (which violates the Generally Accepted

Accounting Principles). You can only accuse him of being groundlessly optimistic. It is the man who feigns optimism in order to postpone losses he expects who is cheating the system. While we can't tell for sure whether NSMC's optimism was feigned or genuine, it appears to have been unjustified.

And now we come to what I would like to call the Killer Footnote. This note points out that if you don't include in fiscal 1969 figures the earnings of companies whose acquisitions were "negotiated and agreed to in principle before August 31, 1969, but closed subsequent thereto . . ." or the earnings of companies whose acquisitions were "agreed to in principle and closed subsequent to August 31, 1969 . . ."—then you have to exclude $3,754,103 in net earnings, leaving a profit of $110,977, or about 4¢ a share (unadjusted). Dig beal, as they say. In other words, if you don't count companies that were not legally part of NSMC in fiscal 1969, then fiscal 1969 barely broke even. (*If* you accept the rest of the creative accounting.)

So why was the stock selling at $140 a share? The company earnings were valued at a multiple about 10 times that of other conglomerates, and those earnings were apparently far from solid. A good time to sell, even though prestigious brokerage houses were still issuing "buy" recommendations.

Brave Alan Abelson dared to point this out in his column in *Barron's,* and the stock fell 20 points the next day. Not so much because of what Abelson pointed out, but because people knew that when Abelson roasted a company, its stock fell about 15%, so they figured they had better sell NSMC until it had fallen about 15%. This is an oversimplification, I admit; but widely read Wall Street columnists surely start as many trends as they discover. Their prophecies are self-fulfilling, too. It was rumored, incidentally, that the NSMC annual report was brought to Abelson's attention by someone who had shorted* 3,000 shares of NSMC stock. If so, that someone made $60,000 the next day, and considerably more thereafter. Abelson had called the cops and the snowball began to melt.

NSMC's reply to the charge that earnings came from companies acquired after the close of the fiscal year was that considerable expenses were incurred in expanding the core company's capabilities in preparation for the acquisition of these companies. If their earnings hadn't been added, neither would the extra capabilities have been necessary. (I thought that might be a euphemistic way of describing the massive costs of running unprofitable programs in plush surroundings in order to have the kind of story that would command a 100-times multiple.) Moreover, the Chairman of Peat, Marwick, Mitchell's Ethics Committee was present at the NSMC annual meeting to read the portions of the accounting principles code that required acquisitions made shortly after the close of a fiscal year to be included in that year's statements.

People had begun to doubt, but Cort kept promising another tripling of earnings and, as you recall from his speech to the New York Society of Security Analysts, predicted that 78% of the higher 1970 earnings would come from internal operations, and only 10% from acquisitions that had not yet been made.

In any case, my first subrationalization for not publishing some kind of dissenting annual report was my not being sure, especially at the time, whether NSMC was exceeding acceptable limits of public relations, creative accounting, and corporate law, though I imagined those limits were being severely strained at the very least. Although I assumed the accountants and law-

---

*Shorting a stock is the opposite of buying it. You sell it first, by "borrowing" it from your broker, and buy it later at a lower price, if you are lucky, to "pay your broker back." While shorts are supposed to be restricted to stocks listed on the exchanges, in practice stocks traded over-the-counter are sometimes shorted also.

yers were given unfalsified records to work with, I really had no way of knowing. All that was handled at the very top where hands are presumably always spotless. I also assumed that major accounting and law firms would not risk bending their standards for the sake of a client, albeit lucrative. While it was obvious that the public image was a rather fanciful description of the company, I presumed that dollars were dollars and documents, documents when it came down to the assets and liabilities of a financial statement.

A second reason for remaining loyal was that it seemed more reasonable and practical for a company to correct an unfortunate situation rather than commit suicide. Should GM encourage class-action suits against its failure to work sincerely toward curbing pollution, or should it simply begin working toward that end? We all complained frequently to Cort's inner circle about the way the story was being told. The inner circle in turn complained to Cort. We kept getting signs that things would improve, such as the appointment of a Chief Operating Officer, Roger Walther, who was a straight talker and who was willing to stand up to Cort. The third annual report would be different.

A third reason was that if I turned out to be *wrong* in my youthful idealism and/or NSMC and its mutual-admiration society withstood my attack, I would have had a rather difficult time being hired anywhere else. Patrick Henry for President, and all that. Fourth, I had already decided how to split most of my imminent fortune over various Eloy Velez-type projects. I was almost ready to believe that my then $400,000 stock options, with 18 months down and 6 to go, would indeed be worth something. It might be stretching things to say I was beginning to see Ecuadorian towns renamed in my honor—but you get the idea. I wouldn't have minded the 20% I was going to keep for myself, either. My ego was raving over its new clothes—Vice-President of the darling of Wall Street. I, too, wanted to believe.

Fifth, I figured that even if Peat, Marwick and White and Case were being fooled, there were a lot of insiders with more information and more experience than I to whom I could pass the buck. We had lured from Time, Inc., a seasoned executive who was billed as being in line for the Publisher's job; we had lured from J. Walter Thompson a Vice-President with a tremendous track record; we had in-house attorneys and financial people; we had computer people from IBM; we had two Harvard MBA's assisting Cort full time. Did I have the nerve to call a press conference and expose the American Business Establishment? Not *this* kid. I would wait and cast the *second* stone. And I do believe I would have been attacking much more than NSMC with such a press conference. I would have been attacking all those wild glamour stocks of recent years, all those highly paid shingle-hanging professionals, and all those aggressive young entrepreneurs who expected to make a fortune in 3 to 5 years, while 60% of the people on earth struggled to get enough to eat. I would surely have been branded as one of the radical left who wear blue jeans.

Finally, I was very proud of and involved with my own projects, which I felt were exciting. In presenting the NSMC story, as I often did, I was enthusiastic about NSMC's legitimate good points—there were and are many—but I don't think I knowingly passed on much of the fiction. Of course, by remaining an employee I tacitly endorsed the company. And I obviously did not stress the seamy side of the story as I have here. In the case of the one tiny acquisition it was my responsibility to complete, I spent hours with the company's President (Yale '68) to expose all the myths—self-fulfilling prophecies, ineffective media, the works. Yale or no, I wanted to be sure he knew everything I knew before betting his little company.

But it turned out there was a lot I, and virtually everyone else with the possible exception of Cort and a few top generals, did not know. Just when serious, secret negotiations were going on to acquire 3 huge companies—National Tape with $60 million in sales, Champion Products with $50 million, and Josten's, listed on the New York Stock Exchange with $70 million—acquisitions that would have assured NSMC's earnings projections and kept the ball rolling, the accountants finally found that something was very wrong, and the lawyers advised NSMC to announce preliminary information to the public. On February 24, 1970, it was announced that there had been a loss of $1.2 million on sales of $18 million for the first quarter of fiscal 1970—September 1 through November 30, 1969—the year for which Randell had been promising tripled profits. Whatever confidence or credibility may have remained was obliterated 2 days later when it was announced that the company had made a "mechanical error in transferring figures from one set of books to another," such that the loss would actually be $1.5 million on sales of $14 million. Where was the sophisticated, computerized management-control system now?

Evidently, the net profit for all the subsidiaries in this quarter had been a respectable, if not synergistic, $2.2 million; but corporate overhead, the campus rep program and others whose losses could be deferred no further, and write-offs of some of the previous year's creative accounting had racked up a deficit of nearly $4 million.

I was in Cambridge on a rare 3-day weekend when I first heard the news from my Yale '68 Subsidiary President. It came as a complete surprise. I had assumed from Cort's profit projections that subsidiary earnings would continue to be large enough to absorb the costs of keeping up the corporate image. Then I saw the silver lining: No doubt this was the great housecleaning! NSMC was paying its debts to the future, getting its accounting back in line, starting afresh with a clean slate. I figured the stock would suffer for a while, but that a profitable second quarter might restore confidence. In any case, it was pretty clear that 1969 earnings had been boosted to Cort's projections only by dumping problems on 1970. Soviet factory managers do the same thing, borrowing a couple of days' production from April to meet March quotas, then borrowing 3 or 4 from May to hit April, and then a week from June to hit May. Since the managers purportedly meet their quotas, they cannot ask for lowered ones. If anything, quotas are raised. When the reckoning comes, as it almost always does, the Manager is sent off to you-know-where.

If 1969 earnings had not been thus boosted, the stock would have fallen that much sooner, before acquisitions like Cliftex could have been made. Cliftex is a sports-jacket manufacturer in New Bedford, Massachusetts, that NSMC managed to buy for about 17 times its $1.2 million earnings, with 100-times-dubious-earnings stock. This one, and a couple of others, brought NSMC sales close to the $100-million level.

If 1968 earnings had not been thus boosted, perhaps NSMC would now have sales of about $8—not $80 —million.

If 1967 earnings had not been similarly increased, NSMC might never have gone public in the first place. (In fact, on the suspicion that Cort's *own* business ventures never made a dollar of profit from the day he started, it was suggested we call this book *How To Succeed in Business Without Really Having One.*)

So the slate had finally been cleared, to the considerable embarrassment of the company. But had it? There was the possibility that this huge deficit was the minimum that creative accounting would allow, that the debt to the future had actually been increased to keep the deficit from being even larger.

The announcement explained at last why NSMC stock had been slipping so badly—from a high of $143 in December 1969 before the *Barron's* article appeared, to $72 the day before the February 24th announcement. The following day the stock dropped only another dollar.

The *Wall Street Journal,* which by now was running articles almost daily about the Street's favorite stock of 1968, asked Jimmy Joy, our appropriately named Financial Vice-President, just when company officers had first known there would be a loss shown in the first quarter. "About January 20th." And had anyone leaked the news to the investment community? "Absolutely not." Joy attributed the market's foresight to widespread speculation and rumor that things were awry.

Nothing affects the price of a stock more than its earnings. The first one to know about the loss NSMC would announce held valuable information. Because the first one to sell a stock trading at $143 a share probably will get about $143. But as more and more people start selling, the market price goes down. By the time the loss was announced to the public, you could only get $72 for your shares. The first kids in the lunch line pick out the best apples. The Securities and Exchange Commission is the lunch-line monitor. They get most upset when company "insiders" act on information before it has been publicly announced. Someone will always be first to buy or sell his stock; but the S.E.C. wants to be sure that Irving Investor has some chance of a good place in line. Otherwise the officers of a company could buy their own stock, announce some good news so it would go up, and sell the stock before they announce bad news. The NSMC officers were probably not guilty of such manipulation when they sold more than $1-million worth of their personal stock as it passed its peak of $143—but it's hard to decide what is insider-trading and what is not. (Insiders are supposed to file monthly reports with the S.E.C. noting any transactions they may have made in their stock.)

If a company officer gets the feeling that long-term prospects are not too good, and so wishes to sell his stock, must he call a press conference to announce his private doubts about the company's future? He might not get much of a Christmas bonus if he did. Must he hold the stock indefinitely and only sell when it has hit rock bottom? If the answer to both questions is "no," then what is the answer to this one: If he is right and the company begins to announce bad news from time to time, will he look bad for having sold out before the fall? Yes.

So it's a sticky area for the S.E.C. to regulate, and a difficult one for insiders to deal with. This insider knew of the Interstate acquisition an hour before it was announced and (wrongly) could not resist the temptation of running down to a phone booth and calling a good friend to recommend purchase of 100 shares. What better gift to a friend than an inside tip likely to be worth a few thousand dollars? What a great way to feel like a Big Shot. What a shame to let such a valuable opportunity go to waste! Who would find out about a measly 100 shares? You just found out. (As it happened, the market had already pretty much "discounted" this news, and had pushed up the stock price in anticipation. It didn't do my friend any good at all. I guess I wasn't first in line, after all.)

At $72, I was only worth $100,000, but I would have gladly taken that paltry sum and retired to the business school or Bermuda if I could have. The Harvard Alumni Bulletin, to whom I had sent proud news of my Vice-Presidency about 8 months earlier, managed to record it in the March number. Randell was having problems of his own. His net worth was down from $48 million to $24 million, but he must have figured the jig was far from up. Even after he knew of the loss, he continued to predict big profits for 1970. He did not know that the people had renounced their faith.

In fact, the day before he was forced to resign, Cort talked optimistically with one of my colleagues and recommended purchase of the stock. If you play hearts, you know it takes *all* the hearts and the queen of spades to "shoot the moon" and score 26 positive points. Otherwise, the more hearts you have the more negative points you suffer. Once you let even a single heart slip, you've lost the moon and should pick up no more hearts. Yet how often have I, having developed the perfect strategy to the moon, let one heart slip but continued to collect hearts, refusing to relinquish the fantasy and return to earth?

On February 10, Randell was reportedly asked whether he was worried that subsidiary presidents and his own key executives now held a majority of the stock and could force him out. He was quoted in *Fortune* as replying: "Who do they respect? Their confidence in me to succeed is what brought them here. Why do people like Morgan Guaranty buy the stock? Because they have talked to Cort Randell and they have confidence in what we are trying to accomplish. As long as I do a good job, I'll continue. If I don't do a job, I don't deserve to be President."

How about this earlier passage from *American Way* magazine:

> We have a late dinner one night in New York at a midtown restaurant. Randell eats very lightly, as usual. He is introspective. "I'm lucky," he says, "but there has to be some reason in life for this whole thing happening other than making money." He comes close to feeling, he says, that providence has some different work for him to undertake someday. "I feel certain I'll know what great project I'm to begin," he says, "I don't know what it is, but I'm sure that someday—within a year, or five years, or even twenty years, I'll be told." As he talks this way it is not difficult to imagine him the founder of a philanthropic foundation, or sponsor of medical research, or college benefactor.

Can you blame a man who is told several times a day he is a marketing genius, a visionary able to turn his vision into reality, and an awfully nice guy—for believing some of it? There is no question that Cort was a self-promoter. Perhaps he was more eager to think great things about himself than most of us. The fact that Cort was "deeply religious" (a church deacon) was probably also mixed into the messianic equation someplace. But the media, the investment houses, the suppliers, the employees, and the hopefuls all did their share to distort Cort's self-estimation.

A week after his confident statement about continuing to run the company as long as he did a good job, Cort was forced by his chiefs of staff to resign. Five of his Board members, with the support of the subsidiary presidents, told him he would have to leave the company if NSMC were to stand any chance of regaining credibility in the investment community. Their meeting was the culmination of several days of tense power maneuvers necessary to execute the coup successfully. Next morning the New York staff was assembled in the conference room to hear Cort, trembling and voice cracking, announce his resignation.*

The announcement was brief, the reaction varied. Some of those present, particularly the secretaries, were taken entirely by surprise. Some may even have believed Cort's statement to the *New York Times* about resigning for personal reasons of health and much-needed relaxation. Everyone seemed to think they should carry themselves as at a funeral. In preparation for the euphemisms and false sentiment I expected to hear at this meeting, I wore my most cynical, detached frown. I heard Walther say something nice about Cort's having given so much to the company and wish him all the best; while I knew Walther must really have been thinking thoughts far less kind. Eloy and I couldn't feel sorry for Cort and his now-$15-million net worth; it seemed to me his comeuppance was deserved and overdue. Yet, of course, I did feel sorry.

---

*In its generally excellent article, *Fortune* said Cort was "remarkably composed" at this meeting. I was there; he was on the verge of tears.

He *had* become used to luxuries he would likely never enjoy again, he *had* been "an awfully nice guy" to me, he *had* been under tremendous pressure from everyone to produce, he *had* worked harder than anyone else, he *had* come to believe his own messianic creed.

Investors lost further confidence when Cort left and the stock continued its slide. Roger Walther was elected President and immediately began reducing NSMC's outrageous overhead—closing offices, firing recently wooed executives, discontinuing unprofitable programs —but trying all the while to keep up a healthy front. Having lost our original glamour, we would now bill ourselves as a terrific turn-around situation, another glamorous image of sorts to investors anxious to "discover" winners among losers. The media that had run glowing articles in the past felt foolish and wrote extra-glaring articles now. The last subsidiaries to be acquired struggled successfully for recision of their agreements, including Cliftex and my friend Yale '68, on the grounds that they had not been informed of the material change in NSMC's condition prior to their joining up. The rest of the subs stumbled around trying to decide who should run the company, now a string of subsidiaries stripped bare of 90% of the corporate umbrella and public-relations mirage.

After two months of Walther's leadership the subsidiaries decided on Cameron Brown, head of the large Interstate Insurance subsidiary, to carry the ball. At 55, Brown had the conservative image Walther, 33, may have lacked. Walther had not particularly wanted the job of cleaning up Cort's mess, either. He had made his fortune selling New England Travel Company, with his 2 partners, to NSMC (converting much of his stock to cash); why not enjoy it? Investors saw the third Chief Executive in 2 months, read of S.E.C. investigations, class-action suits, and suits against the parent by NSMC's own subsidiaries! The *Wall Street Journal* even uncovered a 1964 Post Office mail-fraud investigation of a Randell enterprise. The stock eventually reached a low of $3.50 in August 1970, down almost 98% from its high less than a year earlier.

While *you* had to go pay $3.50 for a share of NSMC stock, *I* had the option to buy it for $37 a share. Actually, by the time the stock was that low I no longer had my options. I was no longer with the company and you have to be an employee for options to be valid. In March, in the midst of wild confusion, the banks withdrew their lines of credit and, of course, no one would buy the company's letter stock. Nor would healthy subsidiaries lend the parent any money, at least for a while, since they were not sure of their own legal positions. This placed NSMC on the verge of bankruptcy. I sat in Jimmy Joy's office more than once waiting to ask for money to operate our refrigerator project and heard him talk on the phone to irate creditors. They sounded remarkably like the kind of conversations we used to have freshman year in my dorm about paying the telephone bill. Only NSMC's phone bill was about 1,000 times larger and there was no one to write home to as a last resort. The strategy had to be to make payments only when the final threat of suit was made (3 creditors owing $1,000 or more each, I learned, must file petitions in order for a company to be thrown into involuntary bankruptcy).

We could not meet the commitments we had made to schools to deliver refrigerators. In the case of Indiana State, I had been assured we would have the funds to deliver the 700 units that had been ordered; the campus paper announced their impending arrival. Then I was told by my boss to tell them we simply could not deliver. Then, he somehow got approval of the expenditure and told me to tell them it was on again. But I had to visit the student-government President and University Legal Counsel personally in Terre Haute to renegotiate the price of the lease now that our cost of capital had to be figured realistically. They were more than understanding and, having already collected $2 deposits from their impatient students, simply requested that we waste no time in making delivery. The refrigerators were actually loaded onto 2 trucks in Sydney before my boss told me that, unfortunately, we would not be able to deliver after all.

I was mortified by what we had done to the student government and the students of Indiana State. Especially when we had been billing University Products Corp. as the reliable, service-oriented company that was big enough to meet its commitments 100%. I decided to resign.

But what of the people who had invested in NSMC partly as a result of my enthusiasm? Didn't I have a responsibility to stick with the company to try to salvage something? A friend at one company that had put $10,-000,000 (!!) into NSMC called me to remind me of my responsibility. I decided to stay.

One of the Directors of Harvard Student Agencies called me from Boston, told me he had heard some nasty stories about NSMC from his friends in the investment community, and told me I would be crazy, perhaps irresponsible, to stay. I decided to resign.

The concept of the company was still sound, I had a great job, in a few years my options might really be worth $400,000, things are rarely as bad as they seem, I must learn to have more patience, and so forth. I decided to stay.

I was very, very tired and so forth and so forth, and there were so many more "so forths" on the side of resigning that resign is what I did.

I left in April 1970, just in time for my 23rd birthday.

Bernie, the Supersalesman

15

A controversial figure on both sides of the Atlantic, Bernard Cornfeld was variously called "the most flamboyant businessman of modern times" and "a supersalesman." Actually, he was somewhere in between, like the most flamboyant supersalesman of modern times. A 45-year-old former social worker from Philadelphia, Cornfeld founded Investors Overseas Services in Paris in 1956. The $2-billion complex of mutual funds, banks and insurance companies became one of the most successful financial enterprises of its time, attracting a million investors all over the world who were lured into the market by some 15,000 IOS salesmen. Perhaps the best-known fund was the Fund of Funds. But Americans were prohibited by law from buying IOS shares.

What caused Cornfeld's debacle was a crisis of confidence fed by fear of an inordinate number of redemptions which would dump IOS-held stocks. That plus disclosures of large, company-backed loans to IOS officers and directors and Cornfeld's own high-living ways. But IOS's own investments went sour, and the discovery of serious liquidity problems brought it all to a head. After the crisis reached panic levels, Cornfeld was ousted by his board, but several regimes were to be tried, tested and found wanting before the big losses could be pared.

Yet, two summers later, in 1972, Bernie Cornfeld was still his unabashed self, living in Beverly Hills, oc-

cupying a movie star's former home and still giving
endless parties, still the swinger surrounded by stars,
starlets and starers. If the charges of "flimflam" man
thrown at him disturbed him, he did not show it. He
was still trying to recapture his role at IOS or otherwise
make it back to the big time. How did it all happen?
Savor this July 1970 *Newsweek* report.

What Happened to the Perpetual Money-Making Machine?

It seemed like old times—an invitation to the "picnic
of picnics . . . with food for your epicurean delight."
And, in fact, it was the first big staff bash for the employees of Geneva's Investors Overseas Services since
[the] last Christmas. That was the legendary blast
when IOS founder Bernie Cornfeld laid on 3,000 bot-
tles of Moët et Chandon *brut* and sent his female employees home with $20 designer scarves as mementos
of his munificence. But despite the hyperbolic invitation, [the] frolic on the lawn at the company's Ferney-
Voltaire offices just wasn't up to the Cornfeld standard.
This time the menu was mainly hamburgers and beer
—the wine ran out early. More important, the host
was not Cornfeld, sartorially resplendent in a Cardin
suit with a beauty on each arm, but rumpled Sir Eric
Wyndham White, the new chief of IOS and its complex network of mutual funds, banks and insurance
companies. Where was Bernie? Gone—demoted to a
mere director. And in his place Sir Eric was warning
the revelers: "This is not a happy hour, but an occasion
for reaffirming our faith."

His solemnity was not out of place. For IOS, the
$2.3 billion empire founded by Cornfeld in a Paris
flat fourteen years ago, was sorely troubled. Its stock,
which had soared from $10 to $19 on the day it first

went public . . . could be snapped up . . . for $1.88 a share. Its stable of mutual funds, paced by the flagship Fund of Funds, had encountered prolonged squalls in which clients redeemed more shares than they bought. Its army of 15,000 salesmen was being wooed by rival funds, and was slowly eroding. As ousted president Edward Cowett explained it: . . . "We created a monster, and it devoured us. We thought IOS was infallible —but no company is."

In one of the most dramatic financial stories of the decade, IOS had gone from what seemed a perpetual-motion money machine to a creaking mechanism badly in need of overhaul—and, even as the company prepared for its annual meeting . . . in Toronto, precisely how it had all happened remained a bit mysterious. Cornfeld had one story, Cowett another; John King, the Denver oilman who abandoned an attempt to "rescue" IOS, told yet a third story—and insiders could be found to support any of these views, plus others as well. As rumors swirled about proxy fights, new take-over bids and threatened lawsuits against former IOS executives, the only sure thing was that the story was far from over. But for the first time, a coherent picture of the long crisis could be pieced together.

Oddly enough, IOS itself was still remarkably healthy; the problem was in large part a crisis of confidence alone. There has been no suggestion that any of the company's seventeen mutual funds, twenty fund-management companies, twelve insurance companies, ten real estate firms, eleven banks or assorted miscellaneous enterprises are in actual danger of collapse. For all its visible throes, the parent company counts a net worth of some $90 million and only $8 million in debts. What's more, confidence seems to be slowly rebuilding. Despite torrents of publicity about the crisis, IOS salesmen racked up $117 million in new fund sales in May. Net redemptions, which ran as high as $10 million a day during May, have slowed substantially; in the first two weeks of June, the funds lost a comparatively modest $25 million. As Cornfeld himself expressed it, "The loyalty of our clients has been one of the real gratifications through all this hullabaloo."

Yet in IOS's case, anything worse could have amounted to an international financial disaster. What gives fund managers and government officials nightmares is the specter of a swelling run of redemptions forcing IOS's funds to dump their $1.8 billion portfolios on the already distressed securities markets of the world. Indeed, IOS stock sales . . . are widely believed to have played a substantial role in the long sinking spell on world markets. "Any shake-up in something as big as IOS," warns George Sarlo, vice president of William D. Witter, Inc., "leads to a shake-up in confidence in all mutual-fund operations and the markets in general."

What made IOS vulnerable was in large part its sheer complexity; it was a maze of 81 companies operating in more than a dozen countries. Cornfeld, the founder, had cast himself in the role of the developer of new ideas, and spent much of his time jetting to exotic spots, surrounded by bevies of lissome girls. Cowett, the chief operating officer, is widely regarded as one of the world's sharpest international lawyers, and he had structured the entire IOS complex with the chief aim of avoiding every possible nickel in taxes. But this structure was hardly ideally suited for close day-to-day financial supervision. In fact, despite Cornfeld's boast that IOS had "the largest computer operation in the industry," the bookkeeping was so tangled that its executives had no convenient way to keep track of actual cash flow—a shortcoming that was to lead to unpleasant surprises.

This problem was compounded by IOS's practice, limited to the offshore mutual-fund industry, of counting new sales of long-term fund investment plans as if their full cash value had been received. In reality, many new investors pay only a small down payment. And beginning last year, more investors began to pinch

pennies on the installment plan, all the while reducing
the size of their down payments. Thus cash intake
dropped off sharply, but the face value of new sales remained inflated—and so lulled, the company embarked
on an ambitious program of decentralization. Costs
that had averaged $11 million in each of the first three
quarters suddenly skyrocketed to $21 million in the
fourth. Sir Eric Wyndham White, the former head of
the organization that administers the General Agreement on Tariffs and Trade and the man drafted to replace Cornfeld as IOS's chief executive, recalls that the
aim of the program was to gear up the company for
doubled volume within a year—and this at a time when
the managers of IOS's own funds were beginning to
liquidate their positions to prepare for the bear market.
This "complete inadequacy of management," says
Wyndham White, brought on "a classical liquidity
crisis." In plain language, IOS was close to insolvency.

Meanwhile, some of the funds' investments had gone
even more sour than the general markets; for example,
a $7.8 million block of Giffen Industries shares had
fallen in value to only $2.8 million. Then there was a
series of IOS loans totaling $9 million to Common-
wealth United, a California conglomerate that had sold
a $30 million Euro-bond offering through IOS in Febru-
ary. Commonwealth reported a first-half loss of $23
million only four months later—whereupon IOS helped
out with large loans. As one disgruntled insider
summed it up . . .: "We had so many brilliant guys in
Geneva, but no bookkeepers. They never paid attention to plain economic sense."

These mounting woes, however, were not widely
known within IOS, and certainly not to many of its
board of directors—a distinguished group that included
a former U.N. ambassador, James Roosevelt, Erich
Mende, the former leader of West Germany's Free
Democratic Party, and Wyndham White himself. As a
former German general hired by one of the funds stated
the case: "Sure they took me because of my title. I

don't know too much about finance, but their retainer was all right." As late as the March meeting, the board cheerfully approved a $30 million portion of the expansion plan. For their part, IOS executives were equally cheery; on April 11, Cowett reaffirmed a prediction that profits for 1969 would total $20 million.

Just about that time, quite by accident, the first inkling of trouble came to the attention of the board of directors. Director George von Peterffy, who had been going over the company books as part of a long-range planning project, discovered to his astonishment that IOS was dangerously illiquid, and quickly alerted his fellow directors. They convened an emergency meeting, the first of several. "Our first concern was to overcome the liquidity crisis," recalls Wyndham White. "At that time the money was going out faster than it was coming in."

Detailed examination of the books, however, soon uncovered traces of potentially scandalous dealings—a series of loans made by IOS banks, or guaranteed by IOS through outside firms, to the company's officers, directors and friends. The total, the annual report said later, came to $31 million—roughly a third of IOS's net worth. Cowett, as president, and his family had borrowed $2.9 million, and apparently used much of it to support IOS stock in its slump. Another big borrower was John King, the Denver oilman who was later to mount his effort to "rescue" the beleaguered IOS; King personally borrowed at least $1.7 million, and Bahamian trust funds in the names of his children accounted for another $4.7 million. Another loan of $1.6 million went to three IOS directors to make payments on private planes.

None of this was calculated to reassure stockholders. Nor was confidence bolstered when the IOS annual report, after a long and unexplained delay, finally appeared with an auditors' note stiffly reprimanding IOS for refusing to spell out more details. The company pleaded the necessity for secrecy imposed by European banking laws, but both the Toronto and London stock exchanges banned trading in IOS stock until more details were forthcoming—a ban expected to be lifted now that IOS has disclosed the full list of borrowers. Meantime, Wyndham White has used his considerable powers of persuasion to get most of the loans repaid or shifted to other banks.

Even before the existence of the insider loans became known, investors outside IOS had begun to ask awkward questions about another curious transaction. In brief, an IOS subsidiary, Fund of Funds, had bought a 50 percent interest in 22.4 million acres of oil-drilling leases in the Canadian Arctic from King Resources Co. The price, paid in 1968 and 1969, averaged about $1 an acre. Later in the year, however, because nearby land was selling for higher prices, IOS decided that the leases were undervalued; as Cornfeld put it, "It was unreasonable to continue carrying this acreage at our cost." Accordingly, King Resources sold a 10 percent interest in the IOS holdings, for $14.12 an acre, to a group that included Consolidated Oil & Gas of Denver. Based on this sale, Fund of Funds declared its remaining Arctic holdings worth an average $8 an acre. A month later, after the tax books had been closed on 1969, King turned over the proceeds of the sale to Fund of Funds.

This made the fund's holdings grow by $70.8 million at a stroke of the pen, and entitled IOS, as the fund's manager, to a fee of $9.7 million for its perspicacity. In reality, King Resources had paid Fund of Funds only $779,000 as a down payment for the leases, with the balance to be paid in installents beginning in 1973. Nonetheless, IOS deducted the full $9.7 million performance fee from the fund's treasury last year. Without this transaction, IOS would have had a 1969 profit of just about $500,000.

Are such dealings legitimate? "It's dirtier than hell," said Thomas Petschek, a vice president of Manufacturers Hanover Trust in Germany. "But all the same, it's a lovely way to show high earnings." For their part, IOS insiders argue that the original speculation in oil leases still looks promising (Cornfeld says there has been at least one major gas strike in the area, and leases there have recently traded for as much as $80 an acre). Furthermore, say Cowett and Cornfeld, Fund of Funds investors would have had legitimate complaints if the asset value of their shares had not been raised to reflect the sale price. "Anybody who redeems his shares has a right to cash in on their real value," maintains one of the principals. "We'd be remiss if we didn't try to reassess the value."

If a major oil strike ever is made on the IOS leases, the company could certainly do well. Showing a flash of his old salesman's form, Cornfield put it this way: "Look, leases sold on the North Slope in Alaska for $2,000 an acre. If we just get an average of $100 an acre, we'll have a total profit of $1 billion." What's more, insiders maintained, the timing of the deal had nothing to do with IOS's financial problems in the fourth quarter of last year; in fact, they said, the deal had been under negotiation for at least six months.

That, however, wasn't the way things looked in the jittery marketplace—and in mid-April, as a spate of rumors about IOS's various problems spread, the directors found they had a full-fledged crisis on their hands. They could no longer blink the fact that the expected profits had failed to materialize; indeed, the annual report was to show that even after the controversial Arctic deal, profits for 1969 totaled only $10.3 million, rather than the forecast $20 million. Worse yet, outright losses had piled up in the first quarter of 1970. And IOS stock was becoming distinctly unpopular. Cowett had just returned from a trip to France when he was told that a Swiss bank had asked IOS to repurchase 30,000 shares of stock. When IOS refused, the shares were dumped on the market. That same day, another 15,000 shares went on the block.

Soon IOS salesmen, who had fought in the fall to get

in on the offering, were scrambling to unload their company's stock. Many of them had bought on margin, while others had borrowed the purchase price against their holdings of preferred stock. Now they were unable to meet the margin calls, and more stock hit the market. Only four days after the Swiss bank shares had been turned down, the IOS directors met in the company's somber, gray-stone villa on Lake Geneva to quell the gathering panic—but to no avail. As their personal fortunes evaporated, the IOS board sat almost paralyzed. Even Cornfeld, once a dynamo, was reduced to what one insider describes as a "catatonic trance."

Finally, at the end of April, the beleaguered directors decided to seek outside assistance. A list of fourteen or so potential angels was finally narrowed to two: Banque Rothschild and King Resources. IOS sales chief Allen Cantor went to Paris to talk with Baron Guy de Rothschild; Cowett flet to Denver. Rejecting as too niggardly a Rothschild offer, which amounted to $1.50 a share for IOS, the company opted for King, who agreed to put up $40 million in cash and notes and form a consortium of banks and other financial partners.

But if the arrival of King was intended to lure other big investors to the rescue, it backfired. To the crusty club of European bankers, King seemed just another fast-talking Yankee salesman cut from the same cloth as Cornfeld—and equally unwelcome. Others were alarmed by the hand-in-glove relationship between IOS and King. As one insider put it: "If King is saving anybody, it is himself."

Indeed, one reliable source said income from IOS made up 35 percent of King Resources' 1969 gross revenue of $117.8 million, and IOS has existing commitments that King counts on to play a large part in his company's future growth. But King himself says the bid to take over IOS was made only because "it looked like a great opportunity to take one huge leap into an involvement with the capital markets abroad." Late in May, however, King abruptly withdrew his bid after the Securities and Exchange Commission refused to waive a 1967 consent decree that bars IOS from selling its funds to U.S. citizens. By extension, the ban would have prevented King from selling his own stock and oil-fund shares in the U.S. Beyond that, there was a question whether King actually had the stipulated financial backing to swing the deal. Wyndham White, for one, says he didn't—but King himself insists that it was in the bag.

By now, the IOS board was in open revolt. Cowett and Cornfeld had been ousted; Richard Hammerman, head of insurance operations, was briefly made president, then exiled in his turn. Paralyzed by recriminations and bitter feuding, the directors turned to Wyndham White, who had earned a reputation for masterful negotiation as GATT's head. Working fifteen hours a day, Sir Eric began seeking new partners who would provide fresh infusions of capital and expertise. Although he was again rebuffed by the Rothschilds, Sir Eric remained undaunted. As he told *Newsweek*'s Alan Tillier: "Despite all the craziness that has been going on, the basic idea of a financial service company offering a full range of services to the small- and middle-size man is valid. Now my aim is to integrate IOS more into the financial community—to gain more respect, but not to lose our vitality."

And what of Bernie Cornfeld, that latter-day Elmer Gantry preaching a doctrine of "people's capitalism" while living like a pasha? His lakeshore villa in Geneva is all but deserted, and the dust is settling on the white Cadillac and posh Lamborghini sports job parked outside. Putting all that behind him, Cornfeld, still with an entourage, has been jetting between his London town house and the financial centers of the world, making no secret of his determination to get back into the driver's seat at IOS. And he persists in talking as if he were still part of the IOS executive team—a trait that prompted this harsh judgment from Cowett: "Bernie is like a child; when he wants something, he wants it *now*. Reality isn't allowed to interfere." Wyndham White, for his part, was gentler—though he did slip once, referring to a Cornfeld interview as an obituary. "Mr. Cornfeld remains a director of IOS, and he has offered his services," the new boss said. "I would hope that he could help—on the sales side."

Fighting Back: Bernard Cornfeld States His Case

What went wrong with the dazzling financial empire controlled by Investors Overseas Services, and who was to blame? . . . IOS's founder, Bernard Cornfeld, gave his own version of the story to *Newsweek's* Oliver Moore [in July 1970]:

What caused the crisis?

"Crisis" is your word, not mine.

To begin with, the prolonged decline in the stock markets sharply reduced earnings from the securities portion of the portfolios we manage. Recent legislation, particularly in Germany, reduced the sales-charge structure and made sales considerably less profitable. At the same time, the company was involved in a costly process of decentralization.

These real problems were compounded by the decision of our frightened board of directors to be "rescued" by a group of institutions to be put together by John King. Speculation mounted as to whether this take-over attempt would succeed, and this undoubtedly resulted in a loss of confidence.

What role did the European banks play?

Many European bankers are also brokers, and also manage and sponsor their own mutual funds. Initially they may have been pleased to see their largest competitor having difficulties, and they may have contributed to the problems. It was soon realized, however, that our difficulties also affected the European mutual-fund industry as a whole and hit stock markets everywhere.

Could a collapse of IOS trigger a world liquidity crisis?

There's no question of a collapse of IOS. In the recent market slump, the popular explanation has been that we were "dumping" securities. We were not dumping securities at all. On the other hand, there is little question that the threat of our doing extensive selling had a very depressing psychological effect on markets generally. If the mere threat could do this, consider what would happen if we indeed had to sell securities.

Can you clarify the Arctic oil-lease deal?

The purchase price was about $1 an acre, and a 10 percent undivided interest in this holding was subsequently sold to substantial outside oil interests for about $14 an acre. The fund then had to attribute a fair value to the acreage interest it still held. After extensive consultation with the fund's auditors, a valuation of $8 an acre was agreed upon by the directors. Some time ago the press reported a natural-gas strike close to the area of the fund's holding. I am told that exploration rights in the area of the fund's acreage have been trading recently at prices far in excess of the fund's valuation.

What about the loans to insiders?

Virtually all IOS executives, directors, sales representatives and employees are also IOS stockholders. It is only natural that they did their banking business with one of the IOS banks. To the best of my knowledge, most of the loans made to insiders and friends were made in the course of normal banking business and are neither controversial nor excessive.

Why did King's take-over bid fail?

Because it was viewed as an attempt to take control rather than an attempt to bring institutional partners to the firm. The participation of the financial institutions stipulated in our board's contract with Mr. King did not materialize.

What is the future for IOS?

IOS has nearly 1 million clients, and the investment programs that they are currently maintaining will result in nearly $10 billion being invested in our funds over the next fifteen years.

I won't try to predict whether markets have reached their lows. From the standpoint of the monthly investor, it hardly matters as long as he maintains a regular and systematic program of investing in a diversified portfolio. Over the long pull, the result of systematic investing is virtually certain to be good.

I feel a deep responsibility to our million clients and our 50,000 stockholders, and I will do everything I can to serve their best interests.

The Biggest Derailment of All

16

In the biggest of all corporate busts, Penn Central bankruptcy, it has been generally assumed that the real villain was the giant merger itself. After all, how could there be a successful merging between two vast rail lines, each operating under a different policy supervised by two dominant men? Actually, as the three 1970 pieces from the *New York Times* and the *Wall Street Journal* show, the seeds of chaos were planted in 1963, or five years before the merger took place, when one of the partners-to-be embarked on an acquisition-and-diversification splurge.

The Pennsy, operating on the theory that it would be wise to diversify out of low-profit railroading into high-profit real estate, bought a slew of the choicest industrial parks, amusement centers and commercial buildings from New York to Los Angeles. But while the return on investment on these was good for several years, suddenly everything came apart in the queasy economy of 1969.

Both the real-estate operations and the railroads became cash-poor. Inefficiency in railroad activities, coupled with a growing infighting between the two railroad camps, complicated matters. And the creditors began getting nervous.

Then, in 1970, the White House approved a $200-million loan guarantee through the Defense Department to the struggling behemoth. Nine banks would participate in the financing once the guarantee was sealed.

But, unlike the situation involving Lockheed Aircraft, which was subsequently bailed out by the federal government, Congress balked, and the friendly hand in the White House was withdrawn. The issue was clear: Why should the public pay for the mismanagement of a huge corporation?

The three pieces that follow on the Penn Central bust complement each other—the *Times* story examining the causes, one *Journal* article charting the alternatives open and the other *Journal* story showing how the Penn Central directors kept busy selling their stock as disaster neared.

Pennsy: Bad Management or Ailing Industry Debated

By Robert E. Bedingfield

Was it bad management that forced the Penn Central Transportation Company to file . . . for reorganization under the Federal Bankruptcy Act?

That question was put repeatedly to Secretary of Transportation John A. Volpe . . . by members of both the Senate and House Commerce subcommittees, which in the wake of the filing [were] under pressure from the Administration to report legislation authorizing Federal guarantees for the credit of distressed railroads.

Mr. Volpe's answer:

"I'd like to say that any time a corporation is losing money, I generally think it's poorly managed."

The Penn Central, which had a first-quarter loss of more than $100-million on its railroad operations, had only $7-million in the bank . . . to meet a $20-million payroll. . . .

Moreover, even before the nation's largest rail system was granted its petition for reorganization under Section 77 of the Bankruptcy Act—a special section designed to keep troubled railroads running—Mr. Volpe had reportedly been asked by the Penn Central's bank creditors to insist upon a management change as a condition of their extending new loans.

Wryly defending the management, a close associate of Stuart T. Saunders, who was ousted . . . as chairman of the board and chief executive officer of the Penn Central, remarked, "If bad management drove the Penn Central over the brink, the disease appears to be spreading."

His comment followed Mr. Volpe's statement to Congress that at least three or four other railroads appeared to be "waiting on the doorstep" for Government backing of their credit and that 21 of the nation's 74 major railroads operated in the red last year.

As long as 18 months [before], there were reports in Washington that "somebody at the Interstate Commerce Commission" was involved in pressure for a change in the railroad's management because of its inability to avoid operating deficits. Mr. Saunders, when questioned about this, admitted to a reporter that "a couple" of his directors at times gave him a bad time, but he added that other board members had prevailed on him "not to resign" in annoyance.

Mr. Saunders has refused to discuss his resignation since the board requested it. . . . He had called that meeting of directors himself, and, according to one Penn Central official, "After Stuart had convened the meeting and then was asked with other management officials to leave the session, he certainly didn't expect he was the one who was going to get the gate."

In addition to taking Mr. Saunders's resignation, the board announced the retirement of David C. Bevan, the Vice Chairman of Finance, and it said it had "relieved" Alfred E. Perlman, Vice Chairman and former President, of his duties.

Paul A. Gorman, the 62-year-old retired president of the Western Electric Company, who has hired by Mr. Saunders . . . to take over Mr. Perlman's duties as president . . . succeeded Mr. Saunders as chairman and chief executive officer.

That the "executive suite" at Penn Central was hardly a harmonious one was not a secret, either to close Wall Street followers or to industry observers. "There were two chief executive officers," is the way one railroad president describes the situation that developed at the Pennsylvania Railroad in 1963, when Mr. Saunders left the Norfolk & Western Railway to become the Chairman of the Pennsylvania.

"There was Stuart and there was Dave (Mr. Bevan) with Dave doing pretty much what he wanted about finances and getting the board's support, even though Stuart was supposed to be chief executive officer," is the way this president, who says he is a friend of both men, tells the story. That was the situation the Pennsylvania brought to the merger.

This president insists that Mr. Saunders, "until he was fired, had thought he would be able to make Dave Bevan the scapegoat." Mr. Bevan had been so successful in keeping the "true" financial records and cash balances of the huge carrier confidential that Mr. Gorman is supposed to have admitted to Government officials he wasn't aware . . . how bad off the company really was.

A big question . . . is whether the bankruptcy court will honor the pension awards that had been promised by Penn Central's directors to its former senior officers.

Mr. Saunders, if he had remained on the job until his 65th birthday on July 16, 1974, would have continued collecting his salary of $236,972 a year and then retired with a pension amounting to $114,445 a year.

Mr. Bevan, 63 years old, who was paid a salary of $131,984, was supposed to collect a pension amounting to $88,112.

Mr. Perlman was the only one of the three senior executives with a contract. It was to have expired . . . following his 68th birthday, and under it his salary was fixed at $170,000 till retirement, with payments annually thereafter at $50,000 for 10 years and eight months. His pension was to have been $94,141 a year.

Mr. Gorman did get a contract when he joined the railroad. . . . It pays him $250,000 a year, of which $175,000 is to be in cash and $75,000 in allotments under a contingent compensation plan. Mr. Saunders' contract also provides for a pension of $2,000 a month during his lifetime and $500 a month to his widow during her lifetime.

During Senate Commerce Subcommittee hearings in Washington . . . on the Administration's plans for giving Government guarantees of up to $750-million to troubled railroads, one Senator, Marlow W. Cook, Republican of Kentucky, commented on these salaries. Senator Cook observed that he couldn't get over how $250,000-a-year executives . . . have to ask a bunch of us $42,500'ers (a Senator's pay is $42,000 a year) if we can help them out."

Mr. Perlman, from the New York Central, reportedly was "pretty much ignored" from the time the merger was effected on Feb. 1, 1968, even though as President he was supposed to be the chief operating officer. The responsibility for actual operation of the trains was not handled by a Perlman-trained man, at first, but by the former Operating Vice President of the Pennsylvania.

Not only did many Pennsylvania-trained operating employees belittle many of Mr. Perlman's ideas so long as the overall "chief" was their old boss, but also Mr. Saunders turned his attention more to an aggressive diversification program than to reviewing Mr. Perlman's suggestions for spending large sums to upgrade the consolidated company's transportation plant and expanding the railroad's marketing activities.

It was not until . . . after the bad operations of the consolidated system had become the talk of the industry that the Pennsy-trained executive was transferred to the chairman's office, and the opearting job went to Mr. Perlman's protegé at the Central, R. G. (Mike) Flannery.

Mr. Perlman had been one of the most marketing-conscious rail executives in the country while he headed the New York Central. In the spring of 1966, after his railroad had achieved one of the best showings in its history for any first quarter. Mr. Perlman told newsmen, "This railroad is depression proof." He attributed its earnings power to the efforts of the marketing department, research activities and cost-savings realized from the use of computers and other cybernetic systems.

Mr. Saunders and the former Pennsylvania executives didn't share Mr. Perlman's high esteem for marketing and cybernetics. The Pennsy's marketing organization had been a traditional railroad traffic department, with a market-research arm attached. It was noted for opposing change, not creating it.

In an interview a year ago, Mr. Saunders said the 500 people in the marketing department of the two railroads at the time merger was effected were "far more than we needed." He bragged that within 13 months of consolidation the department had been cut back to 300 people, and he insisted that was "still too many."

Stories about the deteriorating service to shippers, and rumors of spiraling costs and mounting railroad losses spread almost from the first day (Feb. 1, 1968) the two railroads began unified operation. The computers of the two systems were incompatible, and there were horrendous tales for months about the misrouting of freight cars and the mislaying of thousands of waybills, in addition to a serious lack of motive power. There was even the impossible story that one freight train "just disappeared."

And from the first, the consolidated system was short on cash. Making good on a promise that both carriers made to labor unions for their support of the merger, Penn Central immediately had to rehire more than 5,000 furloughed employees to whom it had promised jobs for life, if the merger were effected. The cost of this and transferring employees from one location to another—and giving transferred employees as much as

$1,000 for "lace curtains" for new homes—amounted to more than $29-million. Another $75-million had to be spent right away just to physically connect the two systems. To compound the cash problem a $50-million issue of Pennsylvania Railroad bonds fell due on Dec. 1 and had to be paid off.

It was in the fall of 1968, after having obtained a $300-million revolving bank credit all of which was immediately spent or committed, that Penn Central tried what was then "a first." On Nov. 18, 1968, it secured a $50-million, five-year bank loan in the Eurodollar market. When that wasn't enough, the company's financial wizards began selling commercial paper —unsecured short-term notes.

It was the inability to meet $9,795,000 of these I.O.U.'s that fell due . . . and another $21.9-million of interest payments due on long-term debt and long-term debt maturities that precipitated the road's lawyers' formally filing the papers for reorgnization in the Federal District Court in Philadelphia. . . .

During the hearings . . . both in the Senate and House Commerce Committees on rail legislation and Penn Central's insolvency, the question was raised time and again as to: "How could a company with approximately $7-billion of assets not have sufficient resources to avoid a financial debacle?"

Another question that the Congressional investigators kept asking Transportation Secretary Volpe was: Are all of Penn Central's realty holdings mortgaged? Doesn't it have anything of that $7-billion that it could put up as security for new loans on its own credit, or that it could sell so it wouldn't have to borrow new money?

Mr. Volpe answered by explaining that ever since the railroad's lines were built more than 125 years ago, its right of way, as well as all real assets in the form of real estate and the like had been fully mortgaged. While Mr. Saunders often had explained that the Penn Central's transportation plant couldn't be rebuilt today for less than $15-billion to $20-billion dollars, Mr. Volpe told his questioners although that might be so, the plant generally had no value to anyone except for running a railroad.

"They are assets that would have very little value to the sophisticated investing public," said Mr. Volpe, pointing out that on the New York Stock Exchange the 24 million shares of stock of Penn Central outstanding wasn't even worth $200-million. . . .

Mr. Volpe said he did not mean to defend Penn Central's aggressive purchases of non-transportation businesses in the last few years, which he admitted had helped exhaust its working capital. He and his aides kept explaining to the Congressional questioners that most of those businesses which also have been mortgaged to secure outstanding debts were realty ventures that are not easily liquidated. Particularly in periods of high interest rates such as the present.

"Maybe we shouldn't be too critical of Penn Central," said Senator Cook, after Mr. Volpe stressed that the railroad had been the victim of a real liquidity crisis. "They have been practicing deficit spending for a good many years, like Congress—and they finally found out they couldn't do it any more."

Penn Central Officials Sold Stock as Carrier Was Nearing Disaster

By Fred L. Zimmerman

While the nation's largest railroad plunged toward financial disaster in 1969 and early 1970, 15 Penn Central executives took action that was to save them substantial sums as the company's stock price plummeted in succeeding months.

These corporate insiders unloaded more than 40,000 of their Penn Central shares for an estimated total of more than $2 million. The prices received per share, mostly ranging between $40 and $70, were far above the stock's recent low of $5.62.

This insider selling occurred at a time when the investing public was only dimly aware, if at all, that the Penn Central Transportation Co. was in big trouble—which culminated . . . in the company's decision to seek reorganization under the bankruptcy laws.

The Penn Central officers routinely filed prompt reports of their sales to the Securities and Exchange Commission, as required by law, but the transactions haven't been publicized until now.

Some of the sales took place just a few days before various corporate announcements that further depressed the stock's sliding price. But those executives who are willing to discuss their sales with a reporter insist they sold for personal reasons and not because of inside knowledge of the railroad's worsening financial condition; executives' use of inside information to aid their stock dealings would violate the securities laws.

At any rate, the SEC is understood to be planning a broad study to determine whether any of the transactions might have been prompted by the executives' access to information ahead of the general public. The House Banking Committee, chaired by Democrat Wright Patman of Texas, also intends to examine insider-trading patterns as part of its coming investigation of banks' involvement in the railroad's collapse.

There is no evidence that the executive sellers did anything illegal. Several state that they sold because they were strapped for cash or because they were being pressured by banks to reduce outstanding personal loans secured by Penn Central shares, whose value has dropped rather steadily during the past 24 months.

"The officers didn't know anything the public didn't know," declares William R. Gerstnecker, a [former] vice president. . . . Mr. Gerstnecker, now vice chairman of Philadelphia's Provident National Bank, sold 4,000 Penn Central shares in January and February of 1969 and an additional 1,000 the following May 26—about two weeks after the company's annual meeting had heard a generally optimistic forecast of the railroad's future from Stuart Saunders, who was ousted . . . as Penn Central chairman.

The SEC's Penn Central insider-trading file, standing more than a foot high, includes reports of transactions from nearly 100 corporate insiders, going back to the mid-1930s. The reports are made in compliance with a section of the 1934 Securities and Exchange Act that requires any officer, director, or 10%-owner of a company to notify the SEC of any transactions he makes in the stock.

An analysis of the reports filed in the past 24 months shows that Penn Central directors, with one notable exception, made little change in their holdings of the stock; most of the directors don't hold office in the company. In contrast, many of the company's officers were heavy sellers throughout 1969, and a few also reported major sales in late 1968 and in early 1970.

The reports of the 15 executives show only three purchases, totaling about 4,800 shares, in 1969. The purchases were made in February and March through the exercise of stock options at prices far below the market. Later in the year the three officers making these purchases sold a total of about 5,000 shares.

One director, David C. Bevan, who also was chairman of the Penn Central finance committee until [the] executive shake-up, evidently was the biggest of the insider sellers. In the first six months of 1969, according to the SEC reports, Mr. Bevan sold 15,000 shares, nearly halving his holdings.

He sold 3,000-share blocks on January 6, March 11, April 9 and May 6. Additionally, he sold 700 shares on May 27 and 2,300 on June 25. Based on closing market prices on those days, his 15,000 shares presumably brought him about $840,000. The SEC file shows that Mr. Bevan's major acquisition of Pennsylvania Railroad stock occurred in November 1964, when he bought 20,000 shares on options for an indicated total of about $420,000. (The Pennsylvania and New York Central railroads merged in 1968.)

Mr. Bevan, a director of Provident National Bank, isn't willing to discuss the transactions in much detail. "I sold the stock because my bank asked me to reduce my bank loan," he says, declining to identify the bank or specify the size of the loan. "I sold on a pattern and on the advice of counsel, when I didn't have any information that anyone else didn't have."

Besides Messrs. Bevan and Gerstnecker, the following were among major insider sellers in 1969 and 1970:

—Bayard H Roberts, secretary, who sold 2,300 shares in a seven-month period beginning in mid-June 1969 for a total price of about $109,000.

—Theodore K. Warner, Jr., vice president-accounting and taxes . . . who sold 4,000 shares in September 1969 for about $164,000.

—William A. Lashley, vice president-public relations and advertising, who sold 2,000 shares in March, April and May 1970 for about $34,000.

—Robert Haslett, vice president-investments, who sold 3,000 shares on July 15, 1969, for about $130,000.

—Guy W. Knight, senior vice president . . . who sold 3,910 shares in July 1969 for about $195,000.

—John G. Patten, vice president-freight sales, who sold 1,430 shares in August 1969 for about $60,000.

—David E. Smucker, executive vice president . . . who sold 3,600 shares in July 1969 for about $180,000.

(Messrs. Patten, Warner and Smucker are the three officials who reported Penn Central purchases in February and March of 1969. Mr. Patten bought in February the same number of shares he sold the following August; the other two men bought somewhat fewer shares than they subsequently sold.)

Other Penn Central executives who sold during the period include Henry W. Large, executive vice president . . .; Robert W. Minor, senior vice president-legal and public affairs; Jonathan O'Herron, vice president-finance until . . . he succeeded Mr. Bevan as chief financial officer; Malcolm P. Richards, vice president-purchases and materials; P. D. Fox, vice president-administration until March 1969, and John E. Chubb, vice president-Baltimore. Some of these men sold as little as 500 shares, it shoulld be noted, and several of the 15 executives still hold substantial amounts of Penn Central stock.

In retrospect, the railroad's fortunes can be seen to have steadily declined throughout 1969, but it's doubtful that this was clearly evident to the investing public at the time. Probably it was only after dividend payments were halted in November 1969, breaking a 123-year tradition, and after the company had to withdraw a proposed $100 million debenture offering in May 1970 that the gravity of Penn Central's financial troubles became widely apparent to ordinary investors.

Whether the company's executives could see, well in advance of the general public, that the railroad was headed for a crackup is difficult to determine; they generally deny that they could. All the same, the SEC records reflect several insider sales that appear to have occurred at propitious moments.

Four of the 15 insiders—Messrs. Knight, Haslett, Smucker, and Roberts—sold shares in July 1969, prior to the July 28 announcement that the railroad had suffered an $8.2 million loss in the second quarter, in contrast to a $2 million gain in the year-earlier period.

Four other officers—Messrs. Large, Patten, Warner and Chubb—sold shares in the period between August 27, 1969, when Penn Central directors picked Paul Gorman as the railroad's new president, and September 22, 1969, when the company got around to announcing his appointment.

At the time of the announcement, a Penn Central spokesman explained that the delay had been to allow Mr. Gorman time to submit his resignation as president of Western Electric Co. After the announcement, some institutional holders of the stock expressed disappointment over the railroad's failure to name as president a man with a strong railroad background. In the three trading days following the announcement, the stock's closing market price dropped to $36.25 a share from $38.

Mr. Lashley, the public relations vice president, sold 500 of his shares . . . a week before the company's . . . announcement—in the form of a press release Mr. Lashley recalls having helped prepare—that the railroad had suffered a $62.7 million loss in 1970's first quarter, compared with a year-earlier loss of $12.8 million.

Mr. Lashley says he cannot remember the date when he was informed of the first-quarter loss, but he is sure it wasn't far in advance of the announcement because "the financial types around here stay very tight-lipped." He declares that his only reason for selling the 500 shares—as well as 500 additional shares last March 30 and another 1,000 the following May 22—was that he was under heavy pressure from banks to reduce loans secured by Penn Central shares.

He says that last May 15, for example, he received a telegram from one of these banks stating: "Due to the stock market decline your collateral loan is under margin. Kindly make principal loan reduction of (a specific dollar amount, which he declines to state) or pledge additional collateral, or we will be forced to liquidate your collateral. Please comply by May 20."

Mr. Lashley says he never sold any of his shares on the basis of inside information, but he acknowledges that as the company's chief public relations officer he was exposed to a storm of rumors about the Penn Central's difficulties. At the time of his April 15 sale, he recalls, "I knew the company was having a rough time. I felt, in general, that there was going to be a loss" for the first quarter. "I had been getting calls from papers. By that time a lot of the Wall Street people were beginning to get uneasy about it."

The job duties of another seller, corporate secretary Roberts, put him in a ticklish position. One of his responsibilities is to supervise the preparation and mailing of the insider trading reports that Penn Central executives must file with the SEC. Thus, he acknowledges that when he began in mid-June of 1969 to sell 2,300 of his shares he was aware that many of his fellow executives had been heavily selling off their own holdings.

Mr. Roberts states, however, that this knowledge didn't influence his decision to sell. "I sold because I had to have the money," he says. He was faced with big family hospital bills, he recalls, and also was being pressured by a bank to pay off a loan. He says he told no one that he was selling his shares.

Mr. Roberts, who assumes "there is going to be some criticism" of the insider selling, believes the public should recognize that insiders who wish or need to reduce their holdings face "a hideous problem, a real dilemma" in choosing an appropriate time to sell.

Some of the other executive sellers aren't as interested in philosophizing about their transactions. Mr. Large, for example, briskly states that he "can't conceive" of anything unethical about his sales, which he says were made to pay off bank loans. He adds that a 200-share sale last September 17, shortly before the belated announcement that Mr. Gorman had been named president, had "no connection" with the Gorman appointment. That's all he has to say.

Mr. Smucker, when questioned by a reporter about his sales, replies: "It's not any of your business. I have no problem with the SEC, and I have no problem with you. Because I was an executive, my dealings were of public record. You have access to the record, and that's all I have to say."

A few of the sellers aren't available for comment. Among them is Mr. Patten. But his assistant, Charles Drake, suggests that someone "ought to write a story about us poor guys who were buying right to the end, because we had faith in this company."

Penn Central Faces Lengthy Legal Snarls Under Bankruptcy Laws

By W. Stewart Pinkerton, Jr.

How can a railroad with $4.6 billion in assets, including immense real estate holdings, go broke? How can it keep operating? What's the likely long-term solution to Penn Central's woes?

These are only a few of the complex questions arising from the decision by Penn Central Transportation Co., the nation's largest railroad, to seek help under the Federal Bankruptcy Act. That dramatic move came . . . after an unsuccessful attempt to persuade the Nixon Administration to guarantee $200 million in bank loans.

Railroad officials, Wall Street analysts and legal experts generally agree the ultimate solution for the troubled carrier will probably take years to work out. Many months of hearings, investigations—and probably a few lawsuits—lie ahead. Also impending is a dissection of the railroad's complex financial structure. This consists of an intricate web of securities, bonds and other debt, including obligations of more than 60 subsidiary railroads, leased lines and other affiliates.

But close examination of moves made by some of the nearly 40 other railroads that have turned to the bankruptcy laws for help over the years and talks with experts familiar with the complexities of railroad reorganization suggest some of the possible steps that might be taken to keep Penn Central going.

Among them: The carrier's huge real estate holdings could possibly be tapped to help out—but probably only as part of a long-term plan and not as a stopgap measure. Also, suspension of property taxes and other payments could be permitted by the court to ease Penn Central's cash position and help it meet day-to-day expenses. Transfer of passenger service to some sort of public corporation would be yet another step to keep the road operating. Finally, the court could order a recapitalization, a sort of alchemy whereby certain bondholders and other cerditors could salvage at least part of their investments by receiving securities of a new corporation.

Legal experts hasten to add that any final plan might include all, a few or none of these elements. "It would be foolish for anyone to predict what might happen," says James William Moore, a Yale University law professor and railroad bankruptcy expert. "There are just too many questions involved in a company this big."

One fuzzy legal point is whether or not the railroads' creditors can claim any part of the assets of Penn Central Co., the parent concern. Charles Seligson, a Manhattan attorney and an expert on bankruptcy matters, flatly states that the "filing of a petition by a subsidiary does not bring the parent company into the proceeding in any way." But other attorneys who have been involved in previous railroad reorganizations demur, citing complex legal questions involved.

In any event, the debate could turn out to be largely academic. The parent company's only tangible assets—other than the railroad—are a small oil refinery in Texas and a fuel oil distributor in New York.

The railroad, however, does have sizable assets in real estate. But it's equally uncertain whether it can tap these landholdings to ease the current pinch. The carrier owns some lucrative Manhattan properties, including the Waldorf-Astoria, Biltmore and Commodore hotels. And its subsidiary, Pennsylvania Co., has substantial real estate holdings in California, Texas, Georgia and Hawaii.

But many of these holdings, particularly the New York City real estate, have been pledged as collateral for loans or have liens on them and would be difficult to sell. In addition, many attorneys say that selling the holdings now would be something of a fire sale: It could bring some short-term relief but in the long run it might not be worth it. One reason: Last year, the major real estate holdings in Manhattan generated some $20.2 million in after-tax earnings, much of which, Penn Central says, went toward meeting railroad operating expenses.

Furthermore, lawyers point out any sale now would probably produce a flood of claims by creditors unhappy with the distribution of the proceeds. And attorneys note than in any case, the Securities and Exchange Commission and the Interstate Commerce Commission both tend to frown on selling off substantial assets outside a formal plan of reorganization.

Penn Central occupies a unique position under the bankruptcy statute. It filed under what's called Section 77, which is quite distinct from other parts of the Bankruptcy Act that provide for straight bankruptcy, or liquidation. Section 77, specifically designed for railroads, is more closely akin to chapters 10 and 11, those sections that assume a company has at least the potential for profitable operations. Thus, lawyers say, it's incorrect to say Penn Central has "filed for bankruptcy."

Section 77 was originally established to bail out railroads that had the ability to make money from operations but that were burdened with too much debt. Historically, a railroad going into reorganization has reaped two benefits: First of all, debt payments are suspended, thus increasing cash flow, which is net income after taxes but before depreciation charges. And eventually, through a recapitalization, the overall fixed debt charges are usually cut substantially.

In the classic recapitalization case, court-appointed trustees determine the railroad's potential earnings, before fixed charges. Whatever this amount—say, for instance, it's $10 million—it's capitalized at 5%. Thus, in this instance, total capitalization for the new company would be $200 million.

Trustees then divide this up into new stock and debt so that fixed debt charges can be covered with enough left over to pay cash dividends on the stock. New stock is then issued to the holders of the old securities. In the first New Haven reorganization, which began in 1935 and lasted 12 years, capitalization was cut to $385 million from $489 million. Fixed charges dropped to $9.1 million from $17.6 million. To be sure, a recapitalization would undoubtedly leave at least some creditors unhappy with the size of their stake in the new company.

But even assuming a reduction in fixed debt payments, lawyers agree Penn Central trustees will likely have to take far more drastic steps to assure a profitable company after reorganization. A number of attorneys suggest the only way to get the railroad back on its feet is to eliminate its passenger service, which last year ran up a loss of $104.8 million.

Penn Central officials have already said they would like to do this. . . . The carrier got ICC permission to discontinue 27 intercity passenger trains; it . . . petitioned the commission to discontinue 34 more trains on long-haul routes. The railroad is already negotiating with a number of Eastern states with an eye to takeover of its commuter lines by state transportation agencies. Under such an arrangement, Penn Central would in most cases continue to operate the trains on a contract basis, but it would no longer be burdened with equipment financing and other costs.

Conceivably, trustees might also consider cutting down the number of leased lines Penn Central has, lawyers suggest. These account for some 10,600 miles of the carrier's 20,500 miles of track. Bonds and other debts of the leased lines, which include such old carriers as the Battle Creek & Sturgis Railway Co. and the Elmira & Williamsport RR Co., amount to some $365 million. Presumably, if any leased lines were disposed of, Penn Central would continue to operate them on a contract basis, free of long-term debt obligations.

Of prime concern to both Penn Central and the financial community is the railroad's cash position between now and the time trustees would likely issue trust certificates to raise interim funds. . . . The ICC must approve the selection as well. Some lawyers say it could be at least a month before the trustees could actually take title to the railroad.

. . . However, the district court judge handling the reorganization case set wheels in motion for the company to raise new money. . . . Acting on a petition by Penn Central Transportation, the judge, in effect, ordered that the company could issue debtor or trustee certificates of up to $50 million, following the court hearing. . . .

Normally, the ICC would hold another hearing 20 days later to confirm the court's selection of trustees, but some sources have pointed out that the ICC doesn't necessarily have to hold such hearings. In this case, it's believed, the trustees could be confirmed almost immediately after the . . . court hearing and could begin issuing trustee certificates at that time.

Transportation Secretary John Volpe told the House Commerce Committee . . . that there was no certainty that the railroad could continue to meet payrolls for its 94,000 workers. . . . The payroll runs about $20 million a week, with some employes paid on Tuesday, others on Thursday. One newspaper report . . . quoted Mr. Volpe as saying he had been informed that the railroad had only $7 million in the bank . . . to meet the $12 million . . . payout. The payroll was reportedly met by drawing funds from subsidiaries and by using funds that came in [that week].

In addition to payroll and administrative expenses, the railroad is obliged to make payments on equipment trust certificates and installment purchases of rolling stock. Some $14.5 million in trust certificates and $51.4 million in installment payments are due. . . . These agreements cover a substantial number of the road's freight cars and locomotives. Since the equipment would be subject to repossessing if payments aren't kept up, few lawyers believe they would be suspended.

There are some payouts, however, that the court has ruled the railroad can make at its discretion. Among these are property taxes and interline payments to other railroads. The company hasn't decided yet whether or not to pay all or some of the taxes it owes. Some $1.5 million is due . . . to the city of Philadelphia, where the railroad is headquartered. The city has threatened to withhold a $1.2 million commuter subsidy payment if the tax isn't paid.

The railroad is apparently refusing to pay substantial portions of its interline charges. . . . These are payments made to other lines for their proportionate share of freight revenues on shipments carried over more than one railroad. Generally, most freight goes collect. The delivering carrier collects the entire freight bill, even though its share might be fractional. Near the end of the month, accounts are settled among all the carriers.

The Equity Funding Scandal

17

Auditors who didn't audit, analysts who didn't analyze, inspectors who didn't inspect, insurers who didn't insure—this sad conclusion emerges from the Equity Funding scandal as clearly as does another insistent conclusion: where does greed stop and fraud begin? If Equity Funding Corporation of America, the parent company, hadn't insisted on sharply appreciating earnings from its main life-insurance subsidiary, Equity Funding Life Insurance Company, it is possible—perhaps only barely possible—that the fraud would not have been perpetrated.

The Equity Funding matter will be in litigation for a long time. At this point, it involves not only several federal and state regulatory investigations but also a series of suits and countersuits as buyers of Equity Funding stock sought, after the scandal's exposure, to charge sellers with taking advantage of inside knowledge that trouble was brewing inside the West Coast firm. Many revelations are expected from these hearings and trials and it is not without some sense of perspective that the Equity Funding scandal has been called the Watergate of American business. How many Wall Street firms and lending institutions were fooled, lulled into a false sense of security, and how many investors were influenced to buy a kited stock because of unfounded recommendations?

And perhaps more important, how many people were involved? In the electrical price-fixing scandals of some years earlier there were maybe 100, 200, 300? But in Equity Funding's case, it was at least 1,000—all actively involved in and fostering the fraud.

But there's another deplorable aspect to the case. To the growing list of American types whose reputation for honesty has eroded in recent years—our "friendly" neighborhood auto mechanic, the used car dealer, the appliance repairman, the ghetto merchant, the local short-weight supermarket owner or butcher—must we now add the life-insurance salesman?

The "Y" Business Carried to the NTH Degree

By Isadore Barmash

Late in April 1973, Stanley Goldblum, a muscular, six-foot-three-inch former weightlifter, former butcher, former scrap dealer, and former chairman and president of Equity Funding Corporation of America, sat in a federal courtroom in Los Angeles and listened calmly to the proceedings of a bankruptcy action.

Three weeks earlier, Goldblum himself had been compelled to resign in a scandal that threatened to become one of the biggest financial disasters in decades.

As he listened intently and occasionally jotted some words on a yellow legal pad, Goldblum presented a paradoxical figure.

Attired in a tastefully mod suit of brown and gray, a brown and white striped shirt and a brown and gold silk tie, he seemed detached, even remote from the lurid details recounted in the proceedings. Goldblum was something of a loner, described by associates as "not easy to know" and "a private person." His friends spoke respectfully of him as an introspective type, a student of psychology, and a man given to quoting long passages of Shakespeare.

Yet now he was in the eye of a financial storm of fantastic proportions. Equity Funding Life Insurance Company had been accused of a scheme to create bogus insurance policies by the many thousands. Some 56,000 such policies had already been sold for cash to other major life insurers who considered them bona fide. When Equity Funding Life was forced to file under Chapter 10 of the Federal Bankruptcy Act, no fewer than 100 banks and other lending institutions, many among the best known in the country, found themselves stuck with about 2 million shares of Equity stock.

Potential losses to thousands of small stockholders were estimated to reach as much as $300 million, while dozens of insurance companies were apparently cheated as easily as taking candy from a baby. At least three major auditing firms, not to mention several state insurance departments, were duped as the plan progressed from 1970 through early 1973. But few were sucked in as badly as the many Wall Street analysts and brokers who were already acquainted with earlier financial scandals such as the salad oil and the Texas grain-storage-tank fiascos.

As the details of the plot were unfolded, three individuals found themselves thrust into the glare of the spotlight: Goldblum, the quiet, aloof, alleged mastermind; Ronald H. Secrist, a discharged Equity Funding executive who blew the whistle on the scheme; and Raymond L. Dirks, an expert in insurance stocks who, after being told all by Secrist, traveled from coast to coast checking the charges and alerting those duped by Equity Funding. Goldblum maintained a long silence but the other two were articulate and vociferous. Secrist later intimated that after he had passed on his information his life had been threatened. Dirks found himself in hot water when the New York Stock Exchange charged him with violating its rules by informing his clients of what he knew without first telling the securities exchange.

But these three were hardly the only figures caught in the spotlight. In what may well be the most unbelievable fact in this bizarre case, the widespread fraud was known and carried on at many levels of the company by as many as a thousand people. Most of these—at least those closest to the plan's machinations —covered up the fraud by subterfuge, intimidation, threats of violence, punitive action, illegal scrutiny of auditors' schedules, forgery, and use of doctored computer tapes.

The false insurance policies, put on the books and sold for cash to reinsurers, were long known around the company as the "Y" business or "Department 99." Widely bruited about in Equity Funding Life's offices and lavatories, the scheme gradually assumed the character of a joke, a game, almost a gag. "People laughed and laughed about it," recalled a former Equity executive. All this notwithstanding the fact that the elaborate plot required comprehensive, careful follow-through by many people.

Imagine this kind of wild, Catch-22 shenanigans: Since the "Y" business was a delicate matter at best, extra pains were necessary to keep it under control. Inspectors and auditors had to be fooled. Reinsurers had to be regularly lulled into suspecting nothing. Documents had to be forged. Occasionally, employees had to act as policy-holders. False death claims had to be created to give it all the semblance of reality. And to keep it all successfully churning, new bogus policies had to be continually written.

How long could this fantasy world continue to spin?

This may be the toughest question of all; owing to its very hypothetical nature, the answer must remain conjecture. If Ronald Secrist hadn't been fired, if he hadn't called Dirks, if Dirks hadn't gone to some of the big investors in Equity Funding to alert them, if the auditing firm of Haskins and Sells, once confronted by Dirks, hadn't insisted that Equity Funding report the complaints to the Securities and Exchange Commission —it is impossible to say for sure that the scheme might not still be carrying on undetected.

How did it all happen in the first place?

Stanley Goldblum, a restless, introspective yet physically mobile type, unquestionably set the tone for Equity Funding's success and its fiasco.

He was born in Pittsburgh in 1927, attended the Los Angeles public schools after his parents moved to that city in the 1930s, and served briefly in the United States Army Signal Corps. He was attracted to a career in pharmacy but never went beyond a two-year matriculation at the University of California, where he majored in pre-pharmacy. While attending college he worked as an instructor at a Vic Tanny gym in Los Angeles. He married in 1949, later shedding his wife to marry her sister. He involved himself in a war-surplus business, then spent seven or eight years in his in-laws' meat business.

His association with the insurance world began in 1958. He became a clerk for the Gordon C. McCormick insurance concern in Los Angeles, one of the first companies to offer a combined program of insurance and mutual funds sales. It was the same package which, merchandised to the hilt and carried to the hinterlands by a crack sales crew, turned Equity Funding into a glamor stock earning glowing Wall Street plaudits and recommendations. Goldblum later claimed that he had learned from the McCormick techniques but refined them in his own operation.

Evidently enthralled with this sales package, Goldblum, after only two years with McCormick, started his own company along the same lines.

This is how it worked:

A customer agreed to invest a sum of money in a mutual fund operated by Equity Funding. The shares he received were then used as collateral for a loan to pay for his insurance premium. Equity Funding, of course, handled both the investment and the insurance. In the second year, and the third and afterward, the customer bought mutual fund shares again, making his premium payments with them. At the end of a ten-year period, the plan called for the investor-insuree to cash in enough of his mutual fund shares to pay off his entire debt. If he followed through in the prescribed manner, he should still have had mutual fund shares left while enjoying the security of insurance with cash value.

Through an involved evolution in which Goldblum formed a partnership with three others, Equity Funding was launched on its glory road. The partners were Eugene R. Cuthbertson, owner of the Diversified Mutual Funds of Southern California, Ltd., Long Beach; Raymond J. Platt, who had been McCormick's San Francisco sales manager and had also worked for Equitable Life Insurance Company; and Michael R. Riordan, a former Boston mutual-fund salesman. Shortly after they started their company, the quartet met with McCormick in New York to discuss a five-way partnership in his company. McCormick agreed—reluctantly but not too traumatically, since another business deal beckoned him—and the partners absorbed his operations, too.

Yet despite years of great success and wealth that followed, the partnership virtually broke apart within six years. After being bought out in 1963, Platt sued the remaining partners but died during the litigation. Three years later, Cuthbertson also sold his interest.

During this period, however, Goldblum built his concern into a glittering financial conglomerate that boasted assets of $500 million and earnings by 1971 of more than $18 million on revenues of $131 million.

At its peak, Equity Funding owned four life insurance companies, three mutual funds, a Bahamian bank, and a savings-and-loan association. About 4,000 individuals hawked the services, which were expanded to include investments in real-estate development, oil drilling, and cattle breeding.

Perhaps the big difference between Equity Funding and other firms offering a similar program was a smooth, confident merchandising effort. Salesmen did especially well through receiving double commissions and stock options. Wall Street liked the synergistic nature of the package and was taken in by the smooth presentation. Equity stock rose from $6 a share when the firm went public in 1964 to $80 in 1969.

But there was one problem. The package plan required a constant infusion of cash on the company's part. Cash flow was always tight. Why should that be? Why should a company with so much assets and such a high profit always be cash-poor?

The answer lies partly in the insurance business itself. An ordinary insurer must wait several years to cash in on a life-insurance policy. Sales commissions, which are greater than the first and even the second annual premium, must be paid off first. In the case of Equity Funding Life, the problem was complicated by the fact that profits were lean in the ten-year maturity period. But salaries, the cost of servicing the insured, and overhead costs began right away and continued.

Co-insurance, or selling the policies to another company, a reinsurer, seemed to be the answer to the cash question. This practice is similar to a store selling its accounts receivable (mostly charge accounts) to financial institutions in order to raise cash to buy fresh, seasonal merchandise. In both cases, the original insurer and the store continue to handle the account's paperwork, and even the dunning when necessary. Equity's reinsurers, however, bore the risk of the policies they bought. Little did they know how much risk they bore until the whole scheme was exposed.

The bogus policy venture—the "Y" business—may have grown from an employee insurance program begun by Equity Funding Life a year earlier. This had involved giving employees a "special class" insurance for which no premiums were required the first year. Somewhere along the line—the real answer is probably locked up in the tiniest recesses of the minds of more than a few Equity Funding executives—the urgency to raise cash through co-insurance and the ability to promote co-insurance of the employee policies soon led to the creation of fictitious insurance policies. The bogus policies would be sold for cash to the reinsurers.

The plan was put into effect sometime in 1970. It was, in a way, carrying the "Y" business to the Nth degree. With no commission needed to pay an agent, the company could cash in better than if the policy was real. Of course, the policies were set up to resemble real ones as closely as possible. Most were pegged to actual names or at least close enough to be confused for them. Slight differences were allowed in the amounts of insurance, the spelling of names, and birth dates in comparison to those involved in real policies.

Spurring the "Y" business was the parent company's increasing demand for more earnings from Equity Funding Life. The earnings goals, of course, were intended to present the most favorable face to investors, especially the Bigs of Wall Street, as well as to the millions of small investors. Early in the first investigations of the scandal, charges were levied that earnings reports were sent back to company headquarters in a highly inflated form. Did the parent company know about the false policies? Were Goldblum and cohorts so hot on earnings gains that they condoned the shafting of the reinsurers? With so many people involved in the scheme, it is hard to believe that someone up there at headquarters in Century City, California, didn't know something about it.

Goldblum himself seemed to be alternately delegating responsibility away from himself and then reasserting his own control. Yet, oddly enough, when the questions started popping he either maintained a stoic calm or labelled them as "preposterous." That is, he did until April 2, 1973, when the *Wall Street Journal* exclusively reported the events in a story that bore the headline, A SCANDAL UNFOLDS and ended with "My God, the Audacity of It."

Goldblum resigned the same day.

Actually, as a result of Secrist's telling Dirks and Dirks conducting his own investigation, a growing number of people on Wall Street, the insurance field, and even several state insurance departments were aware of it before April 2. But it wasn't until the *Journal* exposure that things began to happen: the New York Stock Exchange halted trading in Equity stock, the S.E.C. filed a suit against Equity Funding on alleged fraud, the Illinois Insurance Department confirmed that it was conducting an investigation, and a flood of lawsuits began.

Many questions remain to be answered. There is, of course, the matter of how the scheme was conducted so that so many employees allowed their company loyalty to subjugate their honesty. But beyond this, what about the lack of hard-nosed suspicion by the many outside "insiders" who so often proclaim their objectivity? Naiveté seems to have been a way of life among the many stock brokerages, banks, mutual funds, and others who got stung by Equity Funding. Why didn't the three major auditing companies spot anything in such a blatant and widespread scheme? And after so many other stock-kiting situations in the 1960s, when they realized that they had been sucked in before, why did all those security analysts allow that to happen to them once more?

Only three months or so before the scandal was exposed, Goldblum convincingly addressed the New York Society of Security Analysts, the largest group of Wall Street analysts. And at about the same time staff studies by such Wall Street houses as Smith Barney, Burnham & Co., and Werthheim & Co. plugged Equity's stock as a good buy.

Perhaps the ultimate naiveté was demonstrated only a week before the newspaper's exposure of the mess when another big securities house, Hayden Stone, declared in a research study on Equity Funding that it could find "no factual basis" to rumors that government authorities were probing Equity. And Hayden Stone added:

> Several rumors have been circulating which have affected Equity Funding's stock. We have checked these rumors and there appears to be no substance to any of them. At 6.0 times estimated 1973 fully diluted earnings, we believe that Equity Funding is considerably undervalued . . .

Conclusions: Rampant Appetites

18

Now every human action ought to be free from precipitancy and negligence, nor indeed ought we to do anything for which we cannot give a justifiable reason. This indeed almost amounts to a definition of duty. Now we must manage so as to keep the appetites subservient to reason that they may neither outstrip it or fall behind through sloth and cowardice. Let them be ever composed and free from all perturbation of spirit; and thus entire consistency and moderation will display themselves. For those appetites that are too vagrant and rampant as it were, either through desire or aversion, are not sufficiently under the command of reason. . . ."

Cicero (106–43 B.C.)

If the observation from the famous classic Roman jurist and author seems an attempt at irony in view of the foregoing chapters, so be it. For those who still tend to view the recalcitrant, erring, corrupt corporation as some sort of institutional entity, unmanaged by the human touch, the events of the last three decades, the period encompassed here, should be sufficient to remove the last vestiges of such innocence. Corporations are managed by men; and men, never forget, manage corporations to suit themselves. Thus corporate calamities are calamities created by men. And, as we have seen in 15 case histories, the basic cause of the business disaster is greed, human greed, simple and unadulterated.

Of course, the greed would not necessarily have led to a financial crisis, a bankruptcy, a liquidation, a jail sentence, a great loss to investors and lenders, etc., if the greed hadn't stumbled over itself. In that case, it was combined with poor judgment, mismanagement, bad timing, self-deception and just plain stupidity. But then, too, it is probably not an oversimplification to say that in most cases the greed crossed over the line into corruption.

Yet it is obvious, too, that it was in the implementation of the inordinate drive, the greed, that the perpetrator, singular or plural, overstepped—crossed the line, as it were—and the proliferating troubles rushed to a calamity status. Already doing quite well, Billie Sol Estes, Tino De Angelis, Edward Gilbert wanted to do even better and so crossed the line, jamming their thumbs into the eye of fate.

Zeckendorf, Cort Randell and Bernie Cornfeld were basically excellent salesmen who fell captive to their own sales pitch and went sprawling over their own promises and rhetoric.

Ford Corporation, RCA, General Electric, Atlantic Acceptance, Texas Gulf Sulphur, Penn Central and others ran up either huge losses or a vast loss to their prestige because the men at their helm were simply too ambitious to look squarely at the facts that faced them and barreled ahead toward disaster, almost as if they were courting it. Ethically speaking, there is, of course, a big gulf between simply throwing away $350 million at Ford in its Edsel whimsey and conspiring for years to fix prices and limit competition on defense contracts as the GE price fixers did. One action was simply horribly bad judgment, and the other was out-and-out corruption. But the common thread among those corporations was an inability to face up to reality, then a faltering step, followed by a sprint into unreality.

As a business editor and financial writer for more than 25 years, I have been intrigued through some quirk in my nature by the behavior of businessmen, completely aside from the performance of their companies, particularly in regard to ways in which their personal traits at times militated against their functions as owners or chief executives. Most businessmen I know, I am impelled to make clear, are basically honest, basically ethical, basically balanced, but there is a portion that is not, and this can—in restrospect, of course, I freely admit—be seen in the light of their own behavior pattern.

From that standpoint, I would like to describe three businessmen I met over the years and how they behaved and how their companies fared because of their behavior. Had I been astute enough, wise enough, at the time, I might have been able to predict how their companies would suffer on their account. As it is, my comments represent observations made while they were still on top and then after they toppled.

The "Quiet One." He always seemed so deliberate in all he did. No move was made, no comment expressed without his having first carefully considered how it would be taken and how it would affect him. Even when I was introduced to him, he seemed to hesitate in both gesture and greeting before he responded, conservatively and almost inaudibly. But what a powerful, admired company he had built in ten years. Wall Street fell all over itself, while the dealers who sold his goods were proud to be on his list. Quality, detail, workmanship were undeniably all there, as well as a strong national brand name established by a colorful, impressive campaign. I used to wonder how such an introvert could be responsible for such a dominant company. And then he surprised a press conference by announcing that he was diversifying, adding via internal expansion and acquisition half a dozen new product categories. Up till then, he had always been a one-product maker. He gestured at his bright, young financial man, saying, "Jeff will fill you in all about our financing plans," and left.

A few months later, the next phase broke on the sports pages. The executive had put in his personal bid to buy one of the major baseball teams for almost $20 million. That was unexpected. Who would have thought he had such interests? But even more unexpected a few months after that was the announcement by a creditors' committee that his firm was being forced into involuntary bankruptcy because it was delinquent on all its major bank loans and trade debts. What had happened to all the carefully thought out moves?

When last heard of, the "Quiet One" was living on his yacht on the inland waterways, his company in the hands of creditors as his stockholders held batches of almost worthless paper. One of the most disillusioned was his bright, young financial man. It seemed that the "Quiet One" had quietly fooled everyone.

The "Smooth One." An alumnus of one of the major conglomerates, he was bankrolled into running his own company by a friendly investment banker who saw in him a truly creative acquisition talent. A thin, thoughtful man of about 40 with a degree in economics, he evolved a concept of building a group of businesses catering to affluent Americans. Within three years, by dint of an easy, soft-sell approach that generated considerable confidence, he put together a holding company that controlled eight nationally-known companies with snob appeal. Here and there, he reluctantly lopped off acquired executives. In a restrained, agreeable, almost ingratiating way, he sold himself, his company and his concept to the security analysts and the press.

The first hint I got about his real nature came from one of the executives whom he had chopped. "He's a real S.O.B.," the man said. "He called me to his office, offered me a drink and fired me without any warning." Later, when I asked the "Smooth One" about the executive he had fired, he dropped his aplomb for a second and then recovered. "Yes," he said offhandedly, "he just didn't have what it takes. We let him have plenty of rope." Who was telling the truth?

Then there was his behavior on a business panel at a conference. When everyone else admitted that pressures on the top man could become heavy at times, he said that it had never happened to him. And when the others admitted confusion on the 1970 economy, he was so bullish and so serene that everyone was put off.

But even the affluents that year began tightening their belts. When he summarily resigned at the behest of his directors because the company was compelled to report a big deficit for the fiscal year and a promise to try to repay lagging payments on debts as soon as possible, he answered all the calls from the analysts and the press as agreeably as he always had. A "smoothie" to the end—at 43.

The "Brash One." I first ran into this man when he held an important divisional post in a large public company and I was impressed with his bold, enthusiastic approach to his work. Few in his field had his drive, his palaver and his ability to generate action. But I was surprised when his employer discharged him. Some months later, he popped up as the head of his own consulting company. In hardly any time at all, he had a number of good clients and was bragging about it to everyone. It all seemed true, too, and you just had to take him or leave him as the type of man who did things in a noisy, exhibitionist manner.

Those who were familiar with his efforts in his new activity spoke well of him. But, it soon appeared, there was a turnstile aspect to his business. Few clients stayed with him more than a couple of months. He promised the world but let them down with a thud, after taking good fees. And then I began to hear some of the wild stories about his debts. One day I asked him about both the turnover in his clients and the stories about his spotty financial reputation. He grinned. "Son of a bitch," he said with a smile, displaying big, white teeth, "you newspaper guys never miss anything, do you? Look, let me ask you a question—did you ever try something, really try, only not have it work out?"

But within a few months his dossier of experience opened up for me. He had held three top executive jobs. He had swashbuckled his way through them all, expanding, conducting himself in a splashy way and in each case running up such heavy expenses, completely out of line with the need, that he had been fired from each job. In one case, he had operated a $100-million business for a retired owner and had almost ruined him. When asked why he didn't prosecute, the elderly owner had replied, "Oh, I think I could put him behind bars all right, but what good would that do? If you get behind the bull, he's such a nice fellow."

But someone should have stopped the man's habit of leaving a trail of bad debts and losses everywhere he went, as well as a string of disappointed clients, bosses and associates, all taken in by his infectious enthusiasm. A con man to the extreme, the "Brash One" still remains at large. Somehow, society hasn't exacted its toll. But, if you should run into him, go to the other side of the street, quickly.

If anyone has doubts about the importance of the early Seventies as the watershed years in the history of the American business calamity, one need only mention the troubles of the American Supersonic Transport (SST) and its Anglo-French counterpart, the Concorde; the Clifford Irving hoax "autobiography" of industrialist Howard Hughes; and the extraordinary relations between ITT and the Nixon Administration and ITT's allegedly illegal insider trading in common stock.

The SST was grounded even before it had a chance to prove itself by a wave of dissent from Congress. Torn by dissent over the Vietnam War, the solons decided that a giant plane that could travel at more than the speed of sound could wait for a more propitious time and perhaps for a more perfected, economical mode. The support funds were withdrawn, and Boeing Aircraft Corporation, the prime contractor, went into a tailspin from which it only narrowly escaped.

A year after the SST was grounded in 1971, the Concorde, jointly produced by Aerospatiale in France and the British Aircraft Corporation, remained at the center of a four-sided battle. The opponents were the plane's designers, the environmentalists, the international aircraft industry and the airlines. Costing $57 million each, or about double Boeing's 747 jumbo jet, the Concorde is scheduled to enter commercial service in mid-1974.

Clifford Irving, the dapper, jet-set author, was sentenced to 2½ years in prison and a $10,000 fine in mid-1972 for trying to swindle $750,000 from McGraw-Hill, Inc. Irving and his German-born Swiss wife, Edith, had pleaded guilty several months earlier, in March 1972, to trying to foist a bogus autobiography of Hughes on McGraw-Hill. Irving, with the aid of Richard Suskind, a researcher, proposed in 1970 to McGraw-Hill, which had published three earlier Irving books, that he compile an autobiography of Hughes on the basis of 100 secret meetings with the reclusive industrialist. He told the publisher that he had received three letters from Hughes expressing tentative interest in having Irving write the authorized biography.

Over the next ten months, McGraw-Hill's editors received calls from various points, such as Puerto Rico, Mexico, Miami, where the author said he had just interviewed Hughes. Reporting that he had a letter of agreement from Hughes, Irving brought the forged document to New York and received a contract calling for an immediate $100,000 advance. Before the sorry tale was ended, McGraw-Hill paid Irving $750,000 in advances, of which $650,000 was supposed to go to Hughes. The latter wound up in the Swiss account held by "Helga Hughes," which, Edith Irving later admitted, was her own account under a pseudonym.

In September 1971, Irving, who had maintained a complete aura of integrity and credibility, came to his editors with the complete tape transcripts of his interviews with Hughes. The publisher showed them to *Life* magazine, which had taken world syndication rights for $250,000.

Until the first hints of fraud were heard, Clifford Irving had worked a real gimmick into his deal with McGraw-Hill. They were not to meet or contact Hughes, because the recluse might take off into the wild blue yonder if he were confronted and disclaim the entire project.

A handwriting expert, called in by the book publisher, termed the Hughes handwriting "irresistible, unanswerable and overwhelming." But later, when the evidence of a hoax began accumulating, the expert, said McGraw-Hill, "issued a revised report which cast doubt on the authenticity of the documents."

This changeabout proved strategic. Another writer, who had briefly worked on another Hughes book, suspected that the Irving manuscript might have been partly lifted from his own, as yet unpublished, work. He raised the question, which by then simply added to a host of nagging questions and indications that the Clifford Irving project was a big, fat hoax. Of course, what irrevocably put the stamp of conspiracy on the Irving book was the disclosure, forced by some solid detective work of Swiss detectives, that the Helga Hughes who had picked up the $650,000 intended for Howard Hughes was actually Edith Irving. Edith drew two months in jail, and Suskind got six months.

Irving on sentencing said that the consequences "have been a loss of almost everything for me." The question that arises from the business standpoint is how McGraw-Hill, or any other publisher, could avoid a hoax perpetrated by an author. The fact is that publishing tradition has been to accept a submitted book-project in complete good faith, trusting the author implicitly. But there's little doubt that, insofar as any controversial books are concerned, the relationship is due for some major scrutiny.

The ITT incidents were totally different, of course. The first one that surfaced involved an alleged wriggling out of three antitrust suits filed by the Justice Department by allowing one of its subsidiaries to underwrite a sizable share of the expenses of the 1972 Republican Convention slated for San Diego. Part of the charges included pressure put on Assistant Attorney General Richard McLaren by White House sources to softpedal the suits against ITT. Shortly after the Justice Department reached an agreement with ITT, McLaren became a federal judge. The move was controversial in itself. Was he put out to pasture because he was overzealous or because he wanted out? McLaren claimed the latter.

The entire matter started when Jack Anderson, the syndicated columnist, published a memo reportedly written by Dita D. Beard, an ITT Washington lobbyist, indicating that the Justice Department was influenced to settle the three antitrust suits. Mrs. Beard repudiated the memo, and ITT denied it all. The influence issue became perhaps the major one when Congress took up the matter of confirming Richard Nixon's nomination of Richard G. Kleindienst as Attorney General. But Kleindienst was approved, although the stigma lingered around ITT.

In mid-June of 1972, the Securities and Exchange Commission accused ITT and two of its top men of illegal dealings in the conglomerate's stock when they knew, although the public did not, that an antitrust suit against the concern was about to be settled. According to the SEC, the Justice Department indicated its willingness to permit ITT to proceed with its acquisition of Hartford Fire Insurance Corporation on June 17, 1971. The public wasn't told of the decision until July 31. But, said the SEC, two ITT officials sold 2,664 and 1,500 shares in the interim for about $163,000 and $100,000, respectively. When the news was announced, the ITT stock declined seven dollars a share, which meant that a prior sale by an insider with knowledge of the impending announcement would have avoided a loss of value in his stock.

These are some of the hottest business calamities in the most recent years of the three decades covered by this book. Not all are out-and-out disasters, nor is there a common thread to SST-Concorde, Clifford Irving and McGraw-Hill or ITT. All, however, represent calamities generated by the classic causes—uncontrolled expansion, greed, mismanagement.

What's the prognosis for the "rampant appetite" in business—the runaway greed which, combined with poor judgment, mismanagement, bad timing, self-deception and just plain stupidity, results in a business calamity? Personally, as a newspaperman, I can't be very sanguine, for when it comes to business greed I've seen it grow over the years and assume yet newer forms. A couple of decades ago, it was the pseudo- or fraudulent bankruptcy. Now, it's insider trading, government influence, an increase in bribes and kickbacks, vast wastage in terms of ill-suited products, services and corporate mergers, embezzlement through inventories that don't exist and conglomerate-aglomerate takeovers that drain the corporate coffers and stifle the financing availability.

Obviously, what is needed is a stiffening corporate resolve to emphasize the ethic in business, to insist on moral behavior by executives. To make sure that this is carried through, concerned, vigilant federal agencies and legislators must remain alert, with the hope that the private sector, through an attentive, intelligent public conscience, will see that the government sector remains alive to the problem.

Industrial security is becoming much more important and more widely used. But this type of service has been used primarily to catch the small fish. Who is to say that corporate investigators, swindle detectives, cannot be used to take over from our harassed police, to ferret out the big fish? Because, as I see it, the big fish are going to multiply.

You see, developing the rampant appetite is so natural nowadays . . . businessmen being judged by the constant increases in net that they can show . . . so many companies going public and their chief executives feeling the pressure of producing under the prod of the public ownership . . . the greed and acquisitiveness of underwriters, investment bankers and stock portfolio holders always looking for a new hot-shot manipulator to latch onto for their own gains . . . and the status criteria of money, money accumulation, power, market position. How often they entrap the little man whose ethical quotient is insufficient . . . turn the head, warp the conscience and . . .

Disaster.

About the Editor

ISADORE BARMASH is a well-known newspaperman and author of a number of books on business subjects, including a recent novel, *Net Net.* Associated with the *New York Times* as assistant to the financial editor, Mr. Barmash is the author of *Welcome to Our Conglomerate—You're Fired!* and *The Self-Made Man.* As a business editor and financial writer for the last 25 years, during which he was also a financial feature writer for the *New York Herald Tribune,* he is a constant observer of the corporate scene.

COME IN
NUMBER ONE,
YOUR TIME IS UP

Derek Jewell

Jewell has written an insider's novel about the struggle for power at the top of The Prospero Group, a huge conglomerate—a story compulsively readable and as authentic as the front page of today's *Wall Street Journal.*

". . . ought to appeal to every executive in every office . . . I wish a novel as sharp and readable came my way every month."

—Julian Symons
The Sunday Times, London

"The Darwin of the Managerial Revolution."

—Time

C. NORTHCOTE PARKINSON

First there was

PARKINSON'S LAW *And Other Studies in Administration*

The devastatingly accurate description of how administration really works. "Must reading for all determined bureaucrats."

—*New York Herald-Tribune*

Then

THE LAW AND THE PROFITS

Parkinson's Second Law—in which he turns his deadly wit on the further follies of bureaucracy. "How long must we wait before the people take Parkinson seriously."

—Robert Townsend,
the author of *Up the Organization*

And then

THE LAW OF DELAY: *Interviews and Outerviews*

Parkinson's Third Law—in which he poses in a fresh way the eternal conundrum of leadership. "Parkinson at his best, finessing so neatly that even his opponents must cry touché."

—*Business Week*

*The true story of how one man alone
bought his company back from
a giant conglomerate*

DIVORCE
CORPORATE
STYLE

Don Gussow

He sold his company to the Cowles Communication empire—and now, in the middle of a recession, he wanted to borrow a million dollars and buy it back!

In one of the most refreshing and candid behind-the-scenes books written about Big Business as it really is, Don Gussow opens the closed doors to the board rooms and shows you how the top-level decisions are made, decisions often costly and wasteful.

I CAN SELL YOU ANYTHING

Carl P. Wrighter

A renegade ad man's no-holds-barred, money-saving guide to the secrets of his trade.
